NOTORIOUS CASOLINI

ANGELO THOMAS CRAPANZANO

ISBN 978-1-957956-41-1 (Paperback)
ISBN 978-1-957956-42-8 (Ebook)

Inquiries and Book Orders should be addressed to:

Leavitt Peak Press
17901 Pioneer Blvd Ste L #298, Artesia, California 90701
Phone #: 2092191548

DEDICATION

This book is dedicated to the faithful and efficient staff members of the Akron General Hospital.

CONTENTS

ACKNOWLEDGEMENTS

I wish to thank my lovely Sister, Mary, for her tireless and dedicated help, not only in her valuable critiquing of the story line, but also for her chapter by chapter editing.

FOREWORD

My father was born in Sicily in a little village called Barrafranca. He and my mother came to the United States in 1927. My father always liked to talk to me about his childhood. One of his experiences he liked to tell me about was the story of an old man that he had met when he was twelve years old. He repeated the story to me several times as I was growing to manhood.

The village of Barrafranca, like most villages in Sicily, was built on top of a hill. This was the custom in the old days for protection. Although the majority of the people were farmers, they built their houses clustered together in the village…Some of their farms were as far as an hour away by horse back. From the center of town, starting in the piazza, a dirt road wandered on the west side of the town and slowly wound down the side of the hill. At the bottom it split and one road continued south toward Catania and the other road folded back and headed north toward Palermo. From the piazza, about half way along the road was a stone wall which prevented travelers from falling off the edge of the road and down into the olive orchards.

Children liked to play on this wall. It was on this wall that my father met Peppino, the old man. Peppino liked to walk down the road and sit on the wall looking down the valley toward the mountains. One of the larger mountains in the view was Monte Uno. It was in a cave in this mountain that Peppino spent much of his youth hiding from the police. My father was warned to stay away from this man because he had killed dozens of people and had spent most of his life in prison. He didn't listen, and after several months he and Peppino got friendly enough for Peppino to open up and tell his story.

Peppino told the story of when he was a young man of about twenty-five. The larger cities in Italy, during Peppino's Youth, had individual kings that ruled the area around the city which included several smaller towns. The king appointed mayors to rule the smaller cities, usually a relative of the king. When General Garibaldi united Italy, he removed all the kings and put all the cities under Victor Emanuel as King of all Italy. A provincial government was set up in each area. For Barrafranca it was Enna. The mayors however remained in the small towns. All the city officials including the city police were a remnant of the king's relatives. They were all corrupt. The mayor of Barrafranca had a son. The mayor's son wanted Peppino's sister for his wife, but the woman didn't want anything to do with him. The Mayor and his son had Peppino jailed on a trumped up charge to get him out of the way, then his sister was forced to marry the mayor's son when they threatened the lives of her brother as well as the life of her Father. Peppino's father tried to sneak out of the city and inform the provincial government. That started the terror of Peppino's family. The family was eventually destroyed by the mayor and his son. With the help of a friend, Peppino escaped from prison and became one of the most feared outlaws in the providence. The ones that feared him the most were the mayor his son and the police force. Peppino conducted his own form of justice.

The novel you are about to read was written with Peppino's life as the skeleton. Every detail of this story, with the exception of the basic skeleton, is pure fiction. The names, people, places and incidents are all created by the author. The only truth is that the city officials destroyed Peppino's family and that he paid them back in full.

Chapter 1

A SIMPLE LIFE

It was a very hot and humid day for this early in the year in Barrafranca, Sicily. For that matter, it was very hot for most days in central Sicily. Occasionally it became this humid in late summer but only when the winds changed direction and came from Africa across the Mediterranean Sea. The winds generally came from the North West and the air was usually very dry. That was more so in Barrafranca which is located near the center of Sicily. The air is usually so dry that mosquitoes are unknown to the villagers. Peppino wasn't as distressed with the high humid temperature as his dad was, but most seventeen year olds are more tolerant.

This morning Peppino was getting ready to do his daily chores as he did every day. The first task was to get water for the family's needs for the day. The family consisted of his father Salvatore, his mother Mariana, and his sister Stellina. They didn't have indoor running water as we do today. It had to be brought in from the outdoor fountain.

"Let's get going, Peppi," yelled his father. "Why are you so slow this morning? Come on. We have a lot of planting to do. It will take longer with this muggy weather"

"I'm coming," responded Peppino. "You go ahead. I'll catch up to you."

"Well hurry. We will need both horses." Peppino quickly saddled the horse he was going to use and quickly threw on the cuffinas, one on each side of the horse.. These water jug containers were large

1

wicker bushel like containers designed to carry the clay water jugs. They were, however, very useful to carry anything one desired, especially the wheat after harvest. Peppino inserted the 25 liter clay jugs in the containers. He mounted his horse and headed for the natural spring fountain every one in the village used to obtain water for their daily use. The spring was sealed with a cement structure with a single pipe extending through the cement wall horizontally at about four feet high. Below the fountain was a cement trough that was used to water the animals while the owners fill their water jugs. "Hi, Peppino," said Gino, Peppino's best friend. He was a little smaller than Peppino and slimmer but he was as strong as his horse. Gino worked with his uncle. His father had died when he was nine. Everything his father owned was left to him. According to the law at that time everything is left to the oldest son. It was his responsibility to take care of the rest of the family. However, his mother died a year after his father and he had no one except Uncle Guido to take care of him. The uncle wasn't too happy to take care of Gino's land as well as his own. He worked Gino very hard and expected Gino to take care of his own land himself as soon as he was able. Gino's land was just a short way past Peppino's family land. Because of this, they usually rode out to the farms together.

"Are you done already?" Peppino asked Gino "Yea, you are kind of late this morning, aren't you?"

"I went to sleep late last night and couldn't get up this morning" said Peppino. "I got to hurry. Will you wait for me by the school so we can ride to our farms together?"

"Okay, but hurry. My uncle will give me hell if I'm too late." Peppino quickly filled his jugs and headed for home. His mother helped him unload the jugs. His sister came out carrying their lunch.

"Papa left without the food for lunch" explained Stellina. "Thanks Stella," said Peppino. "I'll see you tonight." Peppino loved his sister very much. She was thirteen. There wasn't anything he wouldn't do for her. They had never fought over anything. Stella loved her brother not only because he treated her so well but because she respected and looked up to him. Peppino was very tall for a boy of seventeen. He was a little over six feet tall. He was very muscular. The family members were very fair skinned for Sicilians. Mr. Casollini and Stellina had blue eyes.

Peppino's eyes were hazel. His hair was brown but in the sunlight you could see a tint of red. Peppino's mother was more the typical Sicilian with black hair and brown eyes. Peppino put the lunch in his saddle bags. The lunch usually consisted of a large chunk of bread with several dried olives or a piece of cheese and some times an onion.

"Hurry, Peppino," said his mother. "You don't want to upset your father"

"I'm going," said Peppino as he urged his horse to start moving. A few minutes later, he arrived at the school where Gino was waiting for him.

"Boy, I wish I could go back to school," said Peppino wishfully. "You are very lucky," said Gino being somewhat envious. "You got to go all the way to the sixth grade. I was pulled out of school after the fourth grade. My uncle said learning to read and write and a little arithmetic was all that was needed. I've been working the land since I was nine."

"I'm sorry I brought it up," said Peppino with a smile on his face. They both laughed.

"It's been a bad day already and it has barely started," stated Gino.

"What's so bad about it?" asked Peppino not understanding the comment.

"First it is very humid and I know that Uncle Guido will be miserable to work with. Also you didn't get to see Gina this morning did you?"

"What does that have to do with anything?" said Peppino trying to hide the fact that he was smitten by her.

"Come on now," said Gino kidding him. "I could tell from the change in the way you act when she is around. I can tell you are crazy for her."

"She is only thirteen years old," said Peppino. "And I don't even like girls. They are too giggly, especially Gina, she is silly"

"Who are you trying to convince — me or you?"

"Will you stop by when you are finished for the day so we could go home together?" asked Peppino.

"Don't I always? You're just trying to change the subject," teased Gino.

"Well the subject was getting silly. I'm only seventeen. I don't need a girl in my life." They rode in silence for awhile. Then Gino broke the silence.

"Why do you think the air is so humid? Do you think it is going to rain?"

"I don't think so," responded Peppino. "I think it is just one of those unusual days. You know, where colder air picks up moisture from the hot sea air."

"You are so smart," said Gino with admiration. Neither knew what he was talking about.

"What do you know about Monte Uno?" asked Gino. "I hear that it is enchanted."

"I think it is an old wives tail," responded Peppino. "People need something to talk about."

"That's not true," said Gino, being sure of his information. "I hear that people have gone into the cave in the mountain and never came back out. They were never heard from again."

"Well maybe they fell into a hole in the cave. The tunnels don't all have to be horizontal you know. I think it's all bull," insisted Peppino.

"How about the stories the people who went in half way tell us of their experiences? Do you think they are all lying?" asked Gino.

"What stories are you talking about?"

"I'm talking about the people who went in and when they were about half way in their candles slowly went out. Don't answer," Gino said corrected his thoughts. "I know what you are going to say. You are going to say that an air flow inside the cave blew the candles out even though no one felt any. But how about the people who went in with oil lamps?" continued Gino. "They said that the light from the lamps slowly went out."

"Who knows what the true story is," said Peppino. "It could be it got too cold or the amount of oxygen got too low to sustain the flame. I'm only sure there is a logical explanation, it's not because of some magical or mystical enchantment."

"I give up," said Gino. "You've got your mind made up and I'm not going to change it. Some day when we have free time I dare you to go into the cave with me. Then we will see who is right."

"I accept the challenge," said Peppino. He was laughing at the same time. Gino wasn't too happy that Peppino was laughing at him.

"We'll see," is all that Gino would say. They approached Peppino's farm. Peppino lead his horse off the road and headed toward the shed where his father was working.

"See you later," Peppino yelled back at Gino.

"Okay," said Gino as he continued down the road to his farm. Peppino rode up to his father and dismounted. Since it was just beginning to dawn his father was not upset at him.

"Here I have this horse ready to start plowing," said his father. "Start in the north field. We will both work there. We have to do that first. We have to get the wheat in first. It is already getting too late." Peppino started plowing as soon as he reached the north field. A few minutes later his father joined him. They alternated rows. They worked until about one o'clock. Salvatore then signaled his son to stop for lunch. They ate lunch in silence. Peppino was deep in thought about Monte Uno. Was Gino right?

"Papa," said Peppino breaking the silence. "What do you know about Monte Uno?"

"Why do you ask?"

"Gino and I were talking and he said there is a cave in the mountain that has some kind of strange things going on inside." Peppino's father started to laugh.

"You have been fed that story, have you?" he said still laughing. Peppino liked to see his father laughing, even if it was at him. It happened so seldom. Though his father was a very loving father and husband he was usually so tired and had so much on his mind that laughing was not a normal occurrence with him.

"Gino said that people have disappeared inside the cave and that lanterns have gone out inside."

"At one time there was some mining going on in the mountain. I don't remember what it was. I think it was some kind of chemical. Anyway, I think they started that story to scare people away from there," answered Salvatore. "You know how superstitious most people are. The story just hung on."

"Just what I thought," said Peppino trying to hide the fact that he had a leaning to Gino's story. "I never believed it."

"Let's get back to work," demanded his father. "I would like to finish the north field and do the seeding this afternoon." Peppino didn't need to be told twice. He got up and went back to plowing. It was well into the afternoon when they finished the plowing and started to seed. That generally went faster and was a lot easier on the body. They were about halfway done when Gino showed up. "Gino," yelled out Peppino. "What are you doing here so early?" "Uncle Guido went to plow his own land," answered Gino. "He left instruction on what I had to get done. I finished what he told me to do so I left."

"Papa," asked Peppino. "How soon can I leave?"

"I'll tell you what," responded his father. "I'll make a deal with you. If Gino will help us finish the seeding of the north field you can both leave."

"Sounds great to me," responded Gino. "What do you want me to do?"

"You know what to do. God knows you have done it many times. When we meet our goal you both can leave." It took about an hour and a half to finish the seeding.

"What do you want us to do now?" asked Peppino.

"You kids take off," said Peppino's father. "You two deserve a little time off. Don't forget Peppino, we have to finish plowing the south field tomorrow. And don't go riding your horse around. He needs his rest. Take the horse home so your mom can feed him. Then you can go out and play."

"I'll take care of the horse and I'll be ready for tomorrow Papa," said Peppino as he saddled his horse. Soon Peppino and Gino were on the road on the way home.

"I'll race you home," said Gino slapping his feet on the side of his horse to make it go faster.

"No way," responded Peppino. "We get these horses lathered up and tired I'll have to wipe it down. How do I do that without my mother knowing? You don't have any one to see what you do to your horse but my father will never let me have it again if I mistreat him." Gino was distracted by the sight of two horses being raced through the farmlands and lost track of what they were talking about. "They are tearing out all the little seedlings that are just starting to come up."

"Why would they do that?" said Gino in amazement.

"I recognize the fellow in front," said Peppino. "That is Biachio, the mayor's son. I don't know who the other fellow is."

"I recognize him," said Gino. "I see him by the fountain once in awhile. That's Petro, the Maresciallo's son. You know, the head of the police, the mayor's private army."

"Yes I see him now," said Peppino. "What a bunch of good for nothings"

"Why are they doing that to the poor farmer's land," asked Gino. "Won't they get in trouble?"

"Are you kidding," said Peppino. "They are like little gods. No one will report them."

"Why won't anyone complain?" asked Gino.

"Where have you been?" said Peppino surprised at Gino's ignorance of the working of their government. "No one wants to get the attention of the mayor and his gang of thieves. Anyone who catches their attention ends up in deep trouble. If they don't end up killing them, they will make life miserable for them. Didn't any one ever tell you to stay out of their way? You don't want them to even know that you exist."

"I've heard of their cruelties," said Gino. "But I didn't know that it applied to good and honest people."

"You just don't want to cross them"

"I'm hungry," said Gino changing the subject. "I wish we could stop like we did last fall and get ourselves some oranges"

"Did you forget that we almost got shot that time?" reminded Peppino. "Remember, we stood on our horses to pick the oranges that hung over the wall. I can still hear the sound of the bullets tearing through the leaves. I remember it mostly because you almost fell off your horse."

"I did not," said Gino in defense.

"You did so. You were riding on the side of your horse until we got out of range."

"I didn't want to be shot. I did that so I was hidden by the horse."
"Sure you did," said Peppino laughing out loud at the thought.

"I laughed so loud that I almost fell off my horse."

"You don't know anything," said Gino feeling a little embarrassed. They rode a little way before anything more was said. "You know Gaetano DiFranco don't you?" asked Gino.

"You mean Tano?" asked Peppino. "Yes, I went to school with him. I see him once in awhile. I don't hang around him too much. We are both too busy now that we are out of school. Why, what about him?"

"I see him sometimes in the evenings when I'm not with you. I think he has a thing for you sister, Stella. He is always talking about her. Yesterday he asked me to call him whenever you and I are together. I think he wants to get to know you better because of your sister. Anyway I think he want to hang out with us."

"I think Stella kind of likes him too," said Peppino. "I don't mind hanging out with him. He is a very nice guy. He is a very kind and gentle person. That's why Stella likes him I think. Anyway, they are too young. It's only infatuation."

"Is that what you feel for Gina? Only infatuation," kidded Gino. "Are you singing that song again," said Peppino getting tired of Gino's insinuations. "Don't you know any other tunes?" "No," said Gino with a wide smile on his face.

"You can tell Tano that we would like to hang out with him. In the mean time what are we going to do with the time we have right now?"

"I told you that I'm hungry," said Gino. "I know what. Let's go to the garbage dump at the bottom of the olive orchard. It's not too bad this time of the year. The winter has reduced it to dirt like." The garbage dump was a tract of land that was used to dispose of refuge that was accumulated during the day. No liquids were dumped there. All liquids were usually thrown out the front door onto the cobblestone road. It mixed with the horse droppings, and because of the extreme dry air liquids evaporated in a few minutes. "So you want to go eat garbage," said Peppino mocking Gino.

"Have we fallen that low?"

"No, funny guy. There are a lot of birds that feed there. We can set a trap for a large one and cook it right there. I've done it before." "You're kidding me, aren't you?" said Peppino being very suspicious of Gino's motives. "You can't be serious."

"No I'm serious. I told you that I have done it before." "How are you going to trap a bird?"

"I will use a string trap," said Gino.

"This I have to see," said Peppino, chuckling.

"Follow me," said Gino. He then took off at a slow trot with Peppino following. About ten minutes later, they were at the dump. There were several birds feeding on what ever they could find. Gino got out a long piece of string he had in his pocket. He set up a loop with a slip knot. He then put a piece of bread he found there,and set it in the middle of the loop. He waved Peppino to follow him up the hill till he reached a tree.

"Tie your horse here with mine. I'll be right back." Gino went back to the string and extended it as far as it would go. He then hid behind a small bush that was nearby. He waited for a larger bird to come for the bread. He tried several time with no success. Finally, to Peppino's surprise, by pulling on the string quickly Gino manage to trap a fairly good size bird by the leg. The poor bird tried to fly away and escape but to no avail. Gino pulled it in and before Peppino could object Gino had grabbed it and broke its neck.

"You're a mean kid," said Peppino. "I can't believe you killed the poor thing."

"Well how are we supposed to eat it if I didn't kill it?" responded Gino.

"I'm not going to eat any of it," said Peppino with a look of distain on his face. Gino ignored him and started to collect twigs he found around the area. He pulled out a match from his pocket and started a fire. Gino went to his saddlebags and came back with a large cup and the water bottle. He put the bird in the cup and filled it with water. While the water was heating he searched and found two small branches that looked like a "Y". When the water boiled he pulled the bird out and started to pull all the feathers off of its body. The hot water made the feathers come off easily. Gino pulled out his knife and cut off the bird's head and opening up its belly he removed its guts. He then pushed a stick through the entire body and set it on the "Y" branches that were pounded with a rock into the ground on each side of the fire. Every once in awhile he would turn the bird so it would cook evenly. When it was done Gino offered Peppino half of the bird.

"No way," said Peppino. "That bird has been eating garbage." "Here, just taste it," said Gino, as he offered Peppino a leg.

Peppino hesitated to accept it. Gino started to pick and eat the flesh from the cooked bird.

"What does it taste like" asked Peppino. "It tastes a little like chicken."

Peppino took the leg and took a bite. The bite took most of the flesh from the bone. There was so little meat on such a small bird. "All this will do is make you hungrier," said Peppino. "There isn't enough food here to even consider it an appetizer." Without saying a word Gino went up to his horse, got on and started for home.

When they got to Peppino's home Gino waved back. "Will I see you after diner?"

"Okay," said Peppino. "Come over and we could play cards." After Gino left, Peppino opened the large door to the courtyard and led his horse to the stable which was located in the rear of the courtyard. The Casollini residence was much different then the other houses in the neighborhood. Most houses were single large rooms with a stall attached to it. All the houses had three common walls with their neighbors. The rear wall was shared with the house behind them on the next street. The right wall was shared with the neighbor to the right. The left wall, which was normally the outside wall of the stable, was shared with the neighbor to the left. The only part of the house that belonged exclusively to the owner was the front and the roof. There were usually three doors to the house. First was the front door which had the only window of the house set above it. Then there was the larger door to the stable. The third door was the door between the living area and the stable. The living area consisted of a wood burning stove and a stone oven. The room also had two beds in two alcoves, with curtains covering the openings. Underneath the beds usually was the area that the wheat grain was stored. The stall area was used as the rest room. Peppino's house, however, was different. Having been one of the first houses in the area had a lot more land to build on. It had been built by Peppino's great-grandparents. It had a living area on the left like every one else's except it had a small room next to the stable wall that was normally used for storage. However, when Peppino grew too old to sleep with his sister, they converted it to a small bedroom. There also was a smaller building on the right of the area. The stable was located between them and separated the two buildings and also occupied an area behind the main building. The smaller building, Peppino was told, was originally built for the grandparents. It was only one room. The outside front wall was about four feet thick. On the left side was a small closet-like room where they kept the laundry tub and extra water. On the right were steps that lead to the top of the wall. Of course there was a railing on both sides of the upper area. Because the right side building and the stable were smaller there was a small courtyard between them and the front wall. On the lower right side of the front wall, next to the steps, was a stone oven primarily used to bake bread. Wood was burned inside until the inner stones got hot; they turned a whitish color when sufficiently hot. The ashes were removed, the oven floor cleaned with a wet broom and the bread placed inside. The oven opening was sealed with a wooden door and the bread was cooked.

Peppino brushed his horse, gave it some straw to eat, and went inside the house.

"Hi, Peppi," said Stellina being the first to notice him. "You're home early"

"Yes, we finished seeding and I came home."

"Did your father let you go or did you leave with Gino without your father's permission?" asked his mother.

"Gino helped us do the seeding, so when we finished Papa said we could leave."

"Good, go wash up and help your sister." Peppino went to the stove area and began to help his sister peel potatoes. As they worked, Peppino asked.

"Stella, what do you think of Tano?" "You mean Gaetano DiFranco?" "Yes," "Well, what about him?"

"What do you think of him?" asked Peppino the second time. "I don't think of him at all," responded Stellina. "Why do you ask?"

"He told Gino that he wants to hang out with us. I think he has a crush on you."

"What does hanging out with you have to do with me?" "Come on," said Peppino. "You are smarter than that. Hanging out with me will give him a better chance of seeing you."

"Will you stop that," Stellina hissed. "If mama hears you she won't even let me out of the house."

"Well tell me what you think of him and don't try to hide from me because I've seen your face when you look at him. Tell me the truth and I'll make sure that mama will not know anything. You know I would never do anything to hurt you."

"Okay, so I think he is cute," admitted Stellina. "So what, I'm too young to think of boys? Anyway what can you do about it?"

"Well, sis, dear," said Peppino "I can see that he hangs around here where you can feast your eyes on him and he on you. If I know that you like him I can protect you from anyone finding out especially mama."

"What are you two gabbing about?" asked Mariana, their mother. "Finish up your chores. Your father will want the food on the table when he gets home."

"We're almost done," assured Stellina.

After dinner Peppino went out and found Gino at his house. "Gino, why don't you go find Tano? Tell him you are coming to my house to play cards and that he is welcome to come too. That way Stellina and Tano can see each other. I'll go home and meet you there," suggested Peppino.

"You would do that for your sister?" questioned Gino. Most siblings he knew fought all the time.

"She is my best friend, besides you," added Peppino. "She is family. There is nothing more important than family. And there is nothing I won't do for members of my family."

"I wouldn't know about that," said Gino sadly.

"I'm like family to you," assured Peppino. "I'll do anything for you, besides what about your uncle Guido?"

"I don't think he even likes me. I am nothing but a burden to him. You are the only good friend that I have. I will do anything for you. Remember that when ever you need anything."

"Go get Tano. I feel like beating the pants off both of you. We will play Scuppa." Gino left and came back a few minutes later with Tano. They played cards until dark and then a little while under the lantern. Peppino and Gino enjoyed watching Stellina and Tano look at each other. They were giddy all evening. Peppino knew that Stellina was thrilled and Peppino was very happy for her. He loved his sister very much. They always covered for each other since as far back as they could remember. Stellina never forgot that when she was younger that her brother took a spoon across his butt for her a least a couple of times. Tonight she was also grateful to Peppino. The only difficulty was keeping their parent from realizing what was going on. Fortunately, they were busy with the horses and chickens in the stable to notice anything. Finally, as it got late, their mother came in the room.

"All right you guys. It's getting very late and it's time to wind up your game."

"But mama," objected Peppino. "It's only eight-thirty."

"Yes, but do you know how fast five o'clock comes around tomorrow morning?" she asked them.

"All right, we will just finish this hand," promised Peppino. After Gino and Tano left, Peppino went to his room. It was only a little over four feet wide and he had to walk sideways to get to the head of the bed.. He put on his pajamas and was asleep before his head hit the pillow.

Peppino was up at four-thirty the next morning. He was eager to go get the water and to see Gina this morning. He hadn't seen her for several days. Somehow, he knew this was the day. He also was going to swallow his pride and speak with her. He just hoped he would beat Gino there. He arrived at the well just as Gina was coming out to fill a large clay jug with water. She was carrying the jug on her shoulder.

"Ciao, Gina," he said with a lump in his throat. "You're going for water kind of early this morning aren't you?" he asked.

"No, this is about the time I always go. I may be a little earlier because I have to wash the floors today, but not much." Peppino knew very well what time she came out in the mornings. "Are you going to help your father on your farm today?" she continued.

"Yes, we are going to plow and seed the vegetable area today." She reached the fountain and Peppino helped her fill her jug first. "Is this all the water you will need today?"

We live so close that we can have fresh water any time we need it."

"You're lucky," said Peppino, not knowing what else to say. I'm sure glad today isn't as humid as yesterday," said Peppino trying to keep a conversation going.

"Yes," she said. "Me too." Just then, Gino came around the corner.

"Good morning Peppino," he yelled out. "You are earlier this morning. Are you trying to make up for yesterday?"

"Very funny," said Peppino as he got his jugs and began filling them.

"Ciao," said Gina as she walked away with the jug on her shoulder. "Ciao," said Peppino and Gino in unison. Then when she was out of sight, Gino turned to Peppino, and said, "Got to see her this morning did you?"

"What did you think of Tano?" said Peppino changing the subject. "He was a lot of fun," said Gino. "By the way, I saw him this morning. He was on his way to his farm to help his father. He is going to meet us tonight at your house and is bringing along his cousin Antonio. He will make a foursome for our card game. Do you mind? My uncle will be working his own land. I can leave whenever I feel like it. I'll come by your place about three and see if you can leave." They each filled their jugs with water and headed for home.

After work on Friday, the boys grabbed a ball and headed to the field.

"Hiya fellows," said Tano when he arrived. "This is my cousin Antonio. We all call him Nino for short."

"Hiya," said Peppino shaking his hand. Gino also shook his hand. "How is it that you guys could get away this early?" asked Gino. "Well, we are all done with the seeding and can't do anything until the plants break through the ground." said Tano "It was the same with Gino and me," added Peppino.

"My family doesn't do any planting as such," said Nino. "We own an orchard of pistachios trees, walnut, trees, and olive trees. Our work is heaviest in the fall, same as with you guys. Actually, my father is a builder. He built the addition to the mayor's house. He even built the jail at the end of town by that high cliff. When he is not building he works in the orchard."

"Well let's play ball," said Peppino. "Gino and I will play you two cousins."

In the following days and month, Peppino, Gino, and Tano became very good friends. They hung together almost constantly. Tano made no effort to hide that he had fallen in love with Stellina. Stellina didn't hide her feelings for Tano. Peppino was sure that his parents had become aware of the situation. However, they apparently did not object. They liked Tano very much. He was a hard working and a very pleasant person.

Chapter 2

FIVE YEARS LATER

Peppino got up early as usual. He was preparing to get the water as he did every morning. He was twenty-two. If his mother was still alive she would have made a little fuss about it. But his mother, Marianna Casolini, had passed away almost two years ago. He was in the stable getting his horse ready to leave for the fountain. He had set the jugs in the cuffinas and was ready to mount the horse when Stellina came into the stable.

"Happy Birthday brother dearest," she said. "I'm making some eggs and fried potatoes for breakfast. How do you want your eggs?"

"I'm not very hungry," he responded.

"I know how you feel. It's hard to be happy on any kind of holiday without mama. I miss her terribly too. But mama wouldn't want us to be unhappy," said Stellina with sadness in her voice.

"All right," he agreed seeing that he was making her unhappy. "I'll have something to eat when I get back. Is papa up yet? He is usually up before me."

"He is just getting dressed. You know that he misses mama as much as we do. He feels lost without her. I'm trying to fill in for her as much as I can."

"Sister honey, you are only seventeen. You can't expect to fill all her shoes."

"I'm disappointed in you. I'm eighteen. I thought you would remember my age."

"You are growing so fast. I can't keep track."

"Now get going. I will have breakfast ready for you when you get back. Don't spend an hour with Gina now" Peppino gave her a smile that ended with a wink. He left for the fountain. When he got there Gina was waiting for him. They have been seeing each other almost every day for the last year.

"Good morning Gina," said Peppino as he dismounted his horse at the fountain. "You look like a queen this morning."

"You say that every morning, dear Peppi," she said with a big grin on her face. "But I love to hear you say it. It thrills me as it did when you said it the first time."

"You look more beautiful each time I see you."

"Thank you sir," she responded. "Are you in a hurry to go to the farm this morning?"

"I'm afraid so. We have to separate the grain from the chaff today. It will be a long week. I can't stay to long this morning. My father is waiting for me."

"You're going to leave me hungry for your voice?"

"Where is your mother? You are really going to be hungry for my voice if she catches us."

"My mom is in the kitchen cooking breakfast for us. We haven't done anything to be ashamed of. You haven't even kissed me. Besides she hasn't paid much attention to me since dad died," she said sorrowfully.

"I know, it hasn't been a year yet. How are you and your mother getting along? Do you have enough food? If you need anything let me know."

Thank you for asking," she said with a smile on her face. "Dear Peppi, you ask the same question every morning. The answer is the same. We have enough grain from last year's crop. If we are conservative we can get through this winter. It's next year that I'm concerned with. I can seed, but I will have difficulty plowing."

"Don't worry about that," assured Peppino. "We will cross that bridge when we come to it. I'm sure that Gino and I can help you with that."

"Speaking of the devil, here comes Gino now," noticed Gina. Before Gino got within hearing range Peppino bent close to Gina and whispered in her ear.

"About that kissing stuff, I expect to remedy that soon."

"Oh you cad you," she said acting coy. Then she smiled, "Promise?" "Good morning you two," said Gino. "Am I interrupting anything?"

"Yes but don't you every morning?" answered Peppino. "I know, but I have to keep you two honest."

"Ciao," said Gina and left with her water jug on her shoulder. "See what you did," said Peppino suggesting that Gino had caused Gina to leave.

"You have to go anyway," said Gino in his defense. "You have some grain to bring in."

"You are so right," admitted Peppino. "I haven't eaten breakfast yet." "Who needs food when your in love," kidded Gino. "Go I'll meet you at the school."

Peppino filled his jugs and left for home. When he got home he unloaded the water and sat down to eat.

"Where is papa?" Peppino asked Stellina.

"He ate and left," responded Stellina. "He said you should hurry and catch up with him. I say relax and enjoy your food. It's your birthday."

"What did I do that God gave me such a loving sister. I don't deserve you."

"Be quiet and eat your breakfast," she said lovingly. "I know this is the time of the season that requires a lot of hard work and long hours. Just for this one day try to come home about six. I have a special dinner planned for you tonight."

Peppino was so proud of her. She was only fifteen when their mother died. It was just before Stellina's sixteenth birthday. She didn't even get a happy birthday greeting from anyone. Every one was so sad. Stellina never complained once. She took over the duties of her mother like a trooper. She became like a wife to their father and a mother to Peppino. Peppino wouldn't do anything that would make Stellina unhappy.

"All right," said Peppino resigned to letting her have her way. "I'll try to get papa to come too."

"I'm the one God has blessed, giving me a big brother like you. I love you more then you can imagine."

"I know, almost as much as I love you," countered Peppino.

"If you're finished eating, go, bring some grain in," she said laughingly. Peppino wanted to help with the dishes but Stellina pushed him into the stable. When he was on his horse she handed him a bag. "This is a special lunch for you and papa."

"What is so special about it?" asked Peppino. "Do you have extra large olives?"

"No, silly," said Stellina. "Today, for your birthday, I have wrapped several sardines to go with your bread."

"You're kidding," said Peppino in amazement. "Where did you get sardines?"

"I went to the market yesterday looking for something special for dinner and found these sardines."

"What is the special dinner you are having for us this evening?" asked Peppino, knowing very well that she wouldn't tell.

"It's a surprise," she said tightening her lips as if to suppress any hint. "You will have to wait until tonight. Now you better be on your way if you don't want papa to get upset with you. And by the way, invite Gino if you like."

A few minutes later Peppino met Gino at the school. Peppino was sure since he took so long that Gino would have left without him.

"What are you doing here," asked Peppino. "I thought for sure you would have left without me. To what do I owe this special treatment?"

"Mostly I waited because I forgot to wish you a happy birthday earlier. So, Happy Birthday! Also, after Uncle Guido got sick I kind of became my own boss. I don't need much. I've only been working my own land."

"Your Uncle Guido passed away a few months ago, and left you his house and land." said Peppino.

"So what are you going to do with the other house and the other piece of land? Have you decided yet? Since you are not planning to work it, are you just going to let it sit?"

"You know that my Uncle's land borders on Duke Liborio Casino's land. Maybe he will want to add it to his property?"

"But I hear he is inaccessible to anyone."

"That is true," said Gino "But I have a way to get to him." "And how is that?"

"Do you remember Tano's cousin, Nino?" asked Gino. "Well he works for the Duke Don Casino. He works for him most of the year. That is why we have not seen too much of him. He works for him until the fall when his father needs him to gather the fruit from the orchard."

"What does he do for him?" asked Peppino, surprised at the information.

"He is one of his ranch hands," Gino continued. "He stays there in the bunk house with three other ranch hands. The Duke raises horses. He also has a flock of sheep and I hear he also has some cattle on his ranch. Nino stays there for months at a time. He sleeps there so that if the Duke asks him do something for him in the middle of the night, he's available. He also carries a gun to protect the Duke's property and possessions.

"How do you know all of this?"

"I considered going to work for him," said Gino. "I don't like working or living alone. It wasn't any fun farming all alone after my Uncle died."

"What changed your mind?" asked Peppino.

"I don't know if I have actually changed it. I am delaying it until I figure out what to do with one of the houses and both pieces the land."

"So what are you going to do?"

"I'm going to ask Nino to talk with the Duke and see if he is interested in Uncle Guido's land. I'll decide what to do next after I get and answer from him."

"Well good luck," said Peppino.

"I don't really need much," said Gino continuing. "The land that I inherited from my family is even too much for me. I'm not that interested in having a lot of money. Besides the more I make the more the city gets."

"I know what you mean," said Peppino. "I hate giving them so much of the wheat we work so hard to get. But, I guess we have to support the city government."

"Sure we have to support their big palaces and money hungry relatives," said Gino while making a sad expression on his face.

Peppino laughed. "Life isn't fair."

"Are you going to work until after dark tonight?" asked Gino seeing that they were getting near where they would separate each to his own land.

"No, I have to be home by six tonight for a special dinner Stella is preparing for my birthday. She has also asked me to invite you. So if you are coming, be here by five-thirty."

"Are you kidding," said Gino getting very excited. "The Mayor and his private army couldn't keep me from coming."

"Good, I will see you then," said Peppino as he turned his horse to the left to go into his farmland.

"See you later," responded Gino as he headed toward his own land.

Peppino's father was already cutting down the wheat stocks and binding them into separate bundles. Peppino quickly tied up his horse and without a word started helping his father. It took them most of the morning to bundle the wheat that remained from yesterday's effort. When they were finished Peppino's father started to carry them one by one to a large flat open area. There he spread the wheat bundles evenly across the area. He removed the straw and bundled it separately, leaving only the seed pods.

"Better get your horse ready," said Peppino's father. "The wind is starting to come up strong. We had better take advantage of it while we can." When both horses were ready, they walked them in circles across the pods to tramp them down so the wheat grain separated from the chaff. They did this until most of the wheat grain was free. After removing the horses, they shoveled the trampled material into the air. The wind would blow away the chaff and the wheat grain being heavier fell to the ground. They did this until the grain was free. The grain was then shoveled into sacks and stored in the shed. The remaining straw was also stored as it was food for the horses. This continued until about five in the afternoon.

"Papa," said Peppino. "Stellina is cooking a special dinner tonight and would like us to be home by six."

"What are you talking about," responded his father. "What is this all about?"

"Well, she wants to make a special dinner in honor of my birthday,"

"What kind of nonsense is this," responded his father. "We have a lot of work to do. If we delay too long the fall rain will rot the whole crop."

"Papa, I agree with you," said Peppino truthfully. "I don't want any fussing over my birthday, but think of what she has done for both of us. She has taken care of us without a word of complaining. She has done a great job of it too you must admit. She has been such a happy girl that she could help. She has never acted like it was a burden. She has treated it as if it was her privilege. Papa you know how hard it has been for her since mama died. I don't want to disappoint her, do you?" When his father didn't respond Peppino continued. "Papa what has she ever asked of you or me. All she has ever asked was our love."

"All right," said his father finally. "I guess one evening can't hurt. "She deserves more that this from us."

"Great, Papa," said Peppino with a silent sigh of relieve. "After dinner I would like you to run an errand for me." "What do you want me to do?" asked Peppino.

"Remind me after dinner," said his father. Peppino knew better then to ask again. His father will tell him when he was ready to tell him.

"I talked with Mrs. Fanucci," continued Peppino's father. "She is getting close to running out of grain. I told her we will help as much as we can. We will have to work something out between you, Gino, and Gaetano DiFranco."

"When did you meet Gina's mother?" asked Peppino, greatly surprised by his father's remark.

"I stopped at the shoemaker yesterday before I came home. I met her as she was going to the grocery store. I asked her how she was doing. She told me she had enough from the last crop her husband had planted to see her through the winter, or she would if she could find some way of gathering the grain from that last harvest. However they had depleted her store of grain for winter planting. They had used what was stored for the purpose of supporting themselves since her husband died. Although it probably doesn't matter, she said because she didn't see a way to get her land plowed. Her daughter said she would do the seeding but didn't think she could do the plowing or the gathering of the grain by herself – not that she liked the idea of her daughter going to the farm by herself anyway. I told her I would see if I could work out some way of helping her. She is still a very young woman and so very pleasant. I think we should do everything we can to help them."

"Papa," said Peppino, showing great happiness in his actions, "I'm so glad you are willing to help. I'm sure you know that I want to marry Gina."

"I know, Son," said his father. "But you have to wait until Stellina gets married. I can't carry on without some one to help me. If she marries Gaetano DiFranco then he'll help me and you can leave to marry Gina."

"You have everything planned do you, Papa?"

"Of course," he said with one of his rare smiles. "You think all I can do is work. I'm not a horse you know."

"I know, Papa," said Peppino. "It's just that you are so subtle about your plans." His father didn't answer. He started to place two of the sacks of grain in Peppino's cuffinas. He then placed some hay on his horse. They both placed the remaining sacks of grain and some hay in the shed and locked the door. As they got ready to leave Gino rode up.

"You are just in time to go home with us," said Peppino.

"You know I wasn't going to miss this occasion," said Gino. Then with respect he turned to Peppino's father.

"How are you, Mr. Casolini?"

"I'm fine Gino. How are you holding up? I'm guessing it's been rough since your Uncle Guido died."

"I'm still young enough to handle it all right," said Gino. "I have to admit though that it is pretty lonely working by myself."

"Why don't you get married and have children. Then you will have help when you get older and will need it."

"That's kind of a drastic solution isn't it?" said Gino kidding him. "You don't know what you will be missing," responded Mr. Casolini.

"Gino, I have been talking with Peppi about Mrs. Fanucci. We are going to try to come up with a plan to help her and her daughter. I don't know what we can do yet but I was wondering if you are willing to help in some way?"

"I would be glad to help," said Gino. "I don't even have to plant all my land. Half of it would provide enough for me. On the other hand, I can do it all and give half to them."

"I'm glad to hear that, Gino," said Mr. Casolini. "I'll let you know. When we finish with the winter planting we can all get together and make plans."

"Sound great," said Gino. "If Tano would marry Stellina you would have a helper."

"I don't know what he is waiting for," said Peppino.

"I talked with him yesterday," said Gino. "He has been waiting for his little brother to grow up so he could help his father. They are taking him to the farm with them now to train him. Don't worry. He is crazy for Stella."

They arrived at the Casolini house at a little before six. Stellina was pleased to see them. She was afraid that Peppino would not be able to convince papa to leave the land seeing that there was so much work to be done.

"Thank for being so prompt," said Stellina when they arrived. "I have a great dinner ready for Peppi's birthday. I'm also sure you all can enjoy something different." After washing up they sat down and Stellina began serving them. First, she brought each of them a bowl of soup. After they had finished the soup, she brought each of them a small dish of cavatelli with meat tomato sauce. And last of all she brought out a dish of grilled Sausage. All this was accompanied with a salad and a glass of wine. They ate in silence. After eating plain pasta in a bean soup most every night this was indeed a special treat.

"I've eaten so much I don't think I can move," said Peppino after finishing his salad which he always ate last, as was common in Sicily.

"I don't think I want to move," said Gino, stuffed to his ears. Stellina brought out a bowl of fresh fruit. No one had any. They were too full.

"Peppi," said Mr. Casolini. "That errand I asked you to do, I want you to do now. I would like you to take those two sacks of wheat grain we brought home to Mrs. Fanucci. She is going to need that until we can figure a way to gather her grain for her."

"I'll go right now," said Peppino happily, knowing he would get to see Gina.

"Do you want me to go with you?" asked Gino.

"No, that won't be necessary," said Peppino winking at Gino. "Then I think I will go home," said Gino "I'm so full, all I can think of is going to sleep." Peppino got everything ready and left for Gina's house. When he got there he knocked at the door. No one answered. He knocked again. Still no one answered.

"This is Peppi Casolini," he yelled loud enough for some one inside to hear. He was about to leave when he heard the lock on the door unlatch. The door opened slightly and Gina's face peered through the small opening.

"What do you want?" she asked very demurely. "My mother is not home."

"Open the door," demanded Peppino. "I'm here on business. Your mother and my father talked and my father has sent me to deliver some grain." Gina opened the door and looked out, then glanced at the grain.

"Don't you trust me?" asked Peppino "You know I would never dishonor you."

"I trust you," she said. "It's not that. It's that mama isn't home and I don't think she will like it that I open the door for you."

"Don't you think it's about time she knows about us and learns to trust me? Come out here and help me unload these sacks of grain." She came out then and together they removed the sacks and set them by the door. Then she dragged one inside and Peppino followed with the other.

"Let's put the sacks here next to the bed," she requested. They dragged the sacks to the rear of the room by the bed. As Peppino dragged his sack next to the one Gina had, their foreheads touched. "Gina," called Peppino. As she raised her head, their lips touched.

Peppino pulled her to him so the touching became a full kiss. She didn't resist. After a few minutes their lips parted.

"There, you are now ruined for life," said Peppino kidding her. "No one else will ever want you."

"Since I'm ruined now, I may as well take full advantage of it," she said and planted another loving kiss on him. "I will never want any one else anyway," she added.

"I will never let any one else near you," he said feeling very romantic. "Gina, I love you so much. I never thought I could love so completely."

"I love you too," she responded and kissed him again. "When are you going to make it official and bring your dad to ask permission of my mother?"

"I have already talked with my father. He said he wants Stellina to marry first so he can have her husband as a helper. Then he could let me go so I could take care of you and your mother."

"What is holding up Tano?" asked Gina.

"He says that as soon as his little brother can help his father then he will be free to marry Stellina."

"And when will that be," she asked impatiently. "I want you in my arms so badly."

"I know," said Peppino. "Not as badly as I want you. Tano is taking his brother with him to the farm every day to train him. He says he is almost ready." Peppino bent over and was ready to kiss her again when they heard her mother coming.

"What are you doing here?" she asked of Peppino.

"Ciao, Dona Fanucci," said Peppino with a smile that projected innocence. "My father sent me with two sacks of grain. We put them here near the bed. I didn't know where you wanted them."

"That is fine. And don't call me Dona Fanucci. Call me Dona Maria. That's what everyone knows me by. So you can call me Dona Maria for now. Tell your father I am eternally grateful. He is extremely kind. And thank you for bringing them."

"I will Dona Maria," said Peppino. "Ciao."

"Gina, why don't you walk Peppino to his horse?" When they got outside Peppino looked at Gina and they both laughed a happy laugh.

"Did I hear your mother correctly," asked Peppino. "Did you get that when she said to call her Dona Maria for now? For now? Does she expect that to change to maybe Mama Maria?"

"I know," said Gina with a snicker. "I almost fell over when she asked me to see you to your horse."

"Do you think she wants us to know each other better?" asked Peppino. He then added. "I believe she knows about us. And most important, she approves."

"I know she likes you," said Gina. "She has said that you're such a nice young man."

"Your mother is sneaky, you know that? She is smarter than we think."

"Gina," called her mother.

"I'll be right there," responded Gina. "I guess she feels we've had enough." Peppino pulled her to the side of the door out of sight in the dark. He kissed her.

"Now that I've had a taste of you I'll never be the same." "Ciao" she said. "See you tomorrow." She then quickly slipped into the house. Peppino got onto his horse. He was happier then he had ever been. He knew being married to her would make him happy but he couldn't imagine being any happier than he was right now.

The next morning, Peppino got up early thinking of nothing else except that he was going to see Gina. He got his horse ready and went for the water. When he got there, Gina was waiting by her door. Together they went to the fountain.

"My mother knows about us for sure," she said after they had greeted each other.

"How did she find out?" asked Peppino.

"She could tell by how giddy I was after you left. She said she could tell that I was madly in love with you. She also said she could tell by the way you couldn't take you eyes off of me that you cared as much for me."

"I told you your mother is smarter then she looks," said Peppino. "I love her already."

"You had better. After all she will be living with us."

"You don't know how happy that thought makes me feel," said Peppino. "I'm going to talk with Tano. I bet you can guess what I'm going to talk with him about." Gina smiled and shook her head indicating that she knew. They stood there just exchanging small romantic talk after they had filled their jugs. Gina finally decided she had better go home. Gino showed up a few minutes later and per Peppino's request left after he had filled his jugs.

"I'll meet you at the school. I have to talk to Tano privately," he told Gino. About fifteen minutes later Tano came to fill his jugs with water.

"Hi Peppi," said Tano with a surprised look on his face. "What are you doing here so late? You usually are gone by the time I get here. What's happening?"

"I don't understand why you always come so late," countered Peppino.

"We eat breakfast together and my father and brother leave after breakfast. I catch up to them after I bring the water to my mother. I believe you eat breakfast after you get the water."

"That's right," agreed Peppino. "I waited for you so I could talk with you."

"Is there a problem?" asked Tano.

"In a way there is. My father has promised Mrs. Fanucci he will see that her grain is gathered, her land plowed and the winter seed is planted."

"What is your plan?" asked Tano.

"We haven't really come up with one but perhaps you and I could start one. A lot depends on you."

"What do you want me to do?" said Tano. "I'll help in any way I can."

"I was wondering how far along your brother is? Can you spare any time to help my father?"

"I'd be glad to help your father," said Tano with a smile on his face. "But only if I can meet him at your house."

"I see," said Peppino." So you could see Stellina.""Well you know how much I love her."

"Well perhaps we can find some way to work that out." "Peppi, I was just kidding," said Tano. "When do we start?"

"Well, talk to your father and see how much he can spare you. I'll talk with my father and see what arrangement we can make. Gino Manguso has already offered to help."

"Okay," said Tano. "I'll get back to you as soon as I find out what my father thinks."

"See you later then," said Peppino as he rode away. When he got to his father's land he informed his father of the conversation he had with Tano.

"Very good," said his father. "God willing everything will fall in place."

"What I was thinking," said Peppino "was that if Tano could help you, Gino and I could finish gathering Gino's grain...We could then go to Mrs. Fanucci's land and gather her grain...When I'm finished at Mrs. Fanucci's land, I could go back to help Gino." "Sounds like a good plan," said Peppino's father. They went back to gathering their grain. The wind was brisk and the chaff blew away with little trouble. They worked until it got to dark to see the grain so they packed up and went home. Gino had not gone to see Peppino all day.. He worked until it was dark which was a lot longer than usual...He had to get as much done as he could so he could help Peppino with Gina's land. He left after dark and came into town just behind Peppino and his dad.

"You guys are going to kill yourselves working so late," said Stellina worrying about her men. "Come, I have dinner waiting. It's going to get cold." She had pasta a fagiuolo; pastina and beans. They had that at least three times a week. It was the most common and inexpensive food group. After they had eaten, Peppino filled Stellina in about his conversation with Tano. After she had heard everything that Peppino had to say, she turned to her father.

"Papa," she said. "If Tano comes and helps you, even if it's only in the afternoon, don't you think it would be a good idea for Tano to have dinner with us. There is no sense of him going back and forth. We owe him that much."

Her father smiled. "What back and forth?" he asked. "He just drops off the grain and goes home." Stellina's face grew sad.

"I'm just teasing you honey," said his father. "I think it is a great idea. We will have to see what he wants to do. I will offer it to him. We don't even know if his father can let him go at this time of the season." Just then they heard a knock at the door.

"Who could that be this time of night?" said Peppino. "I'll answer the door." He walked to the door and opened it. He was amazed to see Tano standing there.

"Ciao, Tano," he said with a surprised tone to his voice. "Come on in. What's up?"

"My father said he and my little brother Alexandro can handle what is left to do so he said I could help you all day if necessary.

"That will be great," said Mr. Casolini. "You can come here and have breakfast with us or come after breakfast and we can go together. What ever you decide for breakfast is fine, but when you get home, tell your parents you are going to have dinner with us every night."

"I think I will have breakfast with my family," said Tano. "I have to go get the water for them anyway."

"All right, but tell them you need to get used to Stellina's cooking." "Papa," objected Stellina.

"How are you, Stellina?" said Tano finally very shyly. "I guess I can't hide how I feel about you. When all this work is done my father and mother are planning to come and visit. You have about two week to figure what they want."

"I don't need two seconds to know what I hope they are coming for." Both their faces turned red. "It's my dream." She added.

"Mine too," said Tano. "I'd better go. We have to get up early." After he left, Mr. Casolini turned to his daughter.

"Honey, come here," he asked. "You know that Tano's parents approve of you and Tano getting together." Stellina sat down next to her father.

"How do you know that?" she asked.

"You know that this is the busiest time of the year. His younger son is only thirteen years old. They are going to have a tough time this fall. He would never have let Tano go if he didn't want you and Tano to get together. I think he wants you two to get to know each other better. You take my word for it; Tano will have supper with us every night until the fall seeding is finished. Better bone up on your cooking. I don't suspect we will have pasta a fagiuolo three times a week any more." Peppino and his father both laughed.

"I don't think that is funny," she said. "But papa it is so wonderful to see you laugh again."

"I'm going to bed," said Peppino as he left for his little room. The other two followed his suggestion.

The next few days worked out beautifully. Tano helped Mr. Casolini. He would have dinner with them before he went home. Stellina made great dinners for them. She always had a small bowl of pasta. Following the pasta, she had the main course. One day she would have pizza. One day she would have chicken. Another day she would have sausage. Sometimes she would make lamb if she could get a good price from the butcher. Peppino and Gino finished gathering Gino's grain and went to Mrs. Fanucci's land. That was a lot bigger then Gino's. It was during the gathering of Mrs. Fanucci's grain that Gino came late to the work area one morning. Peppino had to work alone. Trying to free the grain from the chaff was difficult doing it alone. Finally, about two hours later Gino showed up.

"Where have you been?" asked Peppino being a little perturbed.

"I have something very important to tell you. It is urgent that we talk."

"What's the problem?"

"Let's finish this round of wheat chaff and then we will sit and I'll tell you," said Gino. They finished stumping the chaff and after shoveling the chaff to the wind they gathered the grain into sacks. "Now let's talk," said Peppino wondering what Gino was so excited about.

"When I got home last night," began Gino. "I found a note on my door from my friend, Anna Maria Cradoni. She's a maid for the mayor. She lives with a young woman named Rosina Croppo, an orphan, and is also a maid for the mayor. They are kind of trapped.

They are not allowed to go on dates or get married until they are released from the mayor's employment."

"What has all of this have to do with anything?" said Peppino becoming impatient.

"Well let me tell you," said Gino getting excited again. "Like I said, she left me a note on my door. She said that it was very urgent that she see me this morning before she goes to work. She leaves the house at eight o'clock, so I went there at seven-thirty. She told me she heard them say that they plan for the mayor, his wife, and Biachio to go to Peppino Casolini's home and ask for the hand of their daughter, Stellina. They plan to go as soon as the fall planting is done."

"We don't have time to lose," said Peppino getting more excited than Gino. We have to warn Tano. We have to be able to say Stellina has been promised to some one else. That will require a ring."

"What are we going to do?" asked Gino.

"I don't know. We should leave early to catch Tano and my father before they leave for home." The two worked diligently for the next few hours. They filled several bags and finished the last bundle they had put aside for the day about four in the afternoon, then stored them in the shed before proceedung to Peppino's family farm. When they got there, Mr. Casolini and Tano were hard at work. They were surprised to see them.

"What are you doing here?" asked Peppino's father. "I can't believe you have finished gathering all of Mrs. Fanucci's grain."

"No," said Peppino. "We are about one third of the way through, but something important came up. Gino found out that the mayor's family is planning to come to our house and ask for Stellina's hand in marriage. I think we have to give them a reason to change their plans."

"That will require at least an engagement ring to discourage them," said Peppino's father. I'm not sure even that will do it. They are a very stubborn bunch." He then turned to Tano. "Tano, no one will blame you if you decide to forget the complete matter. The Mayor's group is no one to get mixed up with."

"No way," said Tano. "I will never give up Stellina. She is my whole life. We will weather this storm together."

"Are you sure?" asked Mr. Casolini.

"I don't have a doubt in the world," said Tano loudly and force-fully. "I'll fight for her with everything I got."

"I'll be right besides you," promised Peppino.

"Great then we don't have a thing to worry about," said Tano with great determination. "Although we would be very foolish if we thought it will not be difficult. We can't let our guard down or underestimate them."

"Now you're talking like the man I always thought you were," said Peppino's father with admiration. "Let's finish these bundles we have set aside. If you two will help Tano and me we should be done by six." They were done by five. They stored the grain in the shed except the ones that Peppino and his father were going to take home. Tano decided not to carry any sacks with his horse. No one question him. They mounted their horses and started for home.

"Will Stella have dinner ready this early?" asked Peppino of his father.

"I wouldn't be surprised," said Peppino's father. "In fact she asked that we come home a little earlier because she has a very special dinner set up for tonight."

"I'm afraid I am going to disappoint her tonight," said Tano. "I think it will be wiser for me to go straight home from here. I have to talk with my family. First, I would like to talk to my mother in private before my father gets home. Then of course I will have to talk with my father."

"Whatever you think is best," said Peppino's father. "Surely you will need their input."

"No, don't get me wrong," said Tano to clarify his goal. "There is no way they can change my mind. It's not a matter of if; it's a matter of how and when."

"I understand," said Peppino and his father in unison. "Let us know of your plans as soon as you can."

Peppino and his father arrived at their house at about five-thirty. They unloaded their burden and settled their horses in the stable.

When they entered the main room Stellina met them looking around for Tano.

"Where is Tano?" was the first thing she asked. She looked very surprised and disappointed.

"He felt it was best for him to go straight home tonight," said her father.

"Oh no," said Stellina with tears appearing in her eyes. "I made lasagna tonight. He told me that he liked lasagna best of all."

"It was best for him to go straight home tonight," said Peppino. When they had finished eating Peppino turned to Stellina.

"Tell me Stella, have you had any contact with the mayor's son, Biachio?"

"Yes," she admitted. "The other day in the afternoon when I went to the butcher for lamb, he was there with his friend Pietro. Biachio flirted and hassled me, telling me I was very beautiful and I would make a great queen after his father retires and he became mayor. I ignored him and came home. Why do you ask?"

"He is planning to come here and ask for your hand in marriage," said Peppino.

"Oh dear Lord," said Stellina with horror showing on her face. "What are we going to do? Are we in great trouble?"

"I will not let anyone near you," promised Peppino. "We are going to use diplomacy first. Tano knows the whole story. Let's wait until we hear from him."

"Is he thinking of backing out of any relationship with me?" "No, in fact he stated in no uncertain terms that he will never give you up!"

"I'm more afraid for him than anything else," said Stellina, her body shivering with fear...While they sat there thinking of what to do next they heard a knock at the door.

"I wonder who that could be this late at night?" said Mr. Casolini almost to himself. Every one looked at each other. Slowly, since no one else got up he went to the door and opened it.

"Ciao," said Tano.

"Tano, and Mr. and Mrs. DiFranco, how are you?" said Mr. Casolini, very surprised at seeing them at his door.

"We are Luigi and Lina," said Mr. DiFranco as they walked inside. "Mr. DiFranco was my father."

"All right, then I am Salvatore. What brings you out here tonight?" he asked knowing quite well what was happening.

"I'm sorry we are calling so late but after what Gaetano has told us we decided we needed to be in a hurry. We had to get my brother to open his jeweler store for us." Stellina recovering from her surprise and suddenly realizing what was happening and getting tears in her eyes ran up to Tano and hugged him. She didn't care if it was appropriate. Tano reciprocated by kissing her on the cheek. "I see we have very impatient children," said Mr. DiFranco. "I suppose we should declare why we are here. Lina and I wish to ask you for the hand of your daughter in marriage for our son, Gaetano."

"Do you understand the risk that you will be taking?" asked Mr. Casolini. "We can only hope that when the mayor hears of the engagement they will forget it to save face."

"Gaetano says he is willing to take the risk," said Tano's mother. "Well I'm not," said Stellina. "I love you Tano with my whole heart, my whole mind and my whole body, but I'd rather marry that pig than have anything happen to you. Papa, maybe you should say no to the proposal."

"I will never accept a 'no' answer," said Tano defiantly. "I'd rather die then see you in another man's arms."

"Look, we will make a big deal of this," said Mr. DiFranco "We will not only tell everyone we know and many that we don't know. We will get it into the local news paper. If things don't work out we can always cancel the engagement."

"We don't have much money but if we pool our resources together we can throw a big engagement party."

"Sound like a great plan," said Mr. DiFranco. "My brother has connections because of his jewelry store. Today is Thursday. Let's plan it for this Saturday." After that was said Tano took out his little box with the ring and offered it to Stellina.

"Will you marry me?" he asked.

"Yes," she said as Tano place the ring on her finger. With tears in her eyes, she wrapped her arms around his neck and kissed him lightly on the lips. Every one congratulated them.

"We had better be going," said Mr. DiFranco "We have a lot of planning to do. Besides, we all better get a good nights rest. It will be a hectic week."

"I will go see the priest first thing in the morning," said Mrs. DiFranco. "I suppose you will want to get married as soon as it can be arranged." Stellina let go of Tano and hugged her future mother- in-law.

"I love you, Mama," she said with sweetness in her voice. "While you are making arrangements, will you see your brother for another ring for Peppino," said Mr. Casolini. "He has a wedding of his own to plan."

"I'll have one tomorrow," promised Mr. DiFranco. "Will it be okay if it's about the same as the one Stellina has?"

"That will be great," said Peppino. They walked them to the door and said good-night. Tano and Stellina lagged behind. At the door, Tano kissed Stellina good-night.

"See you at the party," said Tano.

"Good night," said Stellina. "I can hardly wait."

The next evening when Peppino and his father got home, his father and Tano from the Casolini land and Peppino from the Fanucci land, they were surprised to see Mrs. DiFranco at the house. She had been talking to Stellina and had her very excited.

"How are you?" asked Peppino being the first to see her. "I hope you have good news for us." He knew from his sister's excitement it was good news. Tano hugged and kissed his mother and Mr. Casolini gave her a warm greeting.

"I have very good news," said Mrs. DiFranco. "First, here is the ring you requested. Please look at it and tell me if it is to your satisfaction. If it isn't we can return it for another one."

Peppino took the ring and looked at it briefly.

"It is just beautiful," he said and kissed her on the cheek. "You have beautiful taste. It is perfect."

"What do we owe you," asked Mr. Casolini.

"Let me tell you of the arrangements first," she answered. We can settle the whole thing altogether. First, everything is ready for a party tomorrow at the Correli's restaurant. We have given the information to the local paper and they promised it would be out today. I have not seen it yet, but I'm sure there is a big story in it. I have personally invited all the guests. We have also had pamphlets made out of the coming engagement and wedding. We are posting them all over town. I talked with the priest at Madonna Di Gracia church. The wedding is scheduled for next Saturday. All is ready. We are all very excited." She started toward the door when Stellina approached her.

"Won't you stay for dinner?" she asked.

"Thank you very much for asking, but I have been running around all day and I have to get home to make dinner for my husband." Stellina kissed her good-by. Tano decided to go with his mother. After closing the door behind her Stellina jumped for joy. "Oh how wonderful life is," she said so loud that the neighbors could hear.

"Settle down and feed your men," said Peppino. "We have a visit to make tonight," he said looking to his father for approval.

"I guess we had better or this house will not be livable," said his father with a big grin. They ate quickly and after grooming himself, Peppino was ready to go. To Peppino's surprise his father had groomed himself also. That was unusual for his father. Peppino wondered if his father had ulterior motives of his own. Peppino wondered what it would be like if his father fell in love with Gina's mother. If they got married would Peppino be marrying his step- sister?

They arrived at Gina's house at about seven-thirty. Peppino knocked at the door "How are you?" asked Gina as she opened the door. It was not hard to see how excited she was. She was a very intelligent woman. That was one of the reasons that Peppino loved her so much. A lot of the women of the village were mere housewives. In fact, most of the residents of the city didn't know how to read or write.

"We are all fine," said Mr. Casolini. "We would like to come in and talk to your mother."

"Of course," said Gina as she let them in. Gina's mother was in the stable washing out some of the utensils she had used to cook with. She had not expected anyone to call. When she heard the knock on the door she stayed in the stable to groom herself as much as she could under the circumstances. "Mama," called out Gina. "We have visitors." A few minutes later, her mother came out and greeted her guests.

"I'm sorry to be calling so late Mrs. Fanucci but I couldn't hold back Peppi."

"I know," said Mrs. Fanucci. "You are very busy with the engagement party, planning for the wedding and all. I'm surprised to see you. We had expected you but we thought that it would be sometime after the wedding of Stellina. Please call me Maria."

"I will call you Maria only if you call me Salvatore. Anyway, we are here to ask you for the hand of your daughter in marriage to my son Peppi."

"You know that they have my blessing. I love Peppino as if he was my own son." She then turned to Gina. "What do you have to say, joy of my heart."

Gina couldn't say a word. She was crying too much. Peppino went over to her and hugged her.

"Will you marry me?" he asked. Since she was still crying he answered for her. "I think she said yes."

Still crying she managed to answer, "Yes," she said. "With all my heart, yes." He wiped away her tears with his lips until is lips reached hers. Her body pressed against his as they kissed.

"Well Peppi," said his father getting impatient, "Give her the ring already."

"Oh, I almost forgot." He took out the little box and taking the ring out of it, he grabbed her hand and slid the ring on her finger. "I love you very much," he said as he kissed her again.

"I understand why you are having a big engagement party. Neither one of us can afford a large party. Can we just have a dinner for the family only?" asked Maria.

"I'm glad you asked," said Salvatore. "I was worried you would feel slighted."

"All I want to do, Mr. Casolini is marry your son," said Gina. "Nothing else matters."

As they walked home, Peppino and his father talked about how wonderful everything was coming together. The whole city was aware of the coming wedding. Tomorrow they will have the engagement party. Peppino was now engaged to the girl he has loved since she was twelve. Everything was perfect. Little did they know that the clear sky they now were seeing was the calm before the storm.

Chapter 3

A MOMENT OF HAPPINESS

Everything was going according to plan. The engagement party took place with great fanfare and joyous entertainment.

Half of Barrafranca was there. A small band played Stellina's and Tano's favorite music. They danced till the wee hours of the morning. The newspaper carried an extensive coverage of the engagement party and the coming wedding of Stellina Casolini and Gaetano DiFranco. Pictures of the couple were on the front page. A description of the engagement party was lengthy and expounded on the great joy and love the couple had for each other. It also gave the history of the couple from the time they first fell in love. It wrote in detail how they had secretly loved each other since she was thirteen and he was seventeen. Posters of the wedding were hung everywhere. Stellina was up early the next morning. She was so excited that she didn't sleep much that night even though she was dead tired and didn't get to bed until after one in the morning. This morning she was as perky as she ever was. Her father heard her fussing around and got up. He would have liked to sleep a little longer.

"What are you doing up so early?" he asked her.

"Papa, don't you know I will be getting married in just seven days? I have a lot of planning to do. I have to figure out what I will be wearing. Should I buy a new wedding dress? Can I even get a new one this late?"

"Honey," said her father, "I was hoping you would wear your mother's wedding dress."

"But papa, mama was about four inches shorter than me and about a foot wider. How can I fit into her dress?"

"Why don't you check with the seamstress and see what she thinks?"

"I would love to wear mama's dress. It is so beautiful. It looks so elegant in the pictures of your wedding. That dress was made for her. I don't know if I would do it justice."

"It would take some of the economic pressure off of us if you could wear it," said her father trying hard not to put pressure on her. "Papa, I have an idea," she said being sly. "Why don't I wear mama's wedding dress? I'm sure we can make it fit."

"Honey, I don't mean to put pressure on you. You will only get married once."

"That's okay papa. Let's see what the seamstress thinks."

"You had better get your brother up," reminded her father. "We will all go to church together and afterwards Tano and I will go to the farm. We have a lot of work to do. Remember we lost much of Saturday and will loose next Saturday also. I asked Tano yesterday and he said he would be ready after church."

After church, as promised, Tano showed up at Peppino's house. Gino came a little after Tano. They ate a light lunch and all left for work. Stellina cleaned up the table and sat down to contemplate her next action. The wedding was scheduled for Saturday afternoon at two o'clock. First, she would have to employ a photographer. They would invite close friends and relatives to the house for dinner. Secondly, since she was getting married she couldn't do the cooking, she would have to make arrangement for some one else to do it.. She would also need flowers. She started to write down all the things that would have to be done in the order of their importance. When she finished the list she started to think about what to plan for after the wedding din-ner. Where were she and Tano going for the first night, and were they going on a honeymoon? Did they have enough money for a honey-moon? Would the city officials let them go out of town? Normally businessmen had to get approval to leave the city limits. They had guards at all the main roads out of town. They apparently also had spies in town because they usually knew of every movement each town resident made. She was wary of asking for permission to leave town. She didn't want to attract attention in that way besides she expected a honeymoon was not a good enough excuse to leave. She will have to talk with Tano and get his input.

The day slipped by faster than Stellina had expected. She had cooking to do for the men when they came home. She had plenty of time because she was sure that they would come home late. She had everything ready when they finally got home. As she expected they didn't get home until after eight.

"I'll bet you guys are hungry," she said as she met them in the courtyard. "I have something special tonight. Since you didn't get some the last time I cooked this dinner, Tano. I made it again especially for you."

"I hope that you didn't go to an expensive dinner?" asked her father.

"Not really," she answered. "I had left over ingredients from the last time."

"Well what is it?" asked Tano being curious.

"There are two things you have to do before I tell you.""And what are they?"

"First you haven't kissed me," she complained. "Is this what our life together is going to be like after we get married?" she said teasing him.

"Come here," he said pulling her into his arms. "I'll give you a small taste of what is in store for you." He then gave her a very passionate kiss. "Now what was the second thing?"

"I don't remember," she said as her head was spinning from the kiss. "I don't remember anything."

"Well then what is for dinner?" he insisted.

"Oh, now I remember," she said. "You have to wash your hands and sit down so I can serve you. I made your favorite dinner."

"You made lasagna?"

"Now why did you go and spoil the surprise?" she said sadly. "It didn't spoil the surprise," said Tano in his defense. "I'm still very surprised. I'm also thrilled that you did it."

"It's Sunday. I will always make something special on Sundays. It'll be a kind of thanksgiving dinner remembering to thank God that he brought me you."

"Now, Papa. isn't that the sweetest thing you ever heard," Tano said to his future father-in-law.

"Yes, now stop this foolishness and let's eat. You have made me hungry for lasagna," said Stellina's father partly in jest. He was really happy to hear the romancing of the two lovers.

"Sorry papa," said Stellina. "You had better get used to it because it is going to go on for at least another fifty years."

"Dear Lord," exclaimed Mr. Casolini. "I should live that long." Stellina served them the lasagna. They all loved it and praised her for the fantastic taste of the sauce.

"Well thank you, gentlemen," she said feeling quite pleased with herself. After some coffee and cookies Peppino and Mr. Casolini decided to go to bed.

"We have to get up early tomorrow. We have to get the job done because not only do we lose Saturday, but Tano will be going on a honeymoon and will not be around for awhile. Then we will be repeating the whole thing with Peppino and his bride."

Stellina walked Tano to the door and slid outside with him away from the door.

"Show me how you are going to say ciao to me when you go to work in the mornings. I know it isn't morning, but we do need to practice so when the time comes we will not get it wrong"

"We may have to do it several times till we get it right," said Tano playing along. He kissed her several times taking plenty of time during the kiss. "We will need a lot more practice," he said finally when he had decided he had better be getting home. He knew Mr. Casolini would only tolerate their behavior for a limited time.

The next morning Peppino got up early as usual and started out to get the water. He was in a hurry to see Gina. He had missed her more than usual because of all the romance he witnessed with Stellina and Tano.

"Don't stay too long with Gina," said his father as he left.

"I won't papa," said Peppino not sure however that he could keep that promise. He got to the fountain and Gina wasn't there. It was a little earlier than he usually came. However, he thought, they were engaged, so why couldn't he just go and knock on the door. He did just that. Gina opened the door.

"Good morning sweetheart," he said. "Are you ready to go and get some water?"

"Yes I am, though you are a little earlier then usual. Let me get my jug." Before she could go in he grabbed her by the arm and pulled her outside. He put his arm around her and kissed her passionately.

"What was that for?" she asked with a silly grin on her face. "I've wanted to do that all day yesterday and all night. It's because I've had to watch Stellina and Tano last night. I overheard them said they needed a lot of practice last night outside our house when he was leaving. They were there for about a half hour. I was so jealous."

"My darling sweetheart," said Gina sorrowfully. He pulled her up tight to him attempting to kiss her again when she stopped him. "Wait before you kiss me again and I loose all of my senses, and I have to tell you something,"

"What is more important then my kisses?"

"Nothing, but I have to tell you that we are all set to have a small engagement party Wednesday evening at six. We have invited just a few friends and relatives. We have invited Tano and his family already and unless you have anyone else, all you have to do is invite your father and sister. Oh and also invite Gino if you see him first."

"Is that all?" asked Peppino.

"Yes that is all," she responded. "Now you can kiss me and make my brain drunk with your addictive love."

"Wow," said Peppino. "Do I do all of that?"

"You certainly do and a lot more! You have a strange affect which is beyond description."

"I know that one," said Peppino. "I feel that one. It is like some kind of magic that has you in its power."

"Added to all the wonderful things you are, I now find that you are also very poetic."

"Honey, you haven't seen anything yet. Just wait until we get married. I will show you magic you never knew existed."

"I can hardly wait," she said. She couldn't say more because his lips and tongue monopolized hers.

On his way home to drop off the water Peppino met Gino going for water.

"Hiya buddy," said Gino. "You are a little early this morning. Wanted 'alone time' with Gina did you?"

"Yes, and I'm kind of confused by her kisses. Where are we going this morning?"

"We are going to the Fanucci farm," said Gino. "I have finished seeding my land and am waiting for the plants to sprout. All I have to do then is dig around them so that the soil will hold water better, but you know all that. We are going to the Fanucci farm to start the seeding. After that, I can handle the rest while you go on your honeymoon. By the way, wasn't Gina supposed to help us with the seeding?"

"Oh my, I forgot to remind her," said Peppino. "I will ask her tomorrow. Oh, and she asked me to invite you to our engagement dinner Wednesday evening at six."

"That will give us even less time to finish the seeding," said Gino. "I'm overwhelmed with what has to be done in just four days."

"I'll postpone my honeymoon if I have to," promised Peppino. "Not on your life," said Gino. "That is a once in a life time thing.

I'll work day and night with a candle if I have to, but you're going on your honeymoon."

"Why do I deserve a friend like you? I don't even know if we will have enough money for a honeymoon. You know, with the cost of Stellina's wedding."

"I had better get going and get my water. I'll meet you at the school. You will have to wait for me for a change."

"I'll be there," said Peppino as he headed for home.

After dropping his water at home Peppino went to the school where he was to meet Gino. He was there only about five minutes when Gino rode up.

"You must have been flying," said Peppino. "How did you get everything done so quickly?"

"Remember, I don't need as much water as you do. I only filled my jugs half full. We need to get going if we are to finish in time." They rode the rest of the way mostly in silence. They were both deep in thought. Peppino was thinking of his coming marriage and Gino was thinking of how he was going to finish all the work by himself. When they got to the Fanucci land they were surprised to see a horse tied outside the shed and the shed door open.

"Who could be here?" asked Gino, worrying it was thieves. "What are you afraid of? asked Peppino.

"I'm only five feet eight inches tall, and not a brave man. You however, are over six feet and weighed over two hundred pounds. You ares the tallest man in town. You are also very muscular. Nothing frighten you."

"Who ever it is, is in great danger," said Peppino, ignoring Gino He jumped off his horse and ran into the shed ready to do battle.

"What has kept you guys?" said Gina as she was setting up the seed bags.

"Gina," said Peppino unclenching his fists and stopping short of running into her. "What are you doing here?"

"I told you I was going to help with the seeding," she answered continuing to prepare the bags.

"I almost jumped on you. I thought you were a thief."

"You will have to wait until we are married. Then I will let you jump on me," kidded Gina.

"Very funny," said Peppino relaxing somewhat. "You have scared the daylights out of Gino."

"I wasn't scared," responded Gino. "I knew I had a little giant to protect me."

"Don't you repeat that outside to anyone else. I would hate to have people refer to me as the little giant."

"I'm glad you are a little giant," said Gina. "Since I am unusually tall for a woman, we fit each other perfectly. I would have a hard time finding a man if it wasn't for you Peppino. No man likes a woman that is taller than him."

45

"You are pretty tall at that," said Gino. "How tall are you?" "The last time I checked, which was about a year ago. I was about five feet, eight inches. I think I have grown some since then. Anyway, let's get to work. How do we proceed with seeding?"

"The usual way," instructed Peppino, "is to take the small bag hang it in front of you with the straps around your neck. We will place the seeds in the furls we plowed earlier. We will each take a row. We will have enough seeds to go up one row and down another. When we get back, we will take the shovel and go back up the rows, cover and pack the dirt on the seeds. When we get back we will refill the bags and repeat the process allover for the next rows. We will each take a row and work up together. We will cover six rows at a time."

"Sounds easy enough," said Gina. "I have already filled the bags so lets get started." They worked together up and down the rows. "I am so happy you came today," said Peppino while they were seeding up the rows. "I like being with you during the day. We work well together."

"I like working with you too," said Gina. "I want to be near you all the time. Get used to it because whether I work or not I will be out here in the field with you. I hate the life of most women who stay home and only see their men at night."

"When or who would cook dinner if you are out here with me?" asked Peppino.

"As long as my mother is alive she will do the cooking. Anyway it will only be for a little while. When we have children it will be a different story."

"I like your thinking," said Peppino with a big smile. They worked until twelve noon. They finished the rows they were onand decided to eat lunch. Peppino pulled out his lunch bag and removed a chunk of bread and a few olives.

"Put that away," said Gina with a sly smirk. "I'm not going to let my men eat bread and water,"

"What do you have for us?" asked Peppino, getting hopeful for something good. She opened a bag and pulled out what looked like a small loaf of bread that looked more like a large bun. "What is this? Are we to eat bread alone?"

"Don't get smart," said Gina. "Just start eating it. The surprise will come later." Peppino took a big bite of the bun and suddenly his eyes opened wide with a look of wondrous surprise.

"What in the world?" he said as he looked at the end of the bread where he had just taken a bite. "What's this inside the bread?" "What does it look like?" asked Gina with a big satisfied smile on her face.

"You baked a link of sausage in the bread? How did you do that?" "It's a Fanucci secret, which was passed down through the ages."

"I know that my mother tried once but the sausage juice soaked the bread all around it and it tasted like wet bread," said Peppino. Then turning to Gino he asked, "Gino, have you eaten anything like this before?" Gino looked up and kept on eating. When asked again he just shook his head.

"See that?" said Peppino to Gina. "It's so good he won't even look up from his food."

"I'm glad he likes it," said Gina. "And how do you like it?" Peppino licked his lips.

"Honey, it is the best lunch I've ever had and on top of that the nicest surprise I've ever had. This is fantastic."

"Well fellows," said Gina. "Wipe your lips and pat your bellies and let's get back to work."

"I think by getting married I will not receive a wife but I will have a new mother," complained Peppino.

"I think you are very lucky to be mothered by some one like Gina," said Gino. "I wish I had some one who loves me enough to mother me."

"Keep quiet, Gino," said Peppino. "You're not helping. You're a fellow. You should be sticking with me. We fellows should stick together. You lie and I'll swear to it."

"Very funny guys," said Gina. "I can give orders now while I'm single. After I'm married, Peppi will be the head of the family and I will obey him." Both Gino and Peppino laughed out loud.

"Sure…" They both said simultaneously, continuing to laugh. Gina continued to work, ignoring them. She knew in her heart that Peppino believed her. He also knew that when she ordered them to get back to work she was just kidding and trying to be funny. They worked the rest of the day and gave up when it got too dark to continue.

"Honey," said Peppino. "I don't want you to travel alone though God knows you can take care of yourself. I don't want to take any chances. So I will follow you home tonight, and please wait for me tomorrow morning."

"You're the boss," said Gina smirking under her breath. Both Gino and Peppino smiled. No one said a word. Peppino did see her home and they agreed on a time for the next day. Peppino went home where Stellina had a nice hot dinner waiting for her men. It was only about ten minutes later that Mr. Casolini and Tano arrived from their work. They sat down to eat. Mr. Casolini said grace and they ate hardily being very hungry from the day's toil.

After dinner, they sat for awhile trading small talk about the day's events. Stellina kept unusually quite. When Tano was ready to leave Stellina walked him to the door. He pulled her outside and hid behind the wall next to the door. He kissed her passionately and after a few more pecks he asked her if everything was all right?" "Yes, please don't worry," she assured him. I'm just tired. I'm also very excited. Today I went and had the final fitting of my wedding dress. You will never believe how beautiful it is. It was my mother's; my dad wanted me to wear it. I wasn't too thrilled at the idea at first, but the seamstress did such a great job. You would never recognize it as the one my mother wore. It's bad luck for you to see it before the wedding otherwise I would show it to you. After you leave, I will show it to my father. You ask him tomorrow. He will tell you how gorgeous it is."

"I can hardly wait," he said impatiently.

"It will only be a couple of days and you will see it as I walk down the isle."

"I'd better leave," he said "I'll go crazy with anticipation."

"Go, I'll see you at Peppino's engagement party tomorrow night." He gave her a good night kiss that lasted several minutes and then he departed.

"Papa," she said getting excited. "I had the last fitting of my wedding dress today. I brought the dress home. If you want to see it I will go and put it on. I'm sure glad I listened to you. It is the most beautiful dress you will ever see."

"By all means. I'd love to see it on you," said her father getting excited also.

"I am dying to see it too," said Peppino. Stellina left and returned about ten minutes later. She looked like a princes out of the fairytale books. Both her father and Peppino stood there with their mouths wide open. Stellina spoke first.

"I can see by the look on your faces that you like it as much as I do," she said being very pleased.

"There are no words to express how beautiful you look," said Peppino. "I have always regarded you as the most beautiful girl in town, but now you are beyond even gorgeous. And it isn't all because of the dress. It is you that makes the dress look fantastic." "You're my brother," said Stellina, very pleased at his remarks.

"You are biased. What do you think papa?"

"Honey, I'm speechless," said her father just coming out of the trance he slipped into at the sight of her. "Your mother was the picture of perfection in that dress. You have out done even her."

"I'm very pleased with it too, Papa. I'm so glad I listen to you." "I can't get over it," said her brother. "I only hope that Gina will look half as good as you do."

"Don't worry," said Stellina. "Your love will make her look twice as good as me no matter what she is wearing."

"Do you really think so?"

"I know so," she answered. "Just wait and remember that I told you so." She then went and changed her dress making sure it didn't get soiled.

The next morning Peppino went for water and stopped at Gina's house. He knocked on the door. Gina answered.

"Good morning, Sweetest Fruit on the HumanTree," he said, feeling romantic. After all they were going to have an engagement dinner tonight.

"Good morning," said Gina laughing. "That was sweet but not to poetic."

"Sweet is okay," he said as he walked inside passed her. "Signora Fanucci," he said to his future mother-in-law. "Is there anything you need that I could do for you before we leave for the farm?"

"All that I need for tonight I have already purchased," she answered Peppino. "You can help Gina get all the water I will need for today. Since she will be gone most of the day she will not be here to refill my jugs. Don't you think it is time you call me mother? It is a matter of days before it becomes official."

"Of course, Mama," he said with a loving smile. "I'll help Gina." "I'm going to come home at noon to help you mama," said Gina.

"I think we have the seeding under control. Between the three of us we should be done by Friday." Peppino and Gina got all the water that she needed and left for Peppino's house to bring water to Stellina.

"Don't worry about your mother," said Stellina to Gina. "After I clean up here I will go to your house and help her."

"Oh Stellina," said Gina gratefully, "You are such an angel. I am going to love being part of this family."

"We are the lucky ones," added Peppino. After unloading the water, Peppino and Gina left for the farm. They met Gino at the school and all three went to work on Mrs. Fanucci's field. They worked all morning.

"I feel like we are already married," said Gina. "I feel the happiness just being with you."

"Yes, we have everything but the best part of marriage," said Peppino with a shy look, as if he had gotten away with something. "Now don't get crude, Peppi," said Gina pretending to be bashful because of his statement.

"I'm talking about the comfort of having a marriage certificate. A certificate gives us the authority to be together forever."

"I understand," said Gina with a look on her face that indicated that she didn't believe him.

"What I am saying is you are only mine for now but tonight you will belong to your mother," said Peppino trying to recover from his embarrassment.

"I understood what you meant the first time," she said trying to prolong his embarrassment.

"You are going to leave before lunch aren't you?" said Peppino changing the subject. "So are we on our own for lunch?"

"Now I wouldn't do that to you," she said with that sly grin Peppino loved to see on her. "First I am going to leave right after lunch," she continued. "Secondly I brought something special for you guys today." She then opened a package that she had brought in her saddle bags. There were four separately wrapped packages. She handed each of the boys a package. Each unwrapped their package and stared at what they found in their hands. It was two slices of bread with something green, brown and yellow all mixed and rather solid squeezed between the bread.

"What is this?" asked Peppino. "I don't recognize the stuff in between the slices of bread."

"That is what my family call frittata di asparagi. It is several asparagus spears fried with eggs. It makes a great sandwich. Taste it. You'll like it I'm sure." Peppino and Gino took a bite of the sandwich.

"Mmmm," said Peppino. "I see I'm going to enjoy marriage with this woman more than I had anticipated."

"I hope that you are going to invite me to dinner often," said Gino. "You almost got me wanting to get married."

"God forbid," said Gina. They all laughed. After they ate, Gina saddled her horse and she left.

"I miss her already," said Peppino. It was almost like the sun went out. Peppino felt hollow inside as if his whole life had lost its luster. The joy he had been feeling was gone. The thought that he would be seeing her tonight gave him the will to go on. The next few hours were empty and lasted much too long…

"Boy, Buddy," said Gino, noticing the change in Peppino. "You really have it bad don't you?"

"You don't know the half of it," said Peppino. "It's like nothing is worth doing anymore. The fun of working is gone."

"Cheer up fellow," said Gino…He thought of saying something funny to raise his spirits but decided that this wasn't the time. "Before you know it we will be at your engagement party."

"I guess you are right," said Peppino. They hastily worked the rest of the day and quit at about four-thirty.

"I want to clean up before I go to Gina's house. I don't really know who will be there."

"Let's go," said Gino. He was glad it was over. The afternoon had been kind of depressing for Gino also. "With Gina's help we have done more than I expected we would have done. We still have Thursday and Friday, but I don't think we will need much of Friday." When Peppino got home his father and Stellina were waiting for him. Tano had already left for his house. Gino had gone straight home to get cleaned up and would meet him at Gina's house. "Hurry and get ready," requested Stellina. "You don't want to be late for your own engagement party, do you?"

"I'll be just a minute," answered Peppino. "Anyway they can't start without me." He took care of his horse first. Afterwards he went inside washed up and changed his clothes. He was ready in just ten minutes. The three of them left for Gina's house. Peppino was surprised at how well his father was dressed. He was too excited and too nervous over his own situation that he didn't make a comment. He also was aware at how beautiful Stellina looked in her sexy black dress.

When they arrived at the Fanucci's house, it was full of people. Peppino noticed that Tano's mother and father were there. Peppino's father addressed them first.

"Ciao, Luigi, Lina," he said. "It's so good to see you both. How are you both? Are you ready for the wedding on Saturday?"

"Can a parent ever really be ready?" said Lina DiFranco. "I suppose not," responded Salvatore.

"Have you met my brother and his wife?" asked Luigi.

"I've seen them but I have not met them socially." Luigi called out to his brother and his wife.

"Michele, Antonietta will you come here a minute." When they came to him he introduced them and their son, Antonio. The Women kissed each other on both cheeks as did the men.

"She sure is a beautiful lady," said Michele. "Gaetano is a very lucky man."

Peppino, Stellina and Nino started their own conversation away from their parents.

"Attention every one," announced Maria Fanucci. "Dinner is ready. If you all will take a seat at the table we will start serving." There was a large table setting that took up most of the main room of the house.

It was an arrangement of three smaller tables set against each other to make one large setting. Every one sat down. As they were sitting Gino arrived and sat down next to Tano. They exchanged salutations and Tano pointed out to Gino who every one was. Gino recognized Nino but few of the others. Maria, Stellina, and Giuseppina a neighbor who offered to help started serving. First, they served a bowl of minestrone soup. Next, they served a dish of spaghetti. When that was consumed a thin steak cooked over a charcoal grill was served, and last was served all different types Italian deserts. The last things placed on the table were several bowls of assorted fruit. When they had finished their desert, Salvatore Casolini got up and raised his wine glass.

"I would like to make a toast for my son Peppino and his lovely fiancée Gina. May they always find laughter and enduring love in their lives." Every one raised their glasses and drank to the young couple. "I also want to show our gratitude to Maria, Stellina, and Giuseppina for the fantastic dinner and the regal way they served it." Every one raised their glass in agreement. Soon every one got up and casually assembled in small groups. In one of the groups were Nino, his father and Gino. Peppino walked up as Gino was talking.

"What's the matter, Nino," asked Gino. "You were always so active when we hung together. Is working for the Duke getting hard on you?"

"No, I'm fine," said Nino. I'm just not in the mood tonight." "Come on, Nino," added Peppino to the conversation. "I know you. I know when something is wrong. What is the problem? Maybe we can help."

"I'll tell you what the problem is," responded his father. "We had planned on going to Angelina LaFonti's house to ask for her hand in marriage. However when Nino mentioned it to Angelina, she said that she couldn't marry him."

"How did you know her?" asked Peppino. "Since you stayed at the Duke's bunk house all week, when did you have time?"

"I met her every morning at the fountain of litica. She gets water for herself and it was my job to get water for the duke's household."

"Wait a minute," said Gino suddenly. "Now that I think about it I know her too. She lives with her mother and two other women, Rosina and my friend Anna Maria. They are all servants at the mayor's household. Nino, she isn't rejecting you. She really can't see you formally. It is a rule of the mayor that all help has to be available at all times and can't get involved with anyone. If they find out that she is seeing any one she would be seriously punished. I know I have strong feelings for Anna Maria and I have to sneak around after dark to see her."

"Really," said Nino. "I feel a lot better. How come she is allowed to live at home?"

"There are only a few that are allowed to live at home. The cook, the butler, and the chauffeur are required to live in the north wing. They don't want any of the other servants milling around. I don't know why. Perhaps the mayor and his wife walk around naked at night. Who knows why? All the servants have to be on immediate call day or night. Do you understand, Nino? Angelina can't get involved with you until she is released from her job."

"When and how could that happen?" asked Nino getting hopeful. "I love her so much. I want to spend the rest of my life with her. I thought that she felt the same."

"I sneak in to see Anna Maria ever-so-often. Let me find out what I can and I'll get back to you."

"Since you are a builder for the city, don't you have some pull with the mayor?" asked Peppino.

"Are you jesting? I'm happy that I'm alive. He treats me lower than one of his servants."

"You have done a lot of work for the city, haven't you?" asked Peppino.

"Yes," he answered. "I built the north wing for the mayor's palace and I built the new city hall. I also built the jail there at the edge of the cliff north of the city. That was the hardest job of all. They even have an isolation cell. It's more like a dungeon. It is hidden so that most of the jailers don't know about it. It is underground, below the other cells. It is accessible through a secret wall at the end of the cell isle. The wall pivots back exposing a stairway that leads to the cell. Now, you fellows keep this under your hats. You never heard of this cell, right?"

"What cell?" said Peppino.

"What did you say about a bell?" asked Gino.

"Good boys," said Nino's father. "What are your plans?"

"After my sister gets married to Tano, they will move in and Tano will take my place helping my father. I will marry Gina and move in with her and her mother and I will take care of their land." "Sounds like a wonderful future for all of you. I surely wish you all a lot of love happiness and luck in everything you do."

"Thank you, sir," responded Peppino. After Michele turned and started to talk to his brother Luigi, Peppino searched out Gina.

"Here it is our engagement party and I haven't seen much of you all night," complained Peppino.

"I know," agreed Gina. "Some of the people are wandering outside. Why don't we join them and quietly sneak around the corner."

"No wonder I love you so much," said Peppino. "I'll meet you outside." As they wandered outside, they spoke a word to each person they met until they both met at the outskirts of the crowd. Separately they slipped around the corner where they were alone in the dark. They didn't say a word to each other. There lips just found each other and feasted passionately. They didn't know how long they were out there kissing. They did notice that the conversational noise around the corner slowly diminished. Apparently, people were going home.

"Should we go inside where people could find us to say ciao," asked Peppino.

"My mother will come looking for us when we are needed." No sooner had Gina finished talking that they heard Gina's mother call out.

"Gina where are you?" she yelled. "People are leaving and would like to say good night." Peppino and Gina slowly went into the house and were greeted by well-wishers who hugged them and wished them a good life. Soon every one was gone and all that was left was a lot of cleaning up to do. Gina's mother didn't say a word about where they were.

"You can leave if you want, Peppino," said Gina's mother. "I know you will have to get up early tomorrow."

"No, Mama," he responded. "I want to help. Besides, with Gina's help we have been able to get more done then we expected. We have about a day and a half day's work left."

"If you want to help, will you fold the tables and make them ready to return to the church tomorrow. My neighbor will help me bring them back." Peppino and Gina worked together to clean up. They were deliriously happy to be working together. When the work was completed it was very hard for the two love birds to part.

"I don't want this day to end," said Gina.

"I don't either," said Peppino. "But if you walk me to the door I'll leave after you say ciao ciao."

"You two had plenty of ciao ciao before so don't delay," said Gina's mother with a knowing smile. Peppino gave Gina a good night kiss that lasted longer then they expected and Peppino left.

"Come get me tomorrow and I'll help with the seeding," yelled Gina as Peppino was walking down the road.

The next morning Peppino was at Gina's door at six. He had filled his jugs with water and hesitated at her door, letting Gina get as much sleep as she could. When he knocked at the door, her mother answered.

"Gina is still sleeping," she said whispering. "I just didn't have the heart to awaken her."

"That's all right," said Peppino. "Why don't you give me your jugs and I will fill them while she sleeps."

"You're a real sweetheart. Do you know that?" said Gina's mother. "I don't know how to thank God for you."

"I'm going to be part of this family pretty soon," said Peppino. "I'm just helping my mother."

"God bless you son." Peppino got the jugs as quietly as he could and went to the fountain and filled them up.

"I'll take the large jug and filled it up too," said Peppino when he got back. "You may need the extra water since Gina will be coming with me." It was a large jug like the one he had on his horse. It was very heavy when it was full. Peppino had a difficult time bringing it back to Gina's house. He told himself that the next time he would get her water first and use his horse to transport it. He would get his water last. When he had finished he heard Gina's voice.

"Mama, why haven't you got me up? What time is it? Peppino will be here soon and I'm not ready."

"He has been here, and he has gotten the water while waiting for you to wake up," said her mother. "Get dressed and I'll get you both some breakfast."

"Do I have time for breakfast?" she said looking at the clock. "Peppino wouldn't let me wake you," said her mother in her defense. "He wanted you to get as much rest as you needed. So did I for that matter." Just then Peppino walked in with the large jug.

"So you are up sleepy head," he said kidding her.

"Go outside while I dress and I'll be ready in a minute," requested Gina. After he had gone outside she turned to her mother. "Isn't he just an angel?"

"Just an angel," repeated her mother. After Gina called him in they ate breakfast and headed to Peppino's house to drop off the water.

They left for the Fanucci land. Peppino's father and Tano had already left for their land. Gino showed up about ten minutes later. He had gone to see Anna Maria before she left for work. He was told that Angelina loved Nino very much and she didn't know what to do. She planned to ask for a release from her job. But her hopes weren't too high.

The day seemed to stretch out longer than usual. Two more days and Stellina would be married to Tano. Then Peppino and Gina could set their date. The thought make them work harder. While they were working, Peppino couldn't take his eyes off of Gina. Even with old clothes and a dirty face, she was so much more beautiful than any one he knew. The only one who came close, thought Peppino, was his sister who was no where near as tall as Gina. The height make Gina look like the slim models he had seen in the magazines.

"What?" said Gina noticing he was staring at her and seemed to be deep in thought.

"What are you asking?" said Peppino shocked out of his thoughts. "What is on your mind?" she asked. "I see that you are deep in thought."

"I was thinking how beautiful you are even when you are not all dressed to kill. I can't imagine how you will look in your wedding dress. It will probably drive me nuts."

"That's what you say now," she countered. "Tell me that when we are married a few years and I have gotten fat and wrinkled."

"You can get fat and ugly and I will still think you are the most beautiful lady in the world. Besides I will never let you get fat." They both laughed and continued working. They were finished with a large section of the land and decided to quit for the day and go home. It was about six.

When they got home, Tano and Peppino's father were already there. Stellina had a very nice dinner ready for them. Gino decided to go straight home. He had a lot to take care of.

"How is it that you got home before us?" Peppino asked his father.

"Tano was driving me crazy, that's why," said his father. "He kept asking me the time every two minutes. We have to get these two married or they will drive us mad."

Tano could only smile shyly. It was true so what could he say. After dinner, Tano left for home and Peppino, his father and Stellina sat back to relax and discuss what they had yet to do to prepare for the wedding. When they were about to go to bed there was a knock on the door.

"Who could this be this late at night?" said Peppino's father. "I'll get it and send who ever it is away," said Peppino.

"Tell them to come tomorrow night," said Stellina. Peppino got to the door and opened it. There was a few minutes of silence.

"I'm sorry to be so late," said the elder man. "But I couldn't dissuade my son. May we come in?"

"Of course Signore DiVincenso, come in. How are you Signora DiVincenso?" Mario DiVincenso, Lucia DiVincenso and their son, Biachio, entered. Peppino's father offered them a chair.

"To what do we owe this honor?" he asked but was afraid of the answer.

"My son has taken a liking of your daughter and we are here to ask for her hand in marriage to my son Biachio."

"That's impossible," said Stellina before any one else could answer. I'm engaged to be married." She said showing them her ring. We are getting married in two days. My fiancé' and I have been in love since I was twelve years old. I can never love anyone else."

"Since you are not yet married that could be changed," said the mayor. "As for love, it will come after the honeymoon. Before you answer, let me explain the benefits. First, you will be treated as a princess. You will live in the palace. Your father will not need to work ever again. Your children will be of the upper class," he added. Lucia, the mayor's wife, didn't say a word. It was apparent that she was not at all happy with the situation. "They will get extra treatment where ever they go. And one of them will become mayor some day," continued the Mayor.

"But I love some one else," said Stellina not wanting to give out Tano's name. She was sure that they knew who he was but she wasn't going to parade it.

"Well look," said the mayor. "Think about it for a few days and we will get back to you."

"I think that you will change your mind," said Biachio in a threatening voice. They left and Stellina ran to her bed in the rear of the room, and fell on it crying.

"What are we going to do?" she said not expecting an answer. "You are going to get married as planned," said Peppino shaking with great anger that carried in his voice. "Two days from now you will be married and that will end it."

"Wait," urged his father. "Let's wait until tomorrow. We will have to discuss this with Tano." After much sadness they all went to bed. Peppino, after several hours of tossing and turning, finally went to sleep to the sound of Stellina crying.

In the morning at about six Tano knocked at the door.

"Is every one still sleeping," he said knocking at the door again. A few minutes later Peppino answered the door. "What's going on here is every one sick?" As soon as Stellina heard his voice she ran and threw her arms around him — still full of tears and still in her nightgown.

"My darling Tano, please hold me tight and never let go," she said with tears streaming down her face. Tano tried to wipe away her tears with his lips but there were too many tears.

"Someone tell me what has happened," said Tano with some tears showing in his eyes. "Please, what is wrong?" Neither Peppino nor his father could talk. They were too choked up. Finally Peppino pulled them both inside and closed the door. He then explained to the terrified Tano what had occurred late last night.

"You understand what that means?" asked Peppino's father.

"It doesn't mean anything," said Tano defiantly. "I am still going to marry Stellina Saturday."

"Well let's think about this, Tano," said Peppino's father. "We will always love you like our own son. Stellina will always love you. However, think about what may happen. If you are married and the mayor's son still wants her then the only way he can have her is if she is a widow. Do you see what I'm saying? Do you want to gamble your life?"

"No, that is not acceptable," said Stellina. "I would rather marry that pig than have something happen to you. Papa, cancel the wedding. I will not risk Tano's life."

"Just a minute," said Tano. "I have something to say about this." "No you don't. I am breaking our engagement."

"Honey, listen to me," said Tano begging Stellina to listen to him. "First of all they may very well back off. They don't want the people of the city to accuse them of murder. That would be a pretty big and dangerous step for them to take. Secondly, I'm the one who is taking the risk. It is not in your hands. But most of all listen to me and believe me with all of your heart. I would rather die then see you in another man's arms. Don't you understand? You are my life. Without you I may as well be dead. I will die just thinking of you in someone else's bed. I could never take it. Could you imagine me in some other woman's bed?"

"Oh, Tano," she said crying again. "I don't know what to do." "There is only one thing to do and that is to get married. If they kill me, so what? I would have died a worse death seeing you in some one else's arms."

"Papa," said Stellina looking for help from her father. "What should I do?"

"I understand perfectly what Tano is saying. I felt the same way about your mother. As long as we trust in God and accept him we will all eventually meet in heaven. But the decision is yours."

"Help me, Peppino," she begged "What should I do?"

"Sweet sister," said Peppino. "It is really only Tano's decision. I will back you up with everything I have, including my life. If the problem was between me and Gina, I would make the same decision that Tano is making."

"Stella, sweetheart," said Tano very seriously. I release you of any fault if anything happens to me. I will never let you go. If they come and take you by force then I will die trying to rescue you. Therefore, if you marry me or not, the risk to my life will be the same. I don't want to live without you."

"Tano," she said with love in her eyes. "Do you mean everything you are saying? Don't you want to think about it for a day or so?"

"Every word comes from my heart. I don't have a day or so. Peppino and I will watch each other's back." Stellina threw her arms around him and kissed him passionately.

"I hope that I will not be sorry," she said and kissed him again. "If we only have a few days, then we will at least have that," said Tano. To me that would be worth the risk."

"Well, until Saturday we are all going to stay home," said their father. "We will take no chances. They are cowards. They will not attack a group. After the wedding, you and Stellina could move into grandpa's and grandma's house. It has been vacant since Grandma died. We offered it to Peppino but he decided to stay in the little room next to the stable." They all agreed.

It was late Friday afternoon when Tano's mother, Lina, came to the house. She came in and sat down at the kitchen table.

"What is it?" said Tano seeing his mother looking sad.

"I went to the church to make arrangements for the flowers," she started. Stellina and her father gathered around upon hearing her saddened voice. "When I got there Father Penisi pulled me aside and told me that the wedding was off. I asked him why. He said that he couldn't perform the wedding because of certain things that had to be cleared up. I asked him if the mayor had gotten to him. Do you know what he said to me? He said he didn't want his church burned down."

"Even the priests bow down to the mayor's gang of thieves," said Peppino being very angry. "I'll go talk to him."

"Don't bother," said Lina. "He is like a scared rabbit. We will have to find another way."

"Are you willing to continue at the apparently increased risk to have Tano marry Stellina?" asked Peppino.

"At some place you have to put your feet down and say that's enough," said Lina.

"How about you Tano and you Stellina," asked Peppino.

"I have already answered that question," said Tano. "I'll fight till the death"

"I wish you would put it another way," said Stellina. "But I'm with my husband all the way. As of right now, he is my husband. I'm willing to exchange vows now before God and you witnesses. God is just and he knows we tried the right way."

"You may not have too," said Peppino. "If you are still set on getting married I have a possible solution. You should get married by the church. You will need a marriage certificate. I'm thinking of Father Nicola. He is retired but I think he can still marry and provide the required documents. I also don't think he is afraid of the mayor's hoodlums. I'm going to see him right now" Peppino was out of the door in less than five minutes.

About an hour later Peppino returned to the house.

"Stellina, go put on your wedding dress," instructed Peppino. "Tano you go home and get your parents. Father Nicola will be here in about an hour. He is getting all the documents ready in duplicate. He says he will send a copy to Rome before anyone knows you are married. Make sure your parents don't tell anyone. We can't trust anyone." Tano left, and Stellina with the happiest smile Peppino had ever seen, rushed to get into her wedding dress. Mama Lina helped her looking beautiful for the ceremony.

The Casolini house was full of people when father Nicola arrived. Peppino had informed Gina, and she and her mother were there. The DiFranco family was there. Gino and Nino were there. Nino had brought his parents. Peppino had rounded up two friends, one who played the guitar and the other played the mandolin. The service was quick and sweet. Stellina's father escorted Stellina to the priest and the waiting Tano. Tano was in a state of shock at seeing Stellina being escorted to him. She was more beautiful in her wedding dress than he had ever imagined. After a few words from the priest, they exchanged rings. When the priest announced that they were husband and wife, everyone cheered. The witnesses signed the documents and a copy given to Tano. Their life long dreams had come true. The happiness showed brightly on their faces. Tano's mother Lina, Gina and her mother served the dinner to all the guests. Tano and Stellina were in heaven. Peppino's friends played beautiful music in the courtyard. Everyone got to dance. Too soon the festivities came to an end. Every one left except Tano's parents and Gina and her mother.

"We have fixed Grandpa's house for you two to live in," said Stellina's father. "Your mother-in-law and Mrs. Fanucci have stocked the cabinets with food for a couple of weeks. I don't know what your plans are but I recommend until a little time goes by that you stay indoors. Let the mayor and his crowd cool off."

"Papa, this was so sudden that we didn't have time for plans," said Stellina. "But I think that you are right. We will stay in grandpa's house for now if that is okay with you, Tano."

"All I want to do is spend the rest of my life with you," said Tano. "Where, is not important. We can lock the door and have our honeymoon in there. Papa and Peppino will see that we are not disturbed."

"You bet," said Peppino. "Even papa and I will not disturb you either. You want something you will have to come out to get it. Also, we have always left the front wall door to the courtyard open. Papa and I are going to install a big bolt lock and the door will be locked whether we are here of not. The courtyard will always be secure. We will have to install some kind of a bell so that people can announce their prescence." Stellina hugged her brother.

"Thanks for everything, big loving brother." She then hugged her mother-in-law tightly. "Thank you mama, thanks for giving me your most precious possession, your son." She then hugged her father-in law. "I'll always love you, Papa." She then turned to Gina and her mother. "How special you two are. What would we do without you?" she hugged them both. "I can't wait until Peppino becomes a part of your family. Everything then will be perfect." Tano was saying his thanks and good-byes as Stellina was finished with Gina and her mother. Tano's parents left and Peppino followed Gina and her mother to the door of the courtyard.

"I'll walk a little ahead," said Gina's mother. "That will give you a little time to say good-bye."

"Have you ever heard of a sweeter mother," said Peppino.

"Never mind the sweet words. Don't take too long. I don't want to be out alone this late at night."

"We will have our eye on you," said Gina. They kissed for a few minutes.

"You know, Peppino. I was jealous of Stellina tonight. I was wishing it was you and me."

"I know I was wishful too, but we will have our day soon. We had better go. Your mother is almost out of sight. I'll walk you both home."

"Where are you going," said Gina's mother after they caught up to her.

"You didn't think I was going to let the two most beautiful and precious ladies in my life walk home alone, did you?"

"I understand," Gina's mother answered. "You are hoping for another chance at a good night kiss. Although I don't think it has ever been just one good night kiss."

"Mama you are just too smart for us," said Peppino. "Don't encourage her," said Gina. They all laughed.

Stellina and Tano did not leave their one room building for two weeks. They didn't even venture into the courtyard. Peppino and his father along with Gino worked the land the best that they could. The joy and happiness that Stellina and Tano had during those two week, were beyond there greatest expectations. The happiness they felt radiated from the walls of their home. Peppino and his father could feel it in the evenings when they got home. Although they didn't spend too much time at home because they were invited to Gina's home most evenings for dinner.

Chapter 4

HEIGHT OF TERROR

Biachio met his best friend Pietro at the police station where Pietro's father was chief of police.

"Ciao, Pietro. What are you up too?"

"Nothing is happening," said Pietro. "I wish there was a robbery or something."

"You're not even a policeman," said Biachio. "What do you care?"

"How are you coming with your girlfriend, Stellina?" asked Pietro changing the subject.

"I'm kind of letting my proposal sink in," answered Biachio. "You know my father reluctantly closed down all the churches so they can't get married. You know that my parents are strongly against this marriage, especially my mother."

"So I've heard. It's been over two weeks now," said Pietro ignoring his own parental problems. He knew Biachio was going to do what he wanted "When are you going to act?"

"I guess it's been long enough. I think I'll go over tonight and apply some pressure, but for now, how about you and I going for a ride out in the country. I feel like getting some fresh air."

"Sound great," said Pietro. "I'll get my horse and meet you at your place." Ten minutes later they met and rode their horses across the country. It didn't matter if they destroyed some plants on the way. No one was going to complain. After all, the owners were just peasants. The land really belonged to the mayor. After their joyride they retreated to their favorite bar and drank themselves silly.

Tano and Stellina finally came out of their honeymoon seclusion. They wanted to meet other members of the family, to share the great joy they were experiencing. No one was home so Stellina decided to cook a great dinner for them all. After all, this was the setting they would be in the rest of their lives. Stellina would cook dinner for her father and her husband and have it ready for them when they come home from working the land.

"You had better go see your mother and Mrs. Fanucci to make sure they don't have anything cooking for them."

"That is a good idea," said Tano. "However I think we should go together. They will want to see us both and also we should keep together for safety reasons. Your brother is going to be very angry with us for even going out. We can stop at the store and get something good for dinner so it will be easier for them to forgive us."

"You're sneaky do you know that, sweetheart," said Stellina. "It's not being sneaky," responded Tano. "I'm being a little prudent. Sometimes it pays to use a little wisdom." "Oh," said Stellina. "Is that what you call it?"

"Yes, now what do you suggest would be a good dinner that will calm their wrath."

"I was thinking of cooking a great dinner anyway. It will be the first of the many I will be cooking for my family. I was thinking of lamb. I hear that there is an abundant of lamb at this time of year." They reached Tano's house and before they could knock his mother ran out and hugged them both.

"I'm so glad to see you both," she said while still hugging them. "We have missed you so much."

"Mama," said Tano being surprised at her actions. "What were you doing, looking out the door for us? You ran out like you knew we were coming. You ended up surprising us rather than the other way around."

"I was just looking out the door when I saw the two of you coming down the street. I was just ready to come outside to get some air. Will you two stay for dinner?"

"No, mama," said Stellina. "We would love it some other time.

Are you cooking for my father-in-law and my brother tonight?" "No, your father wants to stay home. He is usually very tired. He hasn't been here for several days. They have spent several days with Maria and her daughter Gina. Peppino of course wants to spend time with his fiancée. I also think your father has a thing for Maria." "You've noticed that too have you?" said Stellina. "This is our first day out. We haven't seen them or any one for over two weeks. I would like to cook something special for them tonight but I didn't want to spoil some one else's plans."

"We have asked them every day when we can find them. They do make us happy and come sometimes. Tonight is not one of those days. I would recommend checking with Maria before you start a big dinner."

"Thanks, Mama," said Tano. They stayed a little while and visited. After a while however they thought they had better visit with Gina and her mother before they started anything.

When they got to Gina's house everything seemed quiet. Stellina knocked on the door. After a few minutes Gina answered the door. "Ciao, Stella and Tano," said Gina. "It's so good to see you. I'm sorry I can't let you in because my mother is very sick. I think it is the flu."

"That all right," said Stellina. "I'm guessing that my brother and father will not be coming tonight. We just came out of our house today. We haven't seen them for over two weeks."

"You haven't come out even for a minute?" asked Gina, surprised. "You have that secluded courtyard that is nice to sit out in at night." "We needed two weeks alone," said Stellina. "You wait until you and Peppi get married. You will understand then." "I get the picture."

"Well we will have to go and buy some food. I would like to cook something special for our men tonight."

"Our men," said Gina with a smile. "I love the sound of that. Have fun and tell Peppi that I love and miss him very much"

"I certainly will," said Stellina as she waved good-bye. They got to the butcher and found all the meats were on sale. Stellina chose some nice lamb chops. That evening when Peppino and his father came home they got an unexpected surprise. The dinner was fabulous. They all over ate and sat down to some coffee and cookies they had left over from the wedding. They were sitting there enjoying each other's company when they heard a knocking at the courtyard door.

"Ignore it," said Mr. Casolini. Our friends and relatives know where the rope is to ring the bell." No sooner did he finish talking, when the bell rang.

"Who ever it is found the rope," said Peppino. He looked out the door and saw that it was Biachio. "It's that jerk, Biachio. Should we just ignore him?"

"No, said Stellina. "Let's get this over with once and for all. Go let him in." Peppino went to the courtyard door and opened it.

"What do you want?" he asked.

"I just want to talk to Stella," said Biachio. "I will only be a minute." "Stella," Peppino yelled. "He wants to talk with you."

"Just stay here," she asked of Tano. "Let me talk to him alone. Get me the wedding certificate in case he doesn't believe me." After he gave it to her, she walked out to the courtyard door.

"Biachio," she asked innocently. "What are you doing here?" "Can I talk with you for a few minutes?"

"What is there to talk about?" asked Stellina. "I thought you understood what the situation was."

"I was just wondering, have you given any thought about us?" "Biachio, there is you and there is me. There is no us." Besides, I am married now. See my wedding ring."

"You can't be married. I understand all the churches were closed. The priests had some kind of a special meeting requested by Rome." "I didn't get married in church," said Stellina. "We got married here in the courtyard. The priest that married us apparently was not invited to the meeting."

"Are you telling me the truth?" said Biachio being dumbfounded by the information.

"We just got back from our honeymoon," she said. "Here look, here is the marriage certificate. I was just getting ready to put it away. A copy was sent to Rome two weeks ago. You can check with them if you don't believe me. Besides, you know I have been in love with Tano since I was twelve. I could never love anyone else, especially now that we have been married for over two weeks."

"I understand," said Biachio. "Good luck" he said as he walked away.

"His face was very red," stated Peppino who had stood near by protecting his sister.

"I know," said Stellina. "I wonder if it was from embarrassment or anger."

"I don't think that kind ever gets embarrassed. I think he held his anger because he saw me nearby looking mean."

"Thanks big brother. I hope this is the last we will see of him." They went inside and related to Tano and their father all that had been said.

"I don't think it is possible never to see him again," said their father. "I'm sure he is thinking of ways to get even. We have to be very careful from now on."

"I will not let either of them out of my sight," promised Peppino.

Biachio walked back to his house. He was steaming mad. He ran into his mother and told her what had taken place.

"Papa promised me there would be no marriage," complained Biachio. "I understood that he talked to all the priests."

"Apparently he missed one," said his mother. "They are smarter then I thought. They must have gotten to Father Nicola. He is retired but still able to perform marriages."

"Let's shut him up for good," said Biachio in anger.

"What for?" asked his mother. "It's too late now. Every action you take should have a profitable purpose and it should never have only negative results. Killing the priest now has no positive results and could have great negative repercussions. Use your brain. What have I taught you?"

"I understand, mama. What can I do?"

"What is it you really want? Do you want revenge? Do you really still want a woman who is married and doesn't want anything to do with you? Why don't you find a nice upper class woman in our family circle? Why would you want an inferior peasant girl anyway? She is below your station. Not only that but she has been used."

"I know it is silly, but Mama, I really love this girl. She is not only beautiful but she is very intelligent for her station. I get shivers whenever I am near her. I want her more than I have ever wanted anything."

"There is only one way you can ever get her for your own," said his mother. That is only if she is a widow."

"What are the chances of that happening?" said Biachio feeling there was no hope for his desires.

"Now don't go off and do something dumb," she said reading her son's face. "You just can't go off and kill someone. The city would all get up in arms and there would be a revolution. We have been very close to that already. Your grandfather got too arrogant and we were almost unseated. Your father used his head and appeased the peasants. That was the most embarrassing time of our lives. You must plan this out carefully. You can't do it so that family members come after you. You must set it up so you will look innocent. The blame must fall on some one else."

"What are you suggesting Mama?" said Biachio a little confused. "Son, I don't like her. I will understand if you want her for a plaything for a while but not as your permanent wife. However if you insist and come up with a plan bounce it off of me or your father before you act on it."

"I couldn't kill her husband, Mama. She would hate me for life. See you later." He left his house and went to his favorite bar. He found Pietro there. He took him aside and they sat at a secluded booth.

"What's up, Biachio?"

"I'm heart broken," started Biachio. He then explained all that had happened. "How could that be?" asked Pietro. "I thought your father had taken care of that."

"Well he missed one," said Biachio sadly. "The only way I could have Stellina now is if she becomes a widow."

"Why don't we just take Tano out?" asked Pietro coldly. "Pietro, have you seen her brother. He could tear you apart with his bare hands. He's not dumb either. Don't you think he would figure out who did the killing? He would be after us in a blink of an eye. Do you want to go through life looking over your shoulder? No, I wouldn't want to be responsible for his death anyway. She would hate me forever. I would rather just love her from a distance." "Wouldn't it be nice to take out Tano and let Peppi get the blame?" suggested Pietro. "That would make Stellina a widow and at the same time get Peppi out of the way. Think about it." "Forget it," said Biachio. "I don't want any part of that."

"We should think of another thing," said Pietro after giving the situation some thought. "Do you really want this girl that bad? Your parents will hate her. Is it all going to be worth it?"

"Yes, I want her that bad. But there is no hope so why even discuss it. I'm going home to bed. See you later." A few minutes after Biachio left Roberto walked in.

"How are you Pietro?" he said. "You look like you are deep in thought. What's up?"

"Biachio is down in the dumps. It seems that the girl he wanted just got married to some one else."

"Stellina got married?" said Roberto, surprised. "What can we do about it?"

"I would like to help our cousin and my best friend," said Pietro still in deep thought. "The only way that he has a chance with Stellina is if she becomes a widow. We also have to get Peppino out of the way. I'm thinking that we take out Tano and put the blame on Peppino. Are you with me?"

"Pietro, you know that I am with you all the way."

"Good. Then let's work out the details." They sat drinking the rest of the day coming up with and analyzing the different possible scenarios.

The next morning Tano got up with his father-in-law. He got dressed and began saddling his horse.

"Where are you going?" said Mr. Casolini. "I think you should stay out of sight for the time being." Just then Peppino came into the stable.

"What is going on in here?" He asked.

"I don't know." said his father. "Tano is saddling up to go some place."

"I think I should do my part and help you," said Tano. "Peppi has to go and help Gina at their farm. That was the way it was set up."

"I know," said Peppino. "But Biachio could be waiting to get you alone."

"So how will my not going with papa help? All he has to do is wait it out. Whether it is now or later what would be the difference except we could get over confident."

"I think Tano has a point," said Peppino. "You and papa better bring a rifle with you and keep it near at all times."

"That's a good idea son. We will do that. In the mean time why don't you both go get water for Stellina so she could prepare us a fantastic dinner? You know this 'wanting to please her husband' will not last forever." They both smiled and shook their heads in agreement.

Having Tano with him to get water was an inconvenience. He would be limited in his time with Gina. But he wanted to spent as much time with Tano during the dark hours of the day. Keeping close to the buildings would make it a tough shot with a gun. The only way to get to them in close quarters is to physically attack them. Peppino had his trusty knife with him. And with his size no one in his right mind would attack them. When he got to Gina's house Peppino pulled Tano close to him.

"Stay close to me. I don't want any one attacking you while I talk to Gina."

"Why don't I go ahead and fill up the jugs?"

"It's too dangerous," assured Peppino. He knocked on the door. When Gina opened the door Peppino pulled Tano inside and closed the door.

"What's going on?" asked Gina as he wrapped his arms around her.

"I'm guarding Tano." He kissed her and addressed her mother who was standing close by.

"Mama, when can we set a date? I want to move in with you two so I can be more help."

"Soon, but for now we must get the farm work done if we want to eat next year. Gina wants a large expensive wedding. We have to save for that."

"Gina," asked Peppino. "Is that so important to you?"

72

"Not really," she answered. "But let's finish the farm work and then we will get married."

"Okay," said Peppino somewhat disappointed. "Let's get your water and then we can go pick up my father and we all can go out to the farm together."

"Have you fellows had breakfast," asked Mrs. Fanucci.

"No but Gina said she has packed us a big lunch," said Tano. "Gino, Stella, and Peppi can join us for lunch. The two farms are not that far apart." When they got home Gino was already there waiting for them.

"What do you want me to pack for lunch?" asked Stellina. "You don't have to pack lunch," said Gina. "I packed a large lunch for all of us. I have made twelve of my famous sausage buns. "Why so many," asked Tano. "Are you trying to make us fat?" "No silly," said Gina. "Two of them are for Stellina. She is going with us.

"That's right. If Gina can work next to her man so can I."

"I'd like that," said Tano. "That way I don't have to worry about you."

"That's fine but who is going to cook dinner for us?" asked Mr. Casolini.

"I have that all worked out," said Stellina. "But you will have to wait until tonight to find out. Did you think I would have let you all go hungry? Besides, you may not know this, but I get hungry too." No more was said. When they got to the crossroads Mr. Casolini, Tano and Stellina went straight, and Peppino, Gino and Gina turned to go to the Fanucci farm. See you at twelve sharp," said Stellina. "That is if you want us to eat with you."

"We'll be there," said Peppino. "You all have your rifles?" "We are all prepared," assured his father.

"If we get ahead at the Fanucci farm I'll come and help you" said Gino. They parted and each group went to their assigned land.

Pietro and Roberto had come up with a plan they thought would work. They spent the next two days working out all the details. They tried to anticipate the worst condition that could occur and how they would deal with it. When they were ready, they went to Biachio's house and found his mother resting. They relayed their plan and possible solutions to her. The most probable problem was an unexpected witness. The solutions varied from getting rid of the witness to postponing the plan till some other day depending on the witness.

"I like your plan. I don't like the idea," said Biachio's mother.

"But if you are set on it, I suggest you had better not try to get rid of witnesses. If one shows up wait until another day. Just remember this: It's always wiser to be able to come back another day." Later that day they checked with the mayor and he blessed the plan. He told them how proud he was with them for thinking it through so thoroughly. "However, I don't like the reason you are doing it."

When twelve noon came around everyone came together for lunch at Mr. Casolini's farm. Gina brought the food. They had all tasted Gina's sausage buns except Stellina. They ate slowly, savoring every bite. When they had finished they decided they should get back to work.

"Gina, I would like your secret on how to make this sausage bun," said Stellina. "It is the best lunch I have ever had. As a matter of fact it is so good it would be great for dinner."

"All right," said Gina. "Since we are going to be family I can give it to you."

"Gina and Peppino are pretty far along in their farm," said Gino to Mr. Casolini. "If you like I can stay and help you and Tano."

"That would be great. We will be happy to have you. Can you do any work after that fantastic lunch?"

"The thought that I may get it again will drive me to work hard," said Gino. They all smiled and Peppino and Gina left. That evening when they got home they found that Mrs. Fanucci was in the Casolini house. She had cooked a superb dinner for them all.

"Dona Maria," said Salvatore Casolini, "how did you get stuck with this task?"

"I am very happy that I could help," she answered. "What do I have to do at home? It's just Gina and I. It is so much nicer to cook for a whole family. I hope you consider me as part of this family. It's only a matter of time."

"You will always be considered as a part of this family," said Salvatore. "I just feel it's unfair for you to keep two households."

"There is no one at my house. I will spend the mornings there and come here in the afternoon, do a little house cleaning and cook dinner. It's really fun. It gives me variety."

"As long as you're happy, Maria, it is fine with me," said Salvatore. "In fact I'm thrilled to have you here." The dinner was special and after a little small talk with coffee Maria and her daughter left for home. Peppino escorted them. He loved it because he got to say goodnight at Gina's door alone.

The routine was satisfactory and enjoyed by all and continued for several weeks. They kept their eyes open for problems but they encountered no problems. In the mornings Peppino would go with Tano to get water. They would pick up Gina and all go to work.

Pietro and Roberto kept track of Tano and Peppino's movements. looking for a break. They had to get Peppino and Tano together, alone. As long as they worked together in the farms the opportunity couldn't materialize. Pietro concluded that the fountain was the best place to execute their plan. They noticed that Tano and Peppino always went to the fountain together. Pietro and Roberto figured that if they could get to the fountain before dawn, they could hide Pietro behind it and no one could see him or discover that he was there. They also realized that Peppino and Tano tied their horses along the side of the fountain, which also helped conceal Pietro. They also noticed that Tano always went first and that Peppino stayed behind…This made it easier for Peppino to protect him. The only problem they had was that Gina would also go with them to fill the water jugs for her mother. Since Gina went to the farm with Peppino she would not be there to fill the jugs during the day as she usually did. These days she filled the small jugs while Peppino filled the large jug. This scene was repeated day after day. Both Pietro and Roberto went home disappointed. But Pietro wouldn't give up. He loved his cousin and had to do this for him. If he had to wait all year he knew the opportunity would eventually materialize.

"Do you know, Roberto," said Pietro one day on the way home. "The only problem we have seen since we started this project is that Gina is always there."

"Have you thought of a way to get her out of the way?" asked Roberto.

"Not really," answered Pietro. "However I was thinking that after they get the land ready for winter the girls will not be needed any more. Then maybe Gina will not need all of that water since she will be home and can get it as they need it."

"Good thinking," said Roberto

"We will just have to wait and see. It gives me new hope. Another thing," added Pietro. "We should get one of my police to be near her house so that if anyone tries to get out he can keep them inside."

"How could he do that?"

"He could just say that there was an emergence and the police are asking every one to stay indoors until it is resolved"

Now that I think of it we will need that anyway." suggested Roberto

"What is your reasoning?"

"Well when the boys don't come back Gina would want to go out to see what had happened."

"That is good thinking," said Pietro. "What would I do without you?"

"You would probably screw up and end up in trouble," said Roberto. They both laughed. "You are thinking like a policeman."

A couple of months went by. The two teams had worked so well together that they hated to see the season end. During lunch one day Peppino reviewed the amount of work accomplished and what was yet to be done.

"Listen guys," he started. "The winter grain is almost all in. The feed for the horses is stacked and stored. We are almost ready for the winter months. All that is left to do is plow the field under to prepare it for the spring planting. We men could take care of this by ourselves. I'm not saying that we haven't enjoyed working with you women but I know you have a lot of work at home you have neglected by helping us. Besides I think Gina's mother could use a break and God knows some help."

"Are you trying to get rid of us?" said Gina in jest.

76

"I will take that as a joke," said Peppino. "I know that both of you know better."

"When do you want us to stop coming?" asked Stellina.

"I think we have about two more days work before we start plowing. At that time we will revise our schedule."

"Stellina," said Gina. "Why don't we get together? My mother and I could take care of our house in the morning. You can take care of your house and in the afternoon we can come to your house and help with your father's house and share our best recipes. We could cook for all our men including our most helpful friend Gino. We can share the work and the costs. It's always cheaper to cook for six than two in three different houses."

"Sound like a great idea," said Stellina. "Do you think your mother will go for it? I would think she will want to go back to the way things were." Gina pulled Stellina aside and whispered softly in her ear.

"If you haven't noticed I think my mother has a thing for your father. I would guess she would love the idea."

"Talk with her and make sure," requested Stellina. "But between you and me I think my father has a thing for your mother."

"I will talk to her," promised Gina. "What makes you think your father is interested in my mother?"

"Are you kidding? Haven't you seen how he dresses up when we go to your house and how he grooms himself?"

"I just thought he was a very nice clean man." "Haven't you seen him at the farm?" asked Stellina. "Yes, but that's different. He has to dress for the job."

"Believe me. He never groomed himself like he does now before he met your mother. He didn't groom himself like that for my mother."

"I hope you are right," said Gina wistfully. "That would make you my step-sister."

"That's right," said Stellina with a sly smile on her face. "That would make your fiancé your step-brother." They both laughed. They knew it wouldn't make a difference.

The farm work in which the girls could help did end in two days and they decided to stay home and be domestic women. The next morning Stellina did go with Peppino and Tano. She wanted to talk to

Gina and her mother to make plans for the coming days. When they got there Gina opened the door. She immediately hugged Peppino and gave him a very passionate kiss.

"I am going to miss you today," she said with a feigned sorrowful look. "Ciao Stellina, Tano. Stellina, I hope you don't mind if I show my affection to your brother. I'm sure you have done a lot of the same thing."

"I think I have shown a lot more affection than you," said Stellina with a smirk.

"I take it you are here to talk about our schedule for the future." "Yes have you talked with your mother?"

"Not yet," said Gina. "Come in and we will discuss it together. First let me get the boys on their way." She gave Peppino the small jugs. "I can get water if we need more."

"Okay," said Peppino. "We will fill your jugs, get a 'see you later kiss', and we will be on our way." Gina gave him a loving smile.

Hiding around the corner in the dark, Pietro and Roberto watched as Tano and Peppino left with Gina's jugs.

"Now let's go through a dry run," said Pietro. "I'll be hiding behind the fountain in the dark. You will approach Tano from the front. You will make some kind of offensive remark. You'll say something like 'look at the coward. Do you always walk with a body guard?' At the same time one of our police will go to the door at Gina's house and keep any one from coming out. Peppino will make a protective remark. You'll pretend to attack Tano with a club."

"Pietro, that's one thing we forgot! What are we going to use as clubs?"

"I will get a couple of used shovel handles and hide one behind the fountain."

"What if that morning someone finds and removes the handle? What will we do?"

"When we are about to pull off our attack if I find that the handle is missing I will call you and we will abort," said Pietro. "Now where was I? Oh yes, you were about to attack Tano. I will sneak up behind Peppino and hit him on the head as hard as you can. Tano will turn around to see what is happening and you grab Tano from behind and hold his hands back. At the same time I'll grab Peppino's knife which he always carries on his right side and stab Tano. After they are both down I will go and get the doctor telling him that Peppino had argued with Tano and in a rage had stabbed him. I tried to help but it took Roberto to stop him with a piece of wood he found by the fountain. What do you think?"

"Are we to kill Peppino so he will not talk?" asked Roberto.

"I'll hit him once unless he doesn't fall unconscious. Then I will hit him again. I don't think we should kill him on purpose. I think Biachio will want him alive for leverage when he talks to Stellina. Her brother is very important to her. We will have witnesses anyway that will verify our story."

"What witnesses?" asked Roberto.

"That's a good point," Roberto. "We will need at least two more witnesses.

"Do you know any of the police besides the one that is to hold back Gina that would help?"

"There are only two policemen I know that I could trust. How about you asking your brother, Gianni"

"I'm sure he will be willing to help," said Roberto. "I know I can trust him. I'll see if I can get him to accompany us when we need him. "I think we are finished here for today," said Pietro. "Everything is looking great."

When Peppino and Tano brought the water Peppino asked to speak with Gina's mother.

"What is it Peppino?" Gina's mother asked. "The work at the farm is almost done," he said.

"What is it, son?" she asked, noticing that he was a little fidgety. "Well since the work is almost done, I wondered, could we set a wedding date?"

"That's a great thought," she answered trying to put him at ease. "I will talk about it with Gina and tomorrow we will go to the priest and come up with a date. Since today is Wednesday this Saturday will be too soon. It will probably be a week from this Saturday"

"I would like it as soon as possible," said Peppino showing his impatience. Gina nodded her head in agreement.

After the men left for work, they all sat down with a cup of coffee to discuss their plans.

"Mama," started Gina. "I suggested we get together to take care of the men."

"What did you have in mind?" asked Gina's mother.

"I thought since I was home now you and I could clean our house in the morning and after lunch we could go to Stellina's house and help her since she had two houses to take care of. After we help her we could take turns cooking for the men."

"You volunteered me, did you?" said Gina's mother in a soft and non-objecting voice.

"Mama," said Gina with a knowing tone, "we all know that you like being with Salvatore Casolini."

"Is it that obvious?" said Maria Fanucci with a slight reddening of her face.

"Yes," said Gina and Stellina simultaneous. "That way we can all be with the men we love," continued Gina.

"Who am I to stand in the way of true love," said Gina's mother. "Cooking for seven will be more efficient and cost effective. We can all help and it will be easier on all of us. Otherwise we would be cooking three different dinners in three different houses. I like the idea girls, but there is one request I have to make."

"And what is that, Mama?" asked Gina.

"Too many bosses can spoil the best of relationships. We need one chief cook."

"That's you, Mama," said Gina. "Do you agree Stellina?"

"I'm for it one hundred percent," said Stellina. They then got serious in coming up with the dinners for the rest of the week and who would do what.

The next three days proved that the girl's plans were not only very workable but fun for them. The situation was also very delightful to the men. Sunday they all went to church together. Stellina sat with her husband, Tano, Gina sat with her fiancé Peppino, and Salvatore Casolini sat with Maria Fanucci. They all seemed to be very happy with the arrangement.

Monday and Tuesday went as smoothly and delightfully as the three days the week before. Wednesday started out the same as the other days. Peppino and Tano arrived at Gina's house early in the morning. Gina answered the door, but before she handed her jugs to them she managed to pull Peppino aside and enticed him to kiss her passionately.

"My Lord, you are very romantic today," said Peppino. "What brought this on?"

"I don't know," she said honestly. "Some how I was thinking this morning how very much I love you. I wondered what I would do without you. My heart had a very strong yearning for you."

"I guess the coming wedding can do that to us," said Peppino not really understanding her desires. "I can hardly wait."

"No it's more than that," she said. "It's more like a fear. Never mind, it's the raving of a woman madly in love. Go get my water. I'll see you before you leave."

Tano walked in front of Peppino who was leading the horses. They tied the horses by the fountain. Suddenly unexpectedly Roberto stood in front of them. Behind Roberto was his brother Gianni.

"Well, well," said Roberto faking that he was drunk. "If it isn't baby Tano. I see you need a baby sitter. What are you afraid of? Is it the dark?" Peppino moved closer to Tano. His right hand was on his knife.

"Why don't you go home and sleep it off," said Peppino. "You're drunk. Did you drink all night or do you start early? Don't start any trouble because you will get the worse of it."

"Well listen to the bodyguard," responded Roberto. "I'm not afraid of you. You're a coward. You're a lot of talk."

"Go home," ordered Peppino. "Go home or someone is going to get hurt. I'll talk to you when you're sober. Take him home Gianni and put him to bed."

"I'll go home when I feel like it," said Roberto "Tano stole my cousin's girl. I can't let him get away with that." Roberto then made a menacing move toward Tano. Peppino drew his knife but Pietro came out from behind the fountain where he was hiding, and hit Peppino on the head with the old shovel handle. Peppino gave out a grunt and fell to his knees. He was still conscious. Tano turned to help his friend. Pietro hit Peppino again as hard as he could and Peppino fell face down on the ground, unconscious. Pietro then grabbed Peppino's knife and attacked Tano. Tano tried to protect himself but Roberto had grabbed his arms from behind and pulled them back so that Tano could not. Pietro buried the knife deep into Tano's chest. As Tano fell backwards into Roberto's arms Pietro pulled out the knife and stuck Tano again near his heart. The last thing that Tano said as Roberto let him fall to the ground was to call out for Stellina. Biachio arrived just as Pietro placed the knife in Peppino's hand.

What have you guys done?" said Biachio. He then ran to call the doctor. Pietro went with him. Giacomo, who was standing a little ways behind the fountain to be a witness, stayed behind with Roberto to watch over Peppino.

Gina and her mother were sitting at the table with a cup of coffee discussing the wedding. After a few minutes Gina got nervous.

"Mama," said Gina showing her concern. "It's been about fifteen minutes since the boys went for water. I wonder what is holding them up."

"They probably met someone and are talking and will be here soon," assured her mother.

"I think I'll go see what is holding them up." Gina put on her shawl and opened the door to leave.

"I'm sorry, signorina," said the policeman in the street. "I am told to keep people off the street until a problem is cleared up."

"What is the problem?" asked Gina in a very shaky voice. She began to worry for Peppino and Tano.

"I'm not sure," lied the policeman. "I think there was a fight between two men. Someone is hurt and we are investigating."

"My fiancé was there to get water. Is he all right?"

"I don't have any information. Once the area is cleared you will be able to come out and find out what happened. Please go back into your house." Gina went back into the house and hugging her mother she began to cry.

"Mama," she cried. "I know something has happened to them. I had an uneasy feeling to day."

"Let's not worry before we know what happened," advised her mother. "Let's not invent trouble."

Biachio requested that the doctor follow him. Gianni went home. He had served his purpose. He had also memorized what he was to say that he saw.

"What has happened?" asked Doctor Bonavista as they left his house for the scene of the trouble.

"My cousin, Roberto, and I were going to fill our jugs with water and we saw these two fellows arguing. The argument got violent and the bigger fellow pulled a knife and started to stab the smaller fellow. We tried to stop it but he was too big. Roberto was to meet me there. We were going on a trip together and he found an old farm implement handle by the fountain and struck the big fellow on the head to try to stop him. He had to hit him twice to stop him he was in such a rage."

"Do you know any of these fellows?" asked the doctor.

"Yes," said Biachio. The big one is Peppino Casolini and the smaller fellow is Gaetano DiFranco. I arrived after it had all happened. "I caught part of the argument," said Pietro "It seems like Gaetano, who is married to Peppino's sister, wanted to desert his sister. He didn't like the idea. I don't know the details."

When they got to the fountain, Peppino was still laying face down on the ground. Tano was bleeding profusely with the knife still in his chest.

"We have to take them both to my office," said the doctor. "How much help do you want me to give them?" The doctor was knowledgeable of the facts about Biachio and Stellina. He also was very wise.

"Give them all the help you can give them," said Biachio knowing there was no help for Tano for sure and he didn't care about Peppino. If Peppino survived, he would be placed in jail anyway. "I want them both alive." They put both of them on Biachio's horses and brought them to the doctor's office.

Gina was out of her mind with worry. She was impatient to find out what has happened. It took all that her mother could do to keep her from screaming at the top of her voice. As her mother tried to calm her there was a knock at the door. Gina ran to the door hoping with all her heart that it was the boys. Opening the door she saw Gino standing there with three horses in tow.

"Gino," said Gina with great disappointment in her voice. "What is going on?"

"I don't know," he said, more puzzled then Gina. "I went to get water and found Tano and Peppino's horses by the fountain. Are they here?"

"No," said Gina starting to cry again.

"What's wrong," asked Gino. "Where are the boys?"

"They went to get water," responded Gina's mother. "When they didn't show up, Gina tried to go and find what was holding them up but a policeman stopped her and wouldn't let her out."

"I didn't see any police around outside," assured Gino. "Look, will you hold on to their horses and I'll try to find out what is going on."

After about a half an hour the doctor came out of his examination room. Biachio and Pietro were waiting.

"I'm sorry I couldn't save the smaller fellow. I think his name is Gaetano. He had lost too much blood. The knife had also done too much damage inside. He never came to. The other fellow, Peppino, is still alive but he is very critical. He has a big cut on the side of his head. He probably will not regain consciousness. Do you want me to stitch him up anyway?"

"Yes," said Biachio, "do everything you can for him."

"You will have to move him to the jail first. You can treat him there," said Pietro. "He will have to stand trial for Gaetano's murder.

After they left Pietro questioned Biachio.

"Why don't you just let him die," he asked. "The doctor could have helped him along. I could tell that the doctor would do what ever you asked."

"How do you know that?"

"I could tell because he kept asking you if he should help them." "Well, I would prefer that he live. I don't like what you have done but since you have done it I want to take advantage of the situation. I don't like what you have done I want to show Stellina that I want to help her by keeping her brother alive." "What are you going to do?" asked Pietro.

"I want Stellina for myself. If she will not come of her own free will then I can entice her with the life of her father and brother."

"I get it," said Pietro. "If he should die, so what, right?"

"Right" They left the doctors office and Pietro instructed the police to put chains on Peppino's hands and feet, incase he does come too, and to lock him up in a cell. Next they went to the city newspaper office. They wanted the story to get out as they had already written it.

Gino headed for the police station to get information on what happened at the fountain this morning. On the way, he met Giacomo, Pietro's friend on the police force.

"What do you know about the happening at the water fountain? asked Gino. Giacomo acted innocent although he had been there. "All I know is that some one was hurt and taken to the doctor's office," Giacomo answered. Gino figured he would get more information from the doctor who was closer anyway. When he arrived at the doctor's office Biachio and Pietro had already left and Peppino had been taken to the jail.

"I would like to speak with Doctor Bonavista," said Gino to the receptionist. Before she could answer, the doctor stepped out of his office.

"Gino," he said How are you? I guess you're here to find out about your friends."

"Yes, doctor they just seemed to have disappeared. No one knows what happened to them." The doctor explained what he was told had happened.

"I'm sorry about Gaetano. I did everything I could but I couldn't save him. I am waiting for the police to notify his wife and then I will deliver the body to her."

"What about Peppino Casolini?" asked Gino. The doctor explained the other man's condition. "Where is he now?

"He was taken to jail, accused of the murder of Gaetano. I'm going to the jail now to see if I can help him."

"Thank you, Doctor," said Gino. "I will have to notify the rest of the family." Gino left and quickly went to Gina's house.

"Gina," said Gino sadly. "I have very bad news."

"What has happened to Peppino?" she asked, tears running down her face. "Please tell me he is all right. Oh God. please." She then bust into loud crying. Gino wrapped his arms around her to comfort her.

"Gina," he said quickly to relieve her anguish. "He is still alive but badly hurt"

"Where is he? I must go to him."

"Listen Gina, you can't go to him right now. Please let me tell you the whole story." Gina's mother came running in from the stable where she was feeding the horses.

"What is happening?" she asked her hands shaking worse than her voice. "Where are the boys?"

"I'm sorry to tell you… but I guess the best way is just to say it," said Gino his voice showing the pain he was experiencing. "Gaetano is dead. Peppino is badly injured. He is in jail accused of killing Gaetano." Gina looked like she was going to pass out. Gino caught her before she could fall. Together her mother and Gino brought her to the alcove and put her in bed.

"That is so ridiculous. Peppino would never hurt Gaetano." "Will you two be all right? I have to go to Stellina. She is going to need her friends more then ever. On the way I should stop by Tano's parents." Before leaving, Gino filled the jugs with water.

Stellina was very worried. Why hadn't Tano and Peppino come back with the water? Her Father tried to comfort her. But the passage of time indicated that something was wrong. She stated to cry.

"Papa, I'm so worried. They would never delay this long knowing how much we will worry."

"Honey," said her father. "Let's not draw any conclusions until we know the truth. Our minds will always conjure the worse. Have faith in God." They stood in each others arms in silence. Suddenly the silence was broken by the sound of the bell.

"Someone is at the courtyard door," said Stellina. They both walked out to the courtyard entrance and opening the door they found a policeman standing there.

"Are you Stellina, wife of Gaetano DiFranco?"

"Yes," said Stellina shaking all the way down to her knees. She knew it was bad news.

"I'm sorry to be the bearer of bad news but I must inform you of the death of your husband." Stellina gave out a loud yell.

"No! no! Oh God, no! Tano please don't leave me," she yelled crying with great sorrow. "I can't go on without you." Stellina's father with tears in his eyes grabbed her and squeezed her hard against his chest muffling the sound of her distress.

"I'm sorry," said the policeman. "The doctor who tried to save him will deliver the body shortly." After making his last statement he left turning his back to the misery he had created. Stellina could not stop her loud wailings.

Gino, trailing the horses behind him, headed to the DiFranco house. When he arrived he heard the sound of sorrowful weeping. Somehow they had already heard of the death of their son. Gino kept on going to Stellina's house. When he got there the courtyard door was open. He tied his horse outside and brought Tano and Peppino's horses into the stable. He settled the horses in and unloaded the water where he knew they kept it. Stellina saw Gino first. She released her father and threw her arms around Gino.

"Gino," she sobbed. "They have taken Tano from me. What am I going to do now? I have nothing to live for. I have no reason"

"Don't say that Stella. You have your father and Peppino to live for."

"Peppino, Oh God what has happened to Peppino. I haven't thought about him. Is he still alive?"

"He is alive and well," said Gino not want to add to her burden by telling her that he was badly hurt.

"But where is he?" Why isn't he here? I need him now more then ever."

"I'm sorry but he has been arrested for the murder of Tano." "That is the craziest thing I have ever heard of. Peppino would die before he hurt Tano. He would never do that to me." It wasn't more than fifteen minutes after Gino got there that Gina and her mother arrived. Stellina and Gina embraced.

"Gina," said Stellina starting her wailing again at the sight of them. "They have taken our men from us," she said mournfully.

"I know," said Gina sorrowfully. "I know." Gina's mother had brought some food for lunch. She brought enough for many people knowing that the house would soon be full. Stellina still holding on to Gina hugged Mrs. Fanucci.

"Dona Maria, thank you for coming and thank you for the food. Although I don't think I'll ever eat again."

"I know my child," she said trying to comfort her. "It will take time." A little later Luigi and Lina DiFranco arrived both deeply grieving. When Stellina saw them she started weeping loudly. She hugged her mother-in-law.

"Mama," she said weeping. "They took our Tano away from us. What are we going to do?" But Lina DiFranco was crying too much to answer. Luigi walked over and hugged them both.

"Stellina," he said. "I hope you don't mind but we ordered a coffin for you. We know how much you must be grieving. It will be here momentarily. You will have to approve it of course. We bought the best Morrelli had in his showroom."

"I don't want a coffin," Stellina wailed. "I want Tano."

The coffin came just seconds before the doctor's carriage came with the body. They placed the coffin in the center of the main room of the old grandparent's house in which Stellina and Tano had settled in. They carried the body onto the bed so they could wash him and dress him. As soon as they laid him down Stellina grabbed him and started to kiss him all over his face.

"Tano," she wailed. "Tano, you're so cold. Get up Tano Please don't leave me. I don't want to live without you. You are everything to me. Please get up." Stellina's father and Gino grabbed her and pulled her away from the body. "Please let me hug and kiss him for the last time," she begged.

"Honey," said her father. "You have to get control of yourself. He is with God and can see everything that is going on. What would he think if he saw you loose control? He knew you as a very strong woman."

She turned and hugged her father.

"I don't want to let him go papa. Don't you understand? I can't let him go. Let me be with him as long as I can." Her father pulled her out of the room.

"Let them clean him up and put on clean clothes on him," suggested her father.

"I have to clean him and dress him. He is my husband. I need to take care of him."

"Honey, that would be too hard on you. Please listen to your father."

Stellina relented and listened to her father. Gino and Tano's father helped wash Tano and get him into clean clothes. When finished, they lifted him gently and placed him in the coffin. Stellina lost control a few times, as did Tano's mother. Stellina wanted to crawl into the coffin. They then both sat in silent grieving. Gina's mother left and returned around dinnertime with much food, but Stellina and Tano's mother couldn't eat.

Doctor Bonavista entered the jail and was led to the cell where Peppino lay on a cot. The doctor turned his head to view the cut. It was still bleeding and the cut was deep. Peppino was still out. Biachio walked in while the doctor was examining Peppino. The doctor looked at him but paid no attention to him while he did his evaluation.

"He will need about eight stitches to close that wound. I'm not sure it will help. He has lost a lot of blood. Besides I don't know what the blow did to his brain. If the brain has swollen then he will probably not make it."

"Doctor," said Biachio. "I want to say we did every thing possible to save him." The doctor took out his tools and after cleaning the wound started to stitch him up. About half way through Peppino opened his eyes and stared at the doctor for a few minutes. He didn't attempt to speak and didn't seem to feel any pain. Before the doctor had finished Peppino closed his eyes and seemed to have died. The doctor checked his pulse. "I feel a pulse although it is quite weak." He then gave him a shot to strengthen his system. "Well he's in God's hands now," he said almost to himself.

The newspaper put out an extra edition that afternoon. It described in detail what Pietro had dictated. It wrote that Gaetano had decided to leave his wife, Peppino's sister, because of his fear of Biachio. It was said that Gaetano had stolen Biachio's girl friend. It clamed that Peppino became very upset and they got into a very violent argument. Peppino became violent and pulled out his knife. Pietro, the son of chief of police, Malavista, tried to stop him. Pietro grabed an old farm implement which he found near the fountain and struck Peppino in the head. It was too late however. Gaetano died in the doctor's office. Peppino was arrested and placed in jail until his hearing. The families have been notified and all are grief-stricken.

Peppino gained consciousness later in the afternoon. Biachio was there when he opened his eyes. Biachio went just to see if he was still alive. Peppino was in a daze. He didn't recognize Biachio. He didn't even know who he was. Biachio assumed it was an indication of brain damage.

Stellina, her father, Tano's parents, Gina and her mother, and Gino, all stayed up all night sitting around the coffin. Weeping and sobbing was heard all night. Sometimes it got loud and then settled into a constant sobbing. Morning came too soon and the church deacons came to take him to church. They let the friends walk by the casket and then wait outside while the family went by. They walked by his casket each kissing their hand and placing it on Tano forehead. Stellina would not leave.

"I can't leave him," she said. "Please let me give him a last kiss." They let her but they had to pull her away. As they walk her outside she yelled back, "Goodbye, my love. Please wait for me, I won't be long." They brought her outside while the deacons closed the casket, and carried the casket to the church. Through the church service and through the procession to the cemetery Stellina was in a state of shock. Everything to her was unreal. She thought that tomorrow she would wake up and she would tell Tano of the terrible dream she had.

Two week later, since Peppino was fully conscious, the police decided to take him to trial. The judge was notified and all the witnesses were called to testify. After the judge heard the testimony of witnesses he declared that Peppino was guilty of murder and sentenced him to life imprisonment. Normally in a murder trail the accused was sentenced to death. However in this case, Biachio wanted him alive to use him as a bargaining chip.

Chapter 5

DEPTH OF DEPRESSION

The next few months were painful for Stellina and her father. They eventually survived the winter with great difficulty. It was spring and the land had to be plowed and the wheat planted. Mr. Casolini had no heart in the work ahead. Besides he didn't want to leave Stellina alone. Stellina still cried when she stopped to think of Tano. She missed him so much. She was in deep depression all winter. She lived because she felt God wanted her to live, but she lived without hope. What was left for her? She would never stop loving Tano. To her he was alive but out of her sight. She wished she had died with Tano, but her deep belief in Jesus kept her from thinking about her own death. She was told by everyone that she should trust in God. She wanted to with all her heart but it was very hard. "Stellina," said her father finding the courage to talk about it.

"The land has to be worked if we are to survive the next year, but I don't want to leave you. What do you think I should do? I don't really want to go."

"Papa, go," she said with the same sadness in her voice she had all winter long. She noticed that her voice seemed to depress him more than when he was by himself. "There is nothing you can do for me. What are you afraid of? Do you think they will come and kill me? I almost wish they would. I don't because I know you need me. If it wasn't for you I would have died naturally. Don't worry they have done their job well. And I would never consider taking my own life."

"I am worried about you," said her father in a loving tone. "You are all I have left. I need you more than I need drink or food. I could live weeks without water and food but I couldn't live a day without you. You are my whole life now."

"I know papa," she said with a forced smile. "I love you too. I won't let you down, besides we have to think of Peppino. He may still be alive and may need our help."

"We haven't heard from him or about him since that dreadful day," said her father. "We really don't know if he is still alive."

"Papa, we can not lose hope. We have to trust in God."

"We trusted him before," said her father with anger in his voice. He was sorry he said that after he had said it. "Forgive me, Lord. We need your help now. Please don't turn your back on us"

Stellina could not answer her father. The whole conversation was driving her in a deeper depression.

"Go, father," she insisted again. "If God wants us to keep on living then we have to have food."

Salvatore stayed with his daughter the rest of the week. Sunday, in church, he prayed for guidance. Monday, his mind told him he had to go to work. It was his duty to support his family no matter how small it was. That morning he went for water. At the fountain he met Gino.

"Mr. Casolini," he said with gladness showing on his face. "How are you? It's so nice to see you."

"Hi Gino. It's nice to see you too."

"What are you doing here this early in the morning?" asked Gino

"I have decided to go and work my land. I should be there by now but I'm having a hard time getting started."

"How is Stellina doing? I have meant to visit but I have been very busy. I am trying to take care of my land as well as Gina's land. It is too much for me. Gina has offered to help me seed both farms. That will help a great deal. I'm just finishing the plowing. I think soon I will have to give up working my land. Mrs. Fanucci has offered to share her harvest. She is feeding me now. That is all I really need."

"You're a good man, Gino. We are so lucky to have you as a friend. I know Peppino would be very proud of you." "Have you heard anything about Peppino?"

"No Gino, we haven't heard a word."

"As soon as I finish plowing I am going to get to the bottom of this.

I promise. I will get information to you." "Thanks, Gino. I know you will."

"Mr. Casolini," said Gino thoughtfully.. "Can I get the water for you in the mornings? I just get a little for myself. I go right by your house anyway. Why don't you leave the jugs by your courtyard door and I'll pick them up in the morning and drop them off in front of the door on the way to work without waking Stellina."

"You don't mind?" asked Mr. Casolini. "That would be a tremendous help."

"I'd be happy too," said Gino. They filled their jugs and both went their own way.

It was two days later after Salvatore had come home from plowing and had eaten a nice dinner that he sat down to talk with his daughter.

"Honey I am so proud of you. In spite of you sorrow you have managed to have a great dinner ready for me every night since I started plowing."

"Papa, you are all I have. You are my whole life now. Besides, I don't know how long I will have the pleasure of cooking for you."

"What does that mean?" questioned her father fearing the worse. "What I mean is that there is another woman who would like to be the cook in your house."

"What are you ever talking about?"

"Papa, I've seen how you groom yourself and how you look at Mrs. Fanucci."

"You're imagining things," he answered getting a little red in the face.

"Papa, there is no shame in loving someone. I'm sure that mama will want you to go on with your life."

"How come that applies to me and not to you? I know it is too soon for you to be thinking of that but you must have hope in the future and that God will guide you to happiness. It took a long time and I will never forget your mother but I have considered moving on."

"With Mrs. Fanucci?"

"Why not," said her father being honest about his feelings. "She is a very sweet and lovable woman. I would be very proud to have her at my side."

"Bravo, Papa," said Stellina smiling for the first time since Tano's death. "As for me the situation is different. I didn't have much time with Tano. I could never care for any one else."

"That is silly, honey. I will never forget your mother or stop loving her, but that does not prevent me from loving some one else too. You will never stop loving Tano and you will never forget him. You love me and you love your brother. And you can also love another."

"I don't think so papa." "We'll see."

Gino finished his daily work and after dinner with the Fanucci's he excused himself and went home. He had to wait until every one was asleep. About midnight Gino went to house of Anna Maria. They had a special knock that would tell Anna Maria it was Gino. He would knock three times delay for a few seconds and then knock twice. If no one answered then the coast was not clear and he would silently and unobserved leave. He gave the door the special knock. The door opened and Anna Maria quickly grabbed Gino and pulled him inside. She spoke to him in a very soft voice which was almost a whisper.

"I was hoping you would come tonight. I have missed you terribly."

"I've been plowing my land and Gina Fanucci's land and it's more than I can handle. Something has to change."

"Why don't you stop doing Gina's land?"

"I can't let them down. They need me," said Gino softly. It was hard to speak past the feeling of helplessness.

"Do you have feelings for Gina?"

"Of course," said Gino feeling out what Anna had in mind. "I love her and her mother."

"You do?" asked Anna looking very hurt.

"I love Gina like a sister. After all she is engaged to my very best friend." Anna looked relieved. "Why are you jealous?"

"Why should I be jealous?" asked Anna, embarrassed. "We aren't involved."

"I would like to change that," said Gino feeling brave. He had been in love with Anna since the first day he saw her. "I have very strong feelings for you. Do you have any feelings for me?"

"What do you think, you idiot." Why do you think I put my life on the line to talk with you? I dream that some day you will fall in love with me."

"You're too late. I have already fallen in love with you."

"Come here," she said pulling him to her. "Why haven't you said anything before? Did you like to see me suffer?"

"Why would you suffer?"

"What do you think a woman does when she loves some one but doesn't know if he even likes her?"

"You should have guessed that by the many times I come here." "How was I supposed to know you just didn't come for the information I can give you?"

"Speaking of information, I would like to know if you have heard anything about Peppino."

"Don't change the subject," she said pulling up so close that their lips touched when they spoke. "You want that information you have to earn it." She said as their lips touched. Several minutes later after their lips parted he thought of her statement.

"What do I have to do to earn it?" he asked.

"You have already earned it," she said with a smile.

"Well let's make sure," said Gino. "I wouldn't want to cheat any one!" He kissed her again. This kiss was more passionate and lasted longer. "I love you so much," he said after they came up for air.

"I love you too," she responded. "Knowing you love me will have to be enough for me. There is no way we can let it go any further. The barbarians will never let me go."

"You had better tell me what you know before we forget what I came for."

"All I know is that Peppino is still alive. I heard Biachio tell his mother he was brain damaged when he was first jailed. He had amnesia. He didn't recognize anyone, not even Biachio. He was in a state of being unaware of anything. However, I heard yesterday that he is slowly beginning to remember things. He may come out of it eventually. It seems to be a slow process."

"Thanks Anna Maria," said Gino. "I think his family and Gina will be glad to hear this."

"Make sure that Biachio doesn't suspect you got the information from me."

"Don't worry. I would never do anything to jeopardize your life. I love you, remember."

"You had better go now," said Anna Maria. "I don't want any one to see you." Gino gave her a quick kiss and left.

The next morning Gino got up early and was at Gina's door by five-thirty. He knocked and waited for a few minutes. When no one answered he started to leave to fill his jugs. Just then Gina opened the door.

"You're here early this morning," she said. "What's up? You know I can get my own water"

"I have a lot of work to do and I wanted to talk with you. First I will be finished with the plowing to day. To do that, I will have to work late. So don't wait for me for dinner. I will have a bite when I get to my house. You said you wanted to help with the seeding." "Yes, I'll be ready tomorrow. Have you plowed your own land?"

"Not yet. I will try to do my land after we finish yours." "Gino, that doesn't seem fair to you."

"What choice do we have?" said Gino. "I'm sure you will not let me starve. You have been feeding me so what else does a man need?"

"I still don't feel right. But until we can figure something else all I can say is God Bless you."

"I also wanted to tell you what I found out about Peppino" Gina grabbed him by the arm and pulled him inside.

"Tell me," she asked getting all excited "How is he?"

"He is alive and as well as could be expected under the present conditions."

"What does that mean?" she asked becoming worried. Gino, seeing how worried she got, decided to keep Peppino's mental health from her.

"It means he is not very happy being in jail for something he didn't do. Beside I understand they are not feeding him too well. I am trying to find a way to get food to him. I have to find out where his cell is. Then maybe I can lower food to him from the window. I'm working on it."

"Gino, you're a real friend. I know that God has sent you."

"I have to go now. I would like to stop at Stellina's house and tell her what I know. She hasn't heard a word about him either. Do you want me to get water for you?"

"No I can get my own. You go and give Stellina the news about her brother. I'll see you tomorrow morning." Gino said good-bye and left.

When he arrived at Stellina's, instead of leaving the water in front of the door as he usually did, he dismounted and rang the bell. No one answered. Gino figured that Mr. Casolini had already left and Stellina had gone back to bed. He rang again and waited. It was too important for him not to stay and wait. After he rang the third time he heard some rustling by the door.

"Who is it?" said a voice that Gino recognized as Stellina's. "It's Gino," he answered. "It's important that I talk with you." "Just a minute," she said and went to put on a robe. She opened the door. "Please," she said in a trembling voice, "don't give me bad news. I couldn't take any more."

"It's good news," responded Gino as he slipped inside. "I found out that Peppino is very much alive." At that, Stellina gave Gino a big hug. "Tell me about him."

"Well he isn't too happy being in jail for something he didn't do." Gino had made up his mind not to tell her anything about his health. "He is getting very thin they tell me. I don't think they are feeding him well. I'm trying to find out what cell he is in so I can lower him food from the cell window."

"How are you getting all this information?"

"I can't tell you that." said Gino. "It would get some one in trouble. And I would request you don't tell any one where you got the information."

"My lips are sealed," said Stellina showing a little happiness for the first time. "How can we find out where his cell is?"

"Don't you try," said Gino worried she might give away his plan. "Trust me. I'll figure a way that will not get us in trouble. If we ask anyone, they may figure out what we want to do. It could even bring harm to Peppino. We have to be very careful."

"I'll leave everything in your hands," she agreed. "Let me know if I can help?"

"I will. I have to get going now. I'm trying to work both Gina's farm and my own. It's an impossible job." Gino unloaded the water jugs and left for the farm. He had no idea on how he was going to find out where Peppino was held.

Mr. Casolini came home late that evening. Stellina had a special dinner waiting for him. He noticed immediately that something was different. Stellina looked almost like her previous perky self.

"Okay, sweetheart," he said finally "What has happened? What has happened that has made you relax from your grieving?"

"Gino stopped over this morning when he brought me the water. He has an informer some where that tells him what is going on in the mayor's organization."

"My God, girl, don't keep me on pins and needles," "Peppino is alive and well," she finally blurted out.

"Thank God," sighed her father. How is his health? Do you know?"

"Just that he is unhappy and Gino thinks he is underfed." "We have to do something about that," he resolved.

"We have to have faith in Gino. He has warned us not to interfere. He will find a way that will not give the effort away. He fears that if they find out what we are planning they may harm Peppino."

"Gino's a good man," he added. "He will do what he says."

Two more weeks went by. Gino had no more information on Peppino. Gina was helping Gino and Stellina was helping her father. Mrs. Fanucci made dinner for both families Mr. Casolini objected but Mrs. Fanucci would not be dissuaded. Everything seemed to be moving along nicely although they did come home pretty tired every evening.

On Friday evening, they had finished eating and the women had cleared the table. They sat for a while and soon Gino, Gina, and her mother left. Stellina and her father were sitting contemplating the work that still had to be done on the farm when the bell rang. Mr. Casolini looked at the clock.

"Who could it be this time of night?"

"I'll go see," said Stellina. She walked out the house across the courtyard to the courtyard door. She opened it and to her surprise, there stood Biachio.

"Ciao Stellina," he said.

"What are you doing here?" she asked rather abruptly.

"I'm sorry to come this late but I have to talk with you." He said with a soft, condescending voice.

"We don't have anything to talk about especially this late," she said. "I'm helping my father so we have to get up early."

"I just want five minutes," he said in a begging tone. "I have to get this off my mind."

"Come back after harvest," she said in a very mean and disgusting manner.

"Please," he begged.

"What is there to talk about?" she asked, getting angry. "You had my husband killed. You had my brother jailed and you expect me to even look at you."

"That's what I want to talk to you about," he said insistently. "I know you think I am responsible for your tragedy. I swear to you I came after it all happened. I wasn't there. I don't really know what happened. Don't you know I wanted to marry you? Why would I go against my parents and pick what they feel is a peasant girl. I've been in love with you since the first time I saw you. I would never do anything to hurt you. I admit I tried to stop your wedding. I am not the most honest person. I admit that, but I would never do anything that would make you unhappy or cause you pain. You will not believe this, but I hurt very much knowing how much you were hurting. I love you too much. You have got to believe that."

"If you mean that, then prove it and get my brother out of jail,"

"I wish I could," he said in the most honest tone he could muster. "I can try but it was the son of the chief police that accused him. He has two witnesses. They would laugh at me. They would know I was just trying to impress you. My parents are against a relationship between you and me. They would never approve of any of our people causing harm to come to Tano. They were thrilled when you got married. That solved their problem."

"I thought your father caused the churches to close," said Stellina She was getting confused. His argument almost sounded like the truth. He sounded very sincere.

"Of course I used my father's name. The priests would never have listen to me,"

"I have to go get some rest,"she said."But you have to understand, I loved Tano with all my heart and I could never love anyone again.""I understand," said Biachio. "I'll always love you that way.

Because I do, I couldn't stand you thinking I would do anything to harm you or make you unhappy."

"Goodnight," said Stellina and closed the door. She walked away confused. Could he be telling the truth? If he was, who else would want to harm Tano and frame Peppino? There was no one she could think that would have any reason. Unless it was some one who wanted Gina and this was a good way to get rid of his competition. She decided that tomorrow when they were having dinner together she would ask Gina what she thought. Her father had already gone to bed so she couldn't discuss it with him.

The next day, after they had worked all morning, Stellina and her father sat down to have lunch. Stellina questioned her father about the possibility that Biachio was telling the truth. She told her father to the smallest detail what had been said the night before between her and Biachio.

"Honey," he said after a few minutes. "That guy is a very great actor. Don't believe a word he says. He is like the devil, a perfect liar. There is no one else that would profit from Tano's death. I don't believe his mother was happy that you got married. She might not like you but I feel she would give Biachio anything he asked for. I also know his father scared the priests. They would never take Biachio's word. They would not take the chance of offending the mayor."

"I guess you are right papa," said Stellina still a little confused. "Still, I think I will bring it up tonight after dinner."

"Sure go ahead," said her father. "What can you lose?" They went back to work.

That evening after they had eaten, they all sat around the table drinking their coffee. Those present included Gino, Gina, her mother Maria, Stellina and her father Salvatore.

"I want to tell all of you what happened late last night. I want to know what each of you think about it."

"What happened?" asked Gina beginning to worry.

"Late last night we heard the courtyard bell ring. I went to answer it and it was Biachio."

"What did he want?" asked Gino getting upset. "Please let me tell it before you ask questions." "Sorry."

"He came to tell me he knew I thought he was responsible for the death of my husband. He said he came to tell me he didn't know anything about it. He said he loved me very much and he would never do anything that would hurt or make me unhappy. He admitted he was the one that tried to stop my marriage. He told the priests using his father's name not to marry me and Tano." She then related his comments about his parents' position. How they were thrilled that she got married.. "He said that he loved me very much and couldn't stand me thinking he had any part of Tano's murder."

"Then why doesn't he get Peppino out of jail," said Gina. "If he cares so much for you, get him to release Peppino."

"Believe me I tried. He said they would laugh him out of the jail. He said it was Pietro who arrested Peppino. He said he had two witnesses that testified that Peppino killed Tano. Biachio swore he wasn't there when Tano was killed. He said he came later."

"The only thing that would support his story," said Gino, "is when I talked to Dr. Bonavista, he said he got Biachio's permission to help Tano and Peppino. He told me Biachio told him to do all that he could to save both of them. He acted like he was worried about Stellina."

"That is chicken droppings," said her father Salvatore.

"Papa, I know what you think. I want to know what the others think. Gina, can you think of any one who would want to hurt Peppino. Is there a possibility that killing Tano was just to get Peppino?"

"First, let me ask Gino a question," said Gina. "Why was Dr. Bonavista told to help Peppino? Was he hurt in the incident also?" "They knocked him out to get to Tano," said Gino, trying to hide Peppino's real mental condition. "That's what they told me.

I understand he came to in jail. He may have had a bruise on his head. I don't really know."

"To answer your question Stella," continued Gina. "I am not aware of any one having trouble with Peppino. Every one we knew loved him. My thoughts are don't trust anything Biachio says. I am willing to bet he will return soon, trying to get on your better side and trying to get you to marry him."

"That whole family is treacherous," said Maria. "I wouldn't believe a thing he says. I am also positive that his mother and father would do anything even kill to please their son. Even if it was something they didn't like."

"That's what papa said," said Stellina. "You and my father think alike. She then turned to Gino. "What do you think Gino?"

"I agree with Gina and her mother. I believe that Biachio orchestrated the whole plan with the help of his mother and father. That said I will ask your permission to leave. I have a few things to take care of at home."

"Go with our gratitude and blessings," said Mr. Casolini. After Gino left Gina turned to Stellina.

"Are you getting soft on Biachio," she asked.

"Good heavens, no. Even if I had never met Tano I could never fall for a guy like Biachio. I don't think he is good looking and besides I don't even like him a little. I feel like throwing up when I look at him. I just wanted to make sure there wasn't any one else that could be an enemy. I wouldn't want to be friends with some one who may have killed Tano. If there is a possibility some one was really after Peppino we should be alerted."

"Good," said Gina. "I was beginning to worry about you." "Well, we better be going," said Gina looking for her mother.

Her mother was at the other end of the room very close to Stellina's father. They were whispering to each other. Their hands were so close that it almost looked like they were ready to hold hands. "Mama, what's going on?" she said with a big grin.

"Nothing," said Maria. "We were just saying good-bye. It's time for us to leave." Gina grabbed her mother's hand and led her to the door.

"Good night everyone," she said. Maria turned to Salvatore and Stellina.

"Good night. See you tomorrow." As the walked down the street toward their home Maria squeezed Gina's hand. "Was that some kind of payback?" she asked.

"What ever do you mean?" asked Gina acting innocently.

"Are you paying me back for the times that I broke up your lengthy good nights with Peppino."

"Did you break up our time together?" asked Gina smiling. "I don't remember anything like that. No mama I think it is very sweet. I really like Mr. Casolini. I think it would be nice to all be in one family. Heaven knows we are almost that now."

"He is very nice isn't he?" she said deciding to confide in her daughter. "He is so gentle and affectionate. I'm sure you didn't see it but he squeezed my hand ever so gently. I get goose pimples when he touches me. I'm glad we are talking. I just had to tell some one how I feel."

"It's pretty obvious how you feel about him. It is also very obvious how he feels about you. And why not? You are very young looking for your age and very beautiful. You have a very nice shape and are very youthful in the way you act and dress. I am always proud to be with you."

"If what you are saying is true why doesn't he make it known to me?"

"Mama," said Gina. "I know that love is very impatient. But think about it. His son-in-law has been murdered. His son is in jail and God only knows what future is in store for him. He can't be thinking of his own happiness."

"I wish he would confide that to me. I would wait forever for him if I knew he cared for me like I care for him."

"Why do you have another suitor you could go to if he makes you wait too long?" said Gina kidded her mother.

"You know what I mean. I would still wait for him but it would be less painful."

"I know, Mama," she said. "You just have to have some patience." Several days went by. The work was progressing satisfactorily with both girls helping. Maria would clean both houses and cook dinner for them all. They all seemed to be as happy as the situation would allow. Every one could tell by looking at Maria and Salvatore, that they were in love. They could see the longing that was in their faces when they sat at the table and looked at each other. Gino had not found out anything more about Peppino and he hadn't figured a way to get food to him. Things changed one day when Salvatore asked Maria to help him in the stable. The children were wise enough to let them go alone.

"What do you want help with?" asked Maria her voice exposing her nervousness.

"I don't need any help," he confessed. "Stellina, the dear sweet heart, thought we should talk. She feels we should clear the air about how we feel about each other." Maria was too nervous to speak. Salvatore continued when he saw that she hesitated. He could tell how nervous she was. He could hardly contain his own nervousness. "Maria, I have very strong feelings for you," he said his nervousness giving Maria some courage.

"What do you mean by strong feeling," she asked.

"I feel happy all over when I'm near you. My heart starts beating at twice its normal rate. I get this knot in the middle of my stomach." "That's probably indigestion,' she said feeling joyful and humorous.

"I guess what I'm saying is, I've fallen in love with you," he finally confessed.

"Well," said Maria with a little tear appearing. I must have eaten the same thing that you ate because I have the same knot in the middle of my stomach."

"Are you telling me that you love me too?"

"Since the first day I saw you," she answered drawing close to him so that their bodies touched.

"Please say it," he requested.

"I love you," she said with great loving tone. Their lips touched gently. They then parted and looked at each other in the eyes. The next kiss was not gentle but was delivered with great passion.

"You understand that nothing could come of this until some time goes by and the fate of my son is known."

"I understand perfectly," said Maria. "Knowing that you love me will keep me happy for a long time. However remember we are not young chickens any more." Salvatore hugged her lovingly and kissed her again.

"We had better go back inside before we set a bad example for our kids. I just want you to know one thing. I am going to ask you to marry me when the time is right."

"I just want you to know one thing. When the time is right my answer will be yes." They both laughed and went inside.

"Was everything cleared up?" asked Stellina. "As clear as the summer sky," said Salvatore.

"We have an understanding between us," said Maria. "And with that settled I think we had better be going home, Gina."

"Mama," said Gina. "It is still very early."

"I would like to get to bed early tonight. I'm very tired." Gina obeyed her mother and they both left after saying good night.

"Mama, why do you want to go home? Did something go wrong with Mr. Casolini?"

"No, honey. Everything went beyond my greatest dreams. I just had to tell you about it. I have the urge to yell it out to the whole world. I have to tell you or I'm going to bust."

"Wow, mama," said Gina being almost happier then her mother. "It was that good. Tell me what happened?"

"He told me that he loved me. He said that when he is near me he gets a knot in his stomach."

"Mama, now you know how it was with me when I was near Peppino."

"Yes I do, and do you know what else he said? He said because of the grieving of Stellina and not knowing the fate of his son that we would have to wait. He said when the time was right he was going to ask me to marry him."

"And what did you say mama?"

"I told him when the time was right that I would say yes." Gina was so happy she hugged her mother and they both stood there in the middle of the street crying with joy.

The next several days went by with little excitement. Every day was just like the day before. They couldn't tell one day from the next. Maria continued making dinner for the whole group. Everything went smoothly. Stellina and Gina could tell that their parents were more calm and happy. While the girls were setting the table or cleaning they would catch Salvatore and Maria whispering to each other as they moved around the room doing what they could to help. Stellina was beginning to accept her fate and once in a while when something funny was said she would smile. She had completely forgotten Biachio. Unfortunately Biachio did not forget Stellina. It was just before the seeding season was over that Biachio came to the Casolini house. There was so little work left to do that the girls were asked to stay home. It was early in the afternoon when Biachio came. Mr. Casolini and Gino had not come home and Maria and Gina had not come to prepare the dinner. Stellina answered the door and was surprised to see Biachio. She had not expected to see him and especially this early.

"Biachio what are you doing here? I can't talk with you now. I have to prepare dinner for my family."

"I know that Gino, Gina, and Gina's mother have dinner with you and your father. Doesn't Gina's mother prepare dinner for all of you?"

"She used to when we all helped in the field. Now that we are home Gina and I cook sometimes."

"I will only take a few minutes. I promise," he said.

"What do you want anyway? I thought I had made my position clear."

"I think that you should be pretty much over your grieving. I know you will never forget Tano. I can live with that."

"Don't you understand," she said starting to get upset. I don't love you. I never will love you. I could never marry you. Isn't that clear?"

"I have enough love for both of us. I believe with all my heart that after a while you will learn to love me. I will treat you like a queen. I will be so loving, you can't help but learn to love me."

"Forget it, Biachio. It will never happen."

"I just ask that you think about it," he said starting to get irritated with her resistance. "I could do so much for you. For one thing I could see that your brother gets proper treatment. I could see that your father is always safe. You know that there are so many notorious thieves out there. Didn't you hear how Mr. Marcelo was robbed and beaten half to death? That could happen to your father or any one for that manner. They wouldn't dare come near the father of Mrs. Biachio DiVincenso. As Mrs. DiVincenso you could get your brother released. They would not refuse the daughter-in-law of the mayor. Do you see the many advantages of marrying me? Don't answer me now. Just think of it. I will come back in a few days and we will speak again." When Maria and her daughter Gina arrived Stellina told them what had occurred.

"I don't trust him at all," said Gina. "He has something up his sleeve."

"Do you think that his comment about Salvatore and Mr. Marcelo's robbery could be considered as a threat?" said Gina's mother. She was worried about Salvatore.

"I don't know Dona Maria.," answered Stellina. "I'm sure he was trying to intimidate me."

"When will this nightmare end?" said Gina feeling sadden by the whole situation.

"What can I do," asked Stellina in utter frustration. "Should I end the problem by marrying Biachio?"

"God forbid," said Gina. "That will only make things worse." "Just think about it," suggested Stellina. "Papa and your mother will be safe and can get married. I, as Mrs. DiVincenso will be in a great position to free Peppino. Then you and he could get married. That would solve everything. Isn't there an old saying if you can't beat them join them?"

"It will be great only you would be sacrificing your life for the rest of us," said Gina. I don't think so. No one will let you do it. That is such a horrible thought."

"Forget it Stellina," said Maria. "Your father and I will never let you do it."

"Never let her do what?" asked Salvatore as he walked in from the stable. "What are you girls talking about?"

"Your daughter wants to sacrifice herself for the good of the rest of us," said Maria as she walked up to him, hugged him and gave him a pecking kiss on the lips.

"How was she going to do that?" he asked.

"She was talking about marrying Biachio," answered Gina. "Your daughter is out of her mind."

"I'm sure she was teasing you," he said. "She would have no reason to do that."

"Papa," Stellina answered her father. "I could help free Peppino and I could see that you are safe."

"Why wouldn't I be safe without you marrying that fool?" "Biachio came to visit me today. He threatened your safety and Peppino's safety."

"He was trying to intimidate you," said her father. "He wouldn't dare do anything to me or Peppino."

"That kind of thinking is what caused Tano's death and Peppino's incarceration," said Stellina getting upset with her father. "I am not going to take a chance. I'm going with you until the spring planting is complete."

"You know," said Maria thinking deeply. "I think we have a spy in the neighborhood."

"What makes you say that, Maria?" asked Salvatore.

"How did Biachio know when Stellina was home alone? There are other things that he does that can't just be coincidence. It wouldn't be hard to pay some one in the area and threaten them at the same time. Any one would submit to the pressure."

"I don't think so," said Salvatore. "I know all my neighbors. I don't think they would do that to us."

"It's amazing what people will do in fear and money," responded Maria.

"As for your comment Stellina," said her father. "You're not going anywhere. I don't need my daughter to be my bodyguard. I can take care of myself."

"That's what you think," said Stellina being disobedient for the first time in her life. "I'm not going to let you out of my sight. I can help dig around the plants until we can both sit and wait for the harvest."

"You're going to disobey me?" said her father not really being surprised or angry. He realized she did it out of love and worry for him.

"Papa," she answered calmly. "I have a house of my own next door. I have been married. I am now a widow. I am not your little girl any more."

"You will always be my little girl even if you are grown up and not under my authority."

"Papa, I will almost always listen to you; just not this time." Stellina was true to her word. The next day she was ready when her father was and went with him.

The next weeks went by like greased lightning. Stellina learned how to dig around the young plants to keep the soil loose so it would keep more water. When they went home Gina and her mother were there to provide a nice dinner for them. Salvatore and Maria seemed happy. They didn't talk any more but they didn't have to. When they looked at each other they knew what the other was thinking. Stellina was happy too. Perhaps she would never find happiness but at least her father would. Gino usually came a little later. They would always ask him the same question.

"Gino have you hear anything else about Peppino." It was usually Gina who asked the question.

"No I haven't," he answered. "What I am trying to find out is where they are holding him."

It was several week later. Mr. Casolini had stayed at home waiting for the time to separate the grain from the chaff. It was at harvest time that Gino got the answer he was looking for. He had gotten home early that day from checking the Fanucci crops. He stopped in at the bar where Biachio and Pietro always go to drink. He had gone as often as he could, hoping that Biachio or Pietro would slip and say something Gino could use. That day Biachio and Pietro were not there. They and a friend, he was told, went with their fathers, the mayor and the chief of police. They went fishing. Gino was about to leave when he noticed one of the jail guards sitting at the bar. He was obviously very drunk. Gino sat next to him at the bar and pretended to be a little high. He struck up a conversation with him and got him talking about his job.

"You're a very lucky guy, do you know that?" said Gino. "I have to dig the land and that is very tiresome especially in this hot weather. You have the job of watching the jail and I understand that there is no one there at this time."

"It is pretty lonely at night," said the jail guard. "It's especially lonely at night."

"If you had a prisoner you could at least talk with him."

"We have a prisoner, but we are not allowed to talk to him." "Well, is he close so you can hear him in his cell?" asked Gino trying to pry the actual location of the cell from him.

"There is only one prisoner and he is located all the way back in the last cell. I think they did it that way so that we couldn't talk with him."

"I understand there are only cells on one side of the building and they are all lined up on the east side so they could hear the noise from the city," said Gino. "That would drive him crazy."

"That would drive him crazy, but actually he is located on the west side. There are cells on both sides of the isle. I don't think it will matter soon because they are not feeding him enough. I think I'm going to fall asleep here at the bar. Could you take me to my horse? He will take me home."

"Sure buddy," said Gino, glad for the excuse to leave. He had gotten what he wanted. "I'd be glad to help an old buddy. I'll see you here again soon." He led him to the horse that the jailer pointed to and saw him off. Gino didn't care if it was the right horse.

Gino headed for Gina's house to catch her and her mother before they left to go to Stellina's house. They usually went together.

Stellina decided she was going to cook for all of them for a change. She and her father had finished up early and went directly to Gina house. Mrs. Fanucci opened the door.

"What are you two doing here?" she asked, totally surprised. "I was just getting ready to cook the food to bring to your house."

"We finished early and I thought that it was time that I do the cooking for awhile. I wanted to catch you before you started cooking."

"Are you sure?" asked Mrs. Fanucci. "I don't mind doing the cooking. I love cooking for the two of you."

"We appreciate that," said Salvatore. "But Stellina would feel better if you let her do it this time. Remember, if things go as I dream they will, you will be doing the cooking on a permanent basis." Maria smiled lovingly at Salvatore.

"What ever makes you two happy," she responded. "You will soon get tired of my cooking anyway." Stellina and her father left to do the shopping. They had not been gone more then five minutes when Gino arrived.

"Ciao Gina," he said as she opened the door What are you doing here so early?" she asked.

"I finished the work at your farm so I came home and went to work on finding out where Peppino was being held."

"What have you found out?" asked Gina looking very concerned. "I found out where his cell is but I have to hurry to get some food to him. The man I got the information from said he wasn't being fed to well."

"Oh dear God," said Gina starting to get tears in her eyes. "What are you going to do?"

"Now that I know where his cell is, I can drop some food down to him. I'm going to try and get in touch with him tonight."

"How are you going to do that?"

"I can drop a line with a bag tied at the other end. The bag will have a note and a pencil in it. We can communicate that way."

"When are you going to do that?" said Gina getting impatient to hear from Peppino.

"I have to do it around midnight. I can't take a chance on some one seeing me."

"The windows are pretty high off the ground. How are you going to reach it?"

"Thanks to Peppino we learned to stand on our horses and steal oranges from the duke's orchard. Actually it was the horses we had to teach to stand still."

"What are you going to do now?"

"I think I'll go and tell Stellina what I have found out."

". Why don't you go get every thing you will need and we will all meet at Stellina's house? You can tell them all then and after dinner you can got to the jail right from there. Perhaps, Mr. Casolini could assist you in some way."

"That's a good suggestion," said Gino. He then stuck his head in the doorway and yelled in to Mrs. Fanucci.

"Ciao, Donna Maria."

"Ciao Gino," she responded. Gino left to get ready for his midnight effort.

That evening they all assembled at the Casolini house. Stellina had prepared a great four course dinner that included thinly sliced chicken breasts fried in egg batter and bread crumbs. Gino then told the Casolini what he had found out and his plan to feed Peppino. "We will wait up for you," said Mr. Casolini. "I don't think Stellina and I could possibly sleep."

"And do you think Gina and I could go home and sleep?" said Mrs. Fanucci. "No chance. We will wait too."

It seemed midnight would never come. They sat around trying to predict the outcome. They were also concerned that they may be too late. Stellina gave Gino some left over chicken to give to Peppino. Finally, at midnight Gino left for the jail. The jail was built on the highest end of town and it sat at the edge of a forty foot high cliff. The cell on the west side of the building was very close to the edge of the cliff. Gino had about ten feet in which to stand on his horse to reach the window. He steadied the horse and spoke to it softly. When he stood on the horse's back he was just barely able to reach the window. He lowered the rope he had prepared that afternoon to communicate with Peppino. He jerked it up and down a few times to get Peppino's attention. He then lowered it until it felt slacken indicating it had hit the ground. In the bag he had placed a note telling Peppino to jerk the rope to indicate that he received the bag. He also included a pencil and a candle with matches so he could read the letter and respond. He waited about ten minutes, but there was no indication from Peppino. After fifteen minutes he pulled the rope back and returned to the Casolini house.

"I couldn't get a response from Peppino. Since he was not expecting me he must have been asleep." No one dared suggest that maybe he wasn't alive.

"Did you leave the chicken for Peppino," asked Stellina.

"No, I didn't know what to do. It would be a risk if they found it before Peppino did. I thought we had better talk about it before I did that."

"That was wise," said Mr. Casolini. "We have to somehow inform him of our plan. One more day can't make that much difference. We will think about it and we will do it tomorrow night if that is what we decide."

"The next day Stellina slept in until seven. When she woke she looked for her father but he wasn't there. When no one answered her call,…she looked in the barn and she noticed that his horse was gone. Only when she went inside again did she notice a note on the table.

"I am going to check to see if the wheat is ready for harvesting. I will be right back. We may have to start harvesting tomorrow if it is ready." Stellina was furious with her father. She didn't want him to go any where without her. She dressed quickly and went looking for him. When she got to the farm and found he wasn't there she returned to town and went directly to Gino's house.

"Gino," she said with tears in her eyes. "My father is missing. Please help me find him. He left a note saying he was going to check on the wheat to see if it was ready for harvest. He never came back." Gino quickly saddled his horse and asked Stellina to follow him. When they got to the road to her farm Gino stopped.

"Listen, Stellina. We have to travel to your farm but let's travel about a hundred feet on each side of the road. If someone robbed him they wouldn't leave him to close to the road. So I'll travel on the left side and you travel on the right side. Let's ride very slowly and keep our eyes open." Stellina agreed. Gino was thinking the worst. If some one attacked him they would drag him off the road on the left side which was more probable due to the rougher landscape on that side and that it was farther from the city. He was correct. About half way to the farm, Gino noticed what looked like a body lying behind a shrub. He quickly dismounted and ran to the body. It was Mr. Casolini. He had blood all over his face. He was apparently beaten and struck on the head. Gino checked his pulse. He was still alive.

"Stellina," Gino yelled at the top of his voice. She heard him and came at a full gallop. She jumped off her horse and ran to her father.

"Papa," she yelled, fearful of the results.

"He is still alive," said Gino trying to calm her fears. "We have to get him to a doctor. I'll put him on my horse and I'll ride with you. I don't think he is too serious. I think they were just giving you a warning." He picked up Mr. Casolini and placed him across his horse. When they got him to the doctor he took him to the examination room and asked them to wait in the waiting room. Stellina was still wailing with grief. The waiting was the worst part of the incident.

"Do you think he will be all right," she asked Gino repeatedly. "Stellina I'm no doctor but I have a lot of experience with sick folks. I felt your fathers pulse. He had a very strong pulse. He is probably going to be laid up for a while recovering, but I am sure he will be as good as new in time."

"What is taking so long?"

"Don't you realize it's good news? The doctor is bandaging him up so we can take him home. I would have worried if the doctor had come out right away." Gino wasn't sure he even believed what he said, but it seemed to be working with Stellina. It was about two hours later that the doctor finally came out to talk with them. Stellina and Gino watched him come out with worried anticipation. "Your father has been seriously beaten. He has a broken arm, a broken leg, a bad bruise on his left side and several bruises on his head. There doesn't seem to be any permanent damage to his head.

It will take time but he should survive with no lasting effects. Stellina cried harder with the news.

"When can we take him home," asked Gino.

"It will be about an hour. He is still unconscious. We would like to check him after he comes to."

Stellina and Gino sat there for the next hour waiting for the final release of Mr. Casolini. Stellina sat there quietly contemplating her situation. She suddenly knew what she had to do. There was no other choice.

Chapter 6

BAD CHOICES

Salvatore Casolini was brought home that afternoon. He had remained unconscious for four hours. Although he had come to at the doctor's office he was in a dazed state for the rest of the day. Gino notified Gina and her mother who both came running to his side. Maria stayed there all evening and slept in a chair all night. She refused to leave his side. The next morning when he awoke he saw Maria. He wasn't in a daze but he didn't remember what had happened to him.

"Maria," he said being surprised to see her. "Why are you here?" "She hasn't left your side since yesterday afternoon," responded Stellina before Maria could answer. Salvatore tried to get up but found it difficult. His head started to spin as he tried to sit up. "What has happen to me?" he asked.

"You were attacked yesterday," said Maria as she placed a new wet wash cloth on his head. She had been placing a new wash cloth on his head every half hour all night.

"Who attacked me?" he asked

"We were hoping that you would tell us," said Stellina.

"I don't remember. What is wrong with me? I don't seem to be able to get up"

"You were beaten pretty badly." said Stellina. "Don't try to get up. You will need a lot of rest. You have three ladies here to take care of you."

"Who else is here?" he asked seeing only his daughter and Maria. "My daughter is here," said Maria. "She won't leave me and I won't leave you. You are stuck with us."

"Did I have to get sick to be so lucky?" he asked, trying to smile. "You're okay," said Gina walking into the room from the stable. "You have your sense of humor back. That is a sure sign that you will be up soon."

"Ciao Gina," said Salvatore trying to reach out to her. "Aiai," he said in pain. "Why does my arm hurt so badly?"

"Papa," responded Stellina. "You have a broken arm and a broken leg. You also have several bruises on your head and a big one on your side. So keep still and let us take care of you."

"When did you start to be so bossy?" asked Salvatore. "When I need to be, to take care of you."

"How long do I have to be laid up?"

"The doctor says it will take about three weeks before he can take off the cast and about six weeks before you can go back to work."

"That's not acceptable," said Salvatore. "The wheat is ready to harvest."

"It could sing Ave Maria but you aren't going to harvest anything." "What are we going to do?" asked Salvatore with great worry in his voice.

"Don't worry Papa," said Stellina calmly. "I will see to everything." "How?" he asked.

"Trust me." She replied. "Just trust me." "Maria, what does she have in mind?"

"I have no idea," she said. She was wondering if Stellina was… still thinking of giving in to Biachio. Maria got a chill up her spine. It was three days later before Salvatore was able to sit up and have a decent meal. Gino had come every evening to visit. He had started to gather the wheat from the Fanucci farm. It was a full time job. He had tried to communicate with Peppino several times, but with no success. Yesterday he decided he couldn't wait any longer so when he went to the jail he dropped a piece of sausage down the window. He decided to wait until tonight to see if he could get any response.

Later that afternoon, after dinner, everyone was around Salvatore's bed enjoying his humor. He was feeling better. Stellina got up because she heard the outer bell ring. She told every one she would take care of it and slipped out to the courtyard. She answered the door and as she had expected it was Biachio.

"Biachio," she said in sort of a cool salutation.

"Stellina, I heard about your father. I'm so sorry. How is he?" "He will survive," she said still acting coolly. "Did you have anything to do with this?" she asked knowing he would deny it. "That's what I thought you would think," he said looking very hurt. "Anything that will happen to your family from now on will be blamed on me. I don't understand why. I would never hurt your father. He never did anything to me. I want him to be my father-in-law. Besides if you want to blame anyone you should blame yourself. I warned you about the high rate of robberies we have been having. We are in a better position to know these things. If you would have agreed to marry me this would never have happened."

"How would you have prevented it," she asked. "I told you my father loves the land and would never give it up."

"If he loves the land and wants to continue working it, that's fine but I would have provided a helper or two so he wouldn't have to work alone."

"Do you still want to marry me?" asked Stellina working out a plan of her own.

"Do I want to marry you?" he asked his countenance brightening like a Chinese lantern. "Does a bear sleep in the woods? I would be the happiest man on earth if you would marry me."

"I have three conditions you have to agree to before I will marry you."

"Name them," he said eagerly. "They will be done before you can finish talking."

"I don't think so," she said. "But that doesn't matter; you have to do them before I will walk down the isle with you."

"What are they?"

"First, you have to send two men to harvest our crop. My father being hurt can not bring in the harvest."

"I already know who I will send. They will work with your father on a permanent basis. What is the next condition?"

"Secondly, you must make arrangement for me to see my brother."

"I hope the third condition isn't going to be as hard as this one." "Well, can you handle it?"

"Yes, I'll take care of it. I'm afraid to ask what the third condition is."

"The third condition is that you have to wait until you actually achieve what you said you would."

"And what is that?" he asked getting suspicious she would set conditions he couldn't meet."

"First, you must tell me that you understand that I still love Tano. You must understand I do not love you and I don't feel I ever will. However, you said you were certain that in time you would get me to love you. Then this is the third condition. There is no romance between us until the time that I can say I love you."

"Wow," he said in desperation. "I knew you were tough, but that is a big condition. If I understand you right I keep my hands off of you until you can say you love me. That is quite a challenge. Then I have a condition. If you have the slightest feeling of affection toward me you must promise to tell me."

"Agreed," said Stellina.

"Then I accept the challenge," said Biachio realizing this was the best he was going to get. I'll go now and inform the men I will send out to your field. I will also set up the meeting with your brother for later today if I can. I will tell my mother to get ready for a wedding."

"Biachio, if you truly love me you will do me one favor." "Anything, my love."

"I want a very small wedding."

"Your wish is my command. How small a wedding do you want?" "I would like just your family and mine. I ask this because of the recent death of my husband. It will not look good. It will look like I didn't love my husband."

"Your husband has been gone for over a year.. However, I guess, to you it seems like it was yesterday, I understand," said Biachio and left to do all she had requested. Stellina went inside. As soon as she got inside she prepared herself to withstand the objections from everyone. She had to brace herself because she wasn't sure she did the right thing.

"Who was that?" asked her father.

"That's not important," she answered trying to keep the information to herself as long as possible. "What is important is that I have two men going out to the farm to bring in the harvest. I also have made arrangement to see Peppino."

"Oh no, Stellina," said Maria. "You haven't made a deal with the devil have you?"

"I have no choice," she answered with tears in her eyes. "What did she do? Maria, please tell me."

"If I understand correctly she agreed to marry Biachio." "She is just kidding you, aren't you Stellina?"

"Yes, papa. You don't have to worry about anything."

"Yes you are kidding or yes you agreed to marry that scum?" "Look, all of you. Listen to me carefully. We can not beat them.

We have lost. I have no other choice. If I had agreed to marry him in the first place Tano would be alive and Peppino would be home."

"You can't blame yourself for that," said her father.

"No, but I can blame myself for you getting hurt. I will not sacrifice your life and most probable Peppino's. They have won. The smart thing now is to accept defeat and make the best of it."

"What good thing could come out of this?" asked her father. "Can't you see Papa? You will be free to marry Maria. You will never guess how happy that will make me. On top of that, as one of the DiVincenso members, I can get Peppino released. They would have no reason to keep him in jail. Then I would be thrilled to see Peppino and Gina get married. You see these events will make me deliriously happy."

"Sure and you will have sacrificed your life," said Salvatore. "I find that unacceptable. So what can they do, kill me? If that is God's will so be it. I have lived a long life. But you are still in your youth. I'm sure that Peppino would beat this craziness out of you." "Papa, didn't you listen to me. I would be deliriously happy to see you and Peppino happy. How many people have you seen where the parents set up a marriage and the people are either unhappy all their lives or they fall in love with the choice. What I'm saying is that there are a lot of unhappy married people. I may just have to be one of them. I will never stop loving Tano. I will feel the same with anyone else as I do about Biachio. Perhaps he will try so hard that I will eventually love him. He could change for me you know." "My life and Peppino's life for yours, is that it? You will be like a dead woman. Being unhappy is like being dead or at lest you will wish you were dead."

"Papa, there is nothing you can say to change my mind. I will not put your life and Peppino's life in jeopardy. And after you and Peppino are gone what will I have. I will either have to marry him or they will eliminate me to."

Biachio was worried about Stellina seeing her brother; therefore he went straight to the jail to confer with the jailers. He was concerned that Peppino might try to talk her out of marrying him After conferring with the jailers who told him that Peppino was still in a state of amnesia, he decided to see Peppino himself. He wasn't going to take any chances. He walked to the cell. Peppino looked at him as if he had never seen him before.

"Peppino, how are you old buddy, old friend." "I'm okay," said Peppino. "Do I know you?"

"Yes, we went to school together. Don't you remember me? I'm your sister's fiancé."

"I'm sorry, please forgive me. I'm having trouble with my memory. I got hit on the head and I'm still a little groggy.

"That's all right," said Biachio, a little relieved. "I just thought I would check to see if you remembered anything about the attack. I'm doing my best to see if I could get you out of here."

"Did you say that I have a sister?"

"Yes, a very beautiful sister she is. I'll bring her to visit you tonight"

"Good, Thank you," said Peppino acting very grateful. "Is she the only family I have?"

"No you have a father too. He will come to visit with you at another time." Being satisfied, Biachio left with the promise he would see him later.

About six-thirty Gino walked in the room.

"How are you Don Casolini?" he asked, not knowing what was going on.

"Not so good," answered Mr. Casolini. "You talk to Stellina. Maybe she will listen to you."

"What's going on?" asked Gino surprised by the gloom that he felt in the room.

"Stellina decided to marry Biachio," blurted out Gina.

"Dear Lord," said Gino. "Please guide Stellina." Then he grabbed Stellina by the arm and pulled her toward the door.

"You and I have to have a private talk, young lady. Let's go outside where we could be alone." Stellina followed with anticipation. She really wanted to hear what Gino thought about it. When they got outside Gino turned toward Stellina.

"Dearest friend, have you lost your mind? You certainly could not like the guy."

"Now listen to me, dear friend," she said mockingly, "they beat up my father. Biachio almost as much promised that Peppino would die. What choice do I have? If I marry him my father will have a chance for a decent life. He will marry Maria. As Biachio's wife I can try to get Peppino out of jail. Gina can marry Peppino and live happy lives. I don't have any other possible future so why not try to help my family?"

"You have this all figured out do you? Have you considered that you are, for one playing right into their hands? Secondly, what makes you think they will let your father live. He knows too much. As for Peppino, they will never let him out. They are afraid of him. He would eliminate them all."

"I know all that. But there is a chance it could work out, even if it is a small one. If I don't marry him it is a certainty that both Papa and Peppino will die. Small as it is I have to take that chance."

"I guess you have made up your mind." "Yes I have, please talk me out of it."

"I've run out of reasons," said Gino being honest. Inside he agreed with her, although he would never let her or any one know. "He has promised me an audience with Peppino. He said it may still be tonight."

"When ever it is if he is able to respond to you, God only knows what they may have done to him, tell him about my midnight attempt to contact him. Tell him to stay awake at midnight. I will send down a note with a pencil. I will also send down a candle and matches. Oh and tell him to jerk the rope twice to tell me that he got the message and that everything is clear. Then I will send down some food. Speaking of food do you have any of that chicken you cooked tonight that I can give to Peppino?"

"I have it all," said Stellina almost starting to laugh at the humor of it all. "We haven't eaten yet. We forgot about eating. Besides we always wait for you."

"Yes, but I told Gina I would be late and to eat without me." "Doesn't matter, no one is hungry" Just then Biachio walked up.

Gino saw him coming up and turned his back to him so he couldn't hear what he was saying.

"I see Biachio is coming. He apparently has made arrangement for you to see Peppino. I'm leaving. Don't forget what I told you"

"Ciao Gino," said Stellina as he started to walk away.

"Don't leave on account of me," said Biachio as he jumped out of his buggy.

"I didn't see you coming up," lied Gino. "I have to leave. I got some work to do, ciao."

"Ciao," said Biachio "Ciao," said Gino as he hurried away. He didn't feel comfortable around Biachio.

"What do you have for me?" asked Stellina, hoping and praying it was permission to see Peppino, but afraid Biachio would say he couldn't arrange it.

"I have an appointment for you to see your brother." Stellina started to cry.

"When?" she asked tearfully.

"Please don't cry," said Biachio. "We can go right now if you wish, but you must stop crying. I can't stand to see you cry,"

"Wait until I get my shawl and I'll come with you." When she came out he helped her into the buggy and they left for the jail.

"Stellina," he said with a very sorrowful tone. "Before we get there I have to tell you something. I had heard a little about it but I didn't pay any attention to it. I'm sorry but since he is your brother I should have cared more. But I did everything I could and pressured the doctor to do all he could at the time of the incident. I hadn't visited him before this afternoon."

"Please don't tell me he is hurt, I couldn't take anymore bad news." She said as she started to cry.

"Please don't cry," he said getting some tears in his own eyes. "He is physically fine it's just that he doesn't remember everything that happened."

"Please hurry," she begged. "I need to see him." Biachio spurred the horses to run at a gallop. They soon got to the jail. Biachio brought her back to the cell where Peppino was being held. As they walked to the cell she saw Peppino holding the bars with both hands looking out from them.

"Are you my sister?" he asked.

"Peppino how are you? I'm your sister Stellina." Stellina then turned to Biachio.

"Biachio dear, may I please be alone with my brother?"

"I don't know if that is wise," he responded not wanting them to be alone together.

"You said you would do anything to make me happy. So the first thing I ask you to do for me you deny?"

"You're right," he said backing down. After all he thought, what harm could it do? "I will leave you alone with your brother."

"Please understand, he may be more at ease if we are alone." "Your wish is my command," said Biachio and left. Peppino looking through the bars watched carefully until Biachio disappeared through the door. He then looked at Stellina through tears. He was crying like a baby. Stellina was shocked and remained silent wondering what was going on.

"Oh my sweet Stellina," said Peppino. "You can't believe what a grand joy it is to see you."

"You don't have a loss of memory?" she said with a joyful smile. "No," responded Peppino. "I don't want them to know I know what really happened."

"The only joy greater than yours is mine to see you are all right. We didn't know if you were dead or alive. But I'm so sad to see how thin you got. But tell me before he comes back. What did happen?"

"It was all skillfully planned. Pietro came from behind the fountain and hit me over the head. I fell to my knees. Though I was dazed I did see Roberto grab Tano from behind and pulled his hands back so he couldn't defend himself. Pietro hit me again and I lost consciousness. But it was Pietro who killed Tano."

"Listen Gino will be here at midnight. He will get on his horse and drops a rope with a note, pencil and paper and a candle with matches. You are to tug on the rope twice to tell him it is clear. Then he will drop you some food."

"Did he drop a piece of sausage last night? I woke up and found the sausage at my feet. I ate it before any one noticed."

"Yes, I guess he did. We talked about it. We did have sausage last night."

"What is this that Biachio told me? He says that you are his fiancée." asked Peppino remembering that Biachio had referred to her as his fiancée.

"Yes that is true," said Stellina. "Before you say anything let me explain."

"You don't have to explain," said Peppino getting upset. "I'm sure you think you are sacrificing yourself for us. But it won't work, believe me."

"Please let me tell you my side," said Stellina cutting him off. "They beat up dad to an inch of his life. He is at home now recuperating. It was just a warning. The next time they will kill him. They are already starving you. Biachio already suggested they will slowly kill you. I don't have a choice."

"They will never let me out alive," said Peppino. "I know too much. The only reason I'm alive now is that I have been able to convince them I have amnesia."

"Listen Peppino," said Stellina realizing she didn't have much more time with him. "I think that Biachio really is madly in love with me. I have to use that to my greatest advantage. Papa and Gina's mother, Maria, have fallen in love. If I take the pressure off by marrying Biachio, then they could get married. After that they may leave them alone. As Mrs. Biachio DiVincenso I may be able to free you. If I could you and Gina could get married. It's the only chance we have. At least I can see you are feed and I could come to see you more often. There is no chance for me."

"It will never work. Too many things could go wrong. How is Gina?

Tell her I miss her very much."

"She is fine. She misses you very much too. Listen, I will have to go pretty soon. Biachio said he could only get me a few minutes." "You're a smart girl. I don't have to tell you what to say when Biachio asks what I said as I'm sure he will." "You can be sure."

"Give my love to Papa and try to come back again soon."

"I sure will." Stellina heard the sound of a door opening. "I will try to get you more food Peppino. I promise."

"It's time to go," said Biachio as he walked up to her. "I'll try to see you again soon," said Stellina to Peppino.

"It was nice to meet you. I didn't know I had a sister," said Peppino putting on his act. "Please come to see me again sister, ah what was your name?"

"It's Stellina."

"Nice to see you, Stellina,"

"See you," said Stellina as she walked away with Biachio. She got tears in her eyes. After they were back in the buggy she started to sob.

"Please don't cry Stellina," he asked.

"What have those animals done to him? He is so thin and he doesn't even remember me or my father. Why can't you do something?"

"I would give my right arm to be able to get him out. I'll try to get him more food. That's all I can do. Don't you understand my parents are not happy about my marrying you? My father will not help me. My mother doesn't care enough. The law is controlled by my uncle, my mother's brother Alfredo Malavista. Perhaps in time as they learn to love you as I do then we can get more out of them."

"Please Biachio, do what you can."

"I love to hear you say my name," said Biachio swooning like a teenager. "By the way, did your brother give you any information that could help us find the real killers of your husband?"

"No, he didn't remember anything at all. He didn't even know why he was in jail. By your statement does that mean you believe me when I tell you Peppino didn't kill Tano?"

"Honey, I love you. I trust your instincts. You know your brother better than I do. The only thing that bothers me is if he didn't do it then who did and why. Who would have a reason besides me?"

"Maybe it had nothing to do with Tano. Maybe he was just a way to get Peppino out of the way. As to why, I have no idea."

"Then you do believe I didn't have anything to do with the death of Tano?" asked Biachio hopefully.

"I haven't made up my mind about that," said Stellina trying to keep him on the hook.

"I can live with that for now," he said being satisfied for the moment. He felt he had made some headway. When they got to Stellina's home she jumped out of the buggy and addressed Biachio with a request.

"Listen, Biachio, I would like to break the news to my family alone.

Do you mind terribly, please? Besides it is terribly late."

"I mind terribly but since you ask so nicely I'll do as you ask. However, I would like to get together soon to plan our wedding. You gave me your word. You're not backing out are you? You would break my heart."

"No I'm not backing out. I gave you my word and so far you have kept yours. I just want my family to learn to accept you. That has to be a slow process. I'll tell them how nice you have been and how much you are doing for me."

"You are cleverer than me. That's one reason why I love you so much."

"Come by around noon tomorrow. We will be alone. We can have lunch together. We should get to know each other."

"You'll never believe how thrilled I am at the thought of seeing you tomorrow."

"We can make arrangement then," continued Stellina. "I also want to talk about my brother. You are going to find out if there is something you can do, aren't you?"

"You bet," he said happy as a man could be. "I'll see you tomorrow." After he left she stood there watching him leave. She wondered about him. Why couldn't he have been a good honest person? Was he getting to her? She went inside. They were all still up waiting to hear what had been going on. "Up" probably isn't the right word. Her father and Maria were asleep in there chairs. Gina and Gino were the only ones that were still awake. Gina had been asleep but heard Stellina come in and awoke. It was after twelve midnight. Gino had come back after Stellina and Biachio had left for the jail.

"Stellina," said Gina excitedly. "How is Peppino? Did you see him?" Her question woke the others.

"Yes, tell us what happened?"asked Salvatore and Maria together. "Yes I did see him and he is fine. Papa, you and Dona Maria seem to think alike. I'm so excited and pleased and happy that you two are together."

"Never mind us," said her father. Tell us about Peppino. What did he say?"

"I saw him and spent about a half hour with him alone. I asked Biachio to wait outside. Peppino is very thin. Gino, he will be awake at midnight. He found the sausage you brought him and ate it. I told him you might bring him something tonight."

"I'll go right now. I'll bring him some chicken. I'll communicate with him tomorrow." Gino left immediately.

"What else did he say?" asked Gina.

"He told me how much he misses you all and especially how much he misses you and loves you, Gina. I also told him that you love and miss him too."

"Did he tell you what happened that night?" asked her father. "Not too much. He was hit over the head as they went for water and woke up in jail with doctor Bonavista patching him up. He doesn't remember seeing anyone. The last thing he remembers is Tano walking in front of him. Peppino was hit from behind." Stellina had decided to lie to them. She was going to marry him. They may as well learn to accept that. Saying anything negative would be counter productive. Every one would be happier if they thought she wasn't unhappy.

"How was it that he let you see him alone?" asked Maria.

"He is like a blind man being led by the nose. He is so in love with me that he is like a little puppy in my hands." She smiled knowing that in reality he was like a little puppy.

"You're not going soft on him are you?" asked Gina.

"Of course not," she responded. "But since I am going to marry him, I may as well be the one in control."

"You're still going through with it then," asked Gina. "Yes, nothing has changed."

"Is there anything else that Peppino said that you want to tell us?" asked her father.

"No, not that I can think of."

"Then I suggest we all go to bed. Come Maria I will escort you girls home."

"You don't have to, besides you can hardly walk" said Maria. "We will be all right."

"I'll not let you go home alone this late at night." "I'm more worried about you,"

"Why, my daughter is marrying the guy. They don't need to harm me."

"As you wish," she answered. Salvatore escorted the girls home using the cane the doctor had given him. He enjoyed it more when Gina went in the house and he was left outside to say ciao to Maria. Early in the morning two men rang the courtyard bell at Stellina's house.

"What can I do for you?" she asked of the two men. She had forgotten about the men Biachio had promised.

I am Bastiano and this is Arturo. We are sent by Don Biachio to help Senor Casolini at his farm."

"He is unable to work. He has been injured. It is two soon." "We know about that. He will only come with us to tell us what to do. We will put him on his horse and take him off at the farm. It will not be necessary for him to walk. We have to get the harvest now or you will lose the crop."

"Why must my father go with you?"

"He has to tell us were the farm is as well as tell us what to do. We have very little experience with farming. We are the mayor's servants."

"Okay then," she said. She helped get her father ready to go with them. He was thrilled to go. "Will you fellows be eating with us tonight?"

"No, we were told to go directly home at six and eat at our regular table." After they left Stellina felt alone. She fussed with the few clothes she had and sat to wait till noon. She found herself looking forward to Biachio's visit.

Biachio showed up at Stellina's house at ten in the morning. Stellina was still in her house coat not expecting Biachio until around noon.

"What are you doing here this early?" she asked.

"I didn't sleep all night with anticipation of being with you. I have thought a lot about us. I have come to a realization and a conclusion."

"Whatever are you talking about?" she said as she let him in. "Please sit out here in the courtyard. I'll go inside and get dressed." "That isn't necessary. You look just beautiful just as you are. I don't want to miss even a second of being with you."

"That's quite a line you have," she said "Have you used it with other girls?"

"I have never said that to anyone else," he said realizing she was teasing him. "Let me ask you a question. If every word of what I said is true, does it still classify as a line?"

"I think so," "Did it work?"

"I think so," she responded. "I'm still here. And I trust you. You wouldn't dare try anything. You're not that foolish. What was that you were saying before about realization and conclusion?"

I came to realize that I am not worthy of you. I have not been an honest man and most certainly not a gentleman. I have been selfish and insensitive to the problems of others. I have done many cruel and evil things that I am ashamed of. I have never killed any one but I have not cared if others did. I don't deserve you. The conclusion that I arrived after this self examination is that I promise you and myself that I will change. From now on I am going to be as honest as a priest. I will be sensitive to others and I will never be ruthless or merciless to others. With your help I want to prepare to be a very good mayor when my father retires. I will do everything I need to do to truly deserve you. What I want most from life besides your love is to have you be proud of me."

"That is quite a speech," said Stellina being impressed by his admission. "How much of it do you mean?"

"Every word, dear Stellina," he promised. "If I do anything that is contrary to this promise I will give you your freedom. I will put it all in writing."

"We will see," said Stellina not knowing if she could trust him. Was this all an elaborate plan? If so, to what purpose? She had already promised to marry him. "Let's talk about our marriage," she said trying to change the topic.

"I have some disturbing information," said Biachio. "My mother will not allow us to live in the main area of the house. She has made that perfectly clear to me. I, therefore, am having the north wing refurbished as our living quarters. It is presently the living quarters for the manager of the house staff. He will be moved to the south wing. It is much smaller. Is that is okay with you?"

"Biachio, can't you see that our wedding is wrong from all angles. Do you want to be at odds with your parents?"

"You still don't fully understand how much I love you. The one thing I know is that I don't want to be anything like my parents. I only want to stay there to fulfill my promise to bring a good mayor to this city. I had strongly considered us moving to a house of our own. I would have no problem learning to farm with your father. We could talk about this but I would like to be the next mayor. If I abdicate my position then I would be letting down the people of this city. They would be ruled by a cruel mayor, my cousin, Cianni." "I don't understand," said Stellina being very confused. "Your parents came down here to ask for my hand in marriage. Have they changed their minds?"

"You don't know how hard and long I begged them to ask for your hand. They don't really want me to marry what they consider a peasant. But I am the only son of my mother and she would do anything to make me happy. That doesn't mean she will accept you as one of us. In her mind she is giving you to me as a sort of pet. It's really only my mother. My father is more reasonable. He says if you are the one I want and having you will make me happy, then I should have you."

"I'll let you figure that out for yourself," she said changing the subject again. It was getting too complicated for her. "As I mention before, I want a very small wedding. I would like it at my house. We will invite only family and very close friends. We can get married in Santa Maria Church."

"Will you go to the church and make arrangements?"

"Yes, she answered. "I'll go tomorrow. Will two weeks from now be acceptable?"

"I would like it to be this afternoon." "Come on now, let's be reasonable."

"What ever date you set is fine with me," he agreed

"How about your parents, are they going to want a say in this? Would they object to it being this soon? Do they want a big wedding at your place or at a hall?"

"I'm not sure that they will even come to our wedding."

"You're kidding," she said being surprised. "If she loves you so much why would she not come to your wedding?"

"I think she feels this is not a real wedding. She doesn't believe in the church or in God, for that matter. She feels I will tire of you and get rid of you."

"But there is no way to get a divorce here in Italy."

"You know how she can get a divorce." he said lifting his eye brows.

"She can give you a divorce like I got. I see that I will never be out of trouble."

"You don't have to worry. I would die before I let anything happen to you. I don't see anyway or anything that anyone can do to make me stop loving you. I have worked too hard getting you. I will never let you go."

"It doesn't matter I gave you my word and as long as you keep your word and your part of the bargain I will keep my promise."

"I will keep my word till I die." He promised.

"What do you want for lunch? How hungry are you?" "I'm very hungry for you."

"I mean food, silly," she said smiling at him. "Do you want a big meal or just a bite to hold you over till dinner?"

"Would you make me a large meal? I didn't have any breakfast and I probable will not have a large dinner. I find it hard to eat when I'm away from you."

"That's chicken poop," she said giving him another of the smiles that cause his heart to stop momentarily. "You don't look like you are wasting away."

"You don't understand. It all began when you said that you will marry me. I've been in a daze since then." Stellina was impressed with his romantic overtures. She only wished she could believe him. She knew he was a smooth liar. He was much more suave than Tano was and more romantic. If only he was some one other than the mayor's son. She cooked him some of the left over chicken from the day before. There was much left over since no one could eat very much last night. She sliced the chicken breast thinly, dipped them in eggs that she had beaten, rolled them in bread crumbs, and fried them. She served him soup she had saved from the day before. A small dish of pasta, she had started just before Biachio came, and then served him the chicken with a glass of wine. That was followed with a salad and a dish of fruit. Biachio ate like he had never eaten before. Stellina was impressed on how neatly and with such elegant sophistication he ate. His mother had trained him properly. Stellina tried to imitate his stile of eating.

"That was the most delicious meal I have ever eaten," he said when finished. "Stella, do you plan on cooking for us after we are married?"

"If that is what you want."

"That would make our marriage extra special. I am so tired of our cook's food. It hasn't changed since I was born. I seldom eat at home anymore." He drank the last of the wine and got up. "I do have to go. I work at my father's office. I'm the financial officer you know. I can't tell you what a great pleasure it's been spending this time with you. I hope we can repeat this again soon. And you don't have to cook for me. I just like being with you. You're so talented and beautiful. I could spend all day just looking at you."

"Go silly, your father wants you.""Ciao," he said giving her a great smile.

"Ciao," she said noticing that he did have a great smile.

That afternoon Maria and her daughter, Gina, came as they always did before. It was their turn to do the cooking.

"Where is Salvatore," asked Maria getting concerned.

"He went to the farm this morning. He will be home soon.""How could he go to the farm? He could hardly walk." Stellina explained everything to her. She was still concerned. Stellina helped with the salad and set the table while Maria and Gina did the cooking. They were always chatting about something or other but Stellina refused to talk about Biachio. She would answer them with "I'll tell you later when the men are here." Salvatore and Gino came within five minutes of each other. The two helpers left immediately. "How was your day, Papa?" asked Stellina. "Did the trip tire you?

Will you be able to do it again tomorrow? Since the helpers now know where the land is and they know what to do, do you really have to be there?"

"Hold on, honey. That is too many questions at one time."

"I'm sorry, Papa. It's that we are worried about you. Don't you know how much we all love you?"

"I know dear," he answered. "Let me see now. Did the trip tire me? The answerer is no. In fact it was good for me. The men treated me like I was their own father. Yes, I can do it again tomorrow and I want to very much. And yes, I have to be there because I enjoy watch and controlling everything from a chair in the shade." Every one laughed at that last remark. Maria finished what she had in her hand and went over to Salvatore and kissed him passionately.

"I love you and I want every one to know it," she said after their lips parted.

"I love you too and I don't care about anyone else knowing it. That you know it is the only thing I'm concerned with."

"Isn't that kind of selfish," said Gina jokingly. "Stellina and I get a lot of joy in hearing about your love. We want to enjoy the thrill of it all too."

"Okay, but only you two matter." He said with a big smile. It was very nice being part of life out there on the farm. There is one thing that is bothering me. I'm starved."

"Sorry," said Maria. "I'll get you something to eat right away..." "You stay right here. We have two young and able daughters to do the waitressing."

"I like to hear you refer me as your daughter although it's not official," said Gina with love in her voice.

"I intend to rectify that as soon as I get better," said Salvatore "Is that a proposal?" asked Maria.

"It will be as soon as I can get to a jeweler."

"I don't care about the ring," she said. "The purpose of a ring is to inform every one else that I am taken. My answer is yes and with your consent I'll start making plans."

"Come here sweet lady. I wanted my proposal to be more romantic. But I'm thrilled at the fact that you want to start planning. What can I do to help?"

"What I want you to do is sit back get well and dream about the day I will become your loving wife."

"I've been doing that for months," he said

"Me too," she said. He kissed her again with passion that was felt across the room. They were so deep in their kiss that they forgot there were others in the room. After a few minutes Stellina and Gina grew inpatient.

"Can you two break it up for a few minutes? Dinner is on the table and it will get cold." said Stellina. They all laughed at the situation. It was almost two years since Tano died and now life began to reenter the Casolini's home. When they finished eating Stellina asked for their attention.

"Listen every one," she asked. "I have a great favor to ask of you all. I have never asked anything of any of you. I have always, and always will love you all. I need a special and very difficult effort from all of you. In two weeks, Biachio and I will be married. I want you all to accept him as my fiancé until then and as my husband after the wedding. You may not agree with my decision and you may not like him personally, but with respect to me I want you to treat him kindly and as part of this family. You don't have to love him. I don't, but he will be my husband. We will be married in a church with vows to God. He has also promised to change not only for me but for himself. I didn't ask him, he volunteered. He realizes that his behavior was bad and he wants to change. He agreed to go to church with me and he wants to learn about the God his parents never told him about. Perhaps it is God's plan that I be placed in the position to save him and maybe others."

"Do you really believe him?" asked her father. "Let's give him a chance," she said.

"That's the man who killed your husband and put your brother in jail," said Gina not convinced.

"I don't know if he did or not. Even if he was involved and repents, will God forgive him? According to the bible he is to be forgiven. Whether he really repents of his sins will become apparent as time goes by. All I ask is that you trust me and give him a chance."

"Are you really going through with this," asked her father. "Papa, please."

"All right I'll hide my feelings." "I'll try," said Gina.

"It will never be said that I turned my backs to one who wants to accept God," said Maria. "I will do my best to make him feel among friends as long as he treats us as with respect."

"My thanks to all of you," said Stellina. "Now how about your wedding Mama Maria. Do you mind my calling you mama?"

"I have never heard more beautiful words," said Maria. "Except the love words I hear from your father."

"Your wedding," reminded Stellina.

"Oh yes, well, if Salvatore agrees we will have your wedding first then after that in about two week we should be ready for ours. What do you think, Sal?"

"It's a long wait, but I don't think we have a choice," he answered. "Stellina has grabbed the good day. Sweet lady, you do all the planning. I am going to sit and dream, remember?"

All right then," said Maria. "That is the plan.

Chapter 7

LOVE BLOSSOMS

The wedding of Stellina and Biachio was very small and simple. Biachio's parents were present at the church service. They did not attend the reception at Stellina's house. Roberto was Biachio's best man. Gina was Stellina's maid of honor. Only a few neighbors attended. Tano's parents, Luigi and Lina DiFranco attended, as did Luigi's brother Michele and his wife Antonietta. Their son Nino was also there. Salvatore Casolini walked his daughter down the isle. After the service, Maria and Fiorella a neighbor served a great five course dinner for the bridal party and the guests. Pietro did not attend. He was very angry that Biachio did not select him as the best man. After all, he was his best friend. Biachio tried to explain that he was trying to get into the best grace of the family and that his being best man would not be wise since it was known he was involved in the death of Tano. The news had carried the story that it was Pietro who had struck Peppino from behind. It was not wise to have anyone involved in the incident as a member of the bridal party. Pietro didn't buy it. In a way Biachio was glad. The life he led with Pietro was what he wanted to change. Pietro was very selfish, arrogant, and self-centered. Biachio decided he was not the kind of friend he wanted to associate with.

The festivities ended about midnight. Gino had a very interesting talk with Nino's father Michele DiFranco. They spoke about the possibility of Peppino getting out of jail.

Don Michele told Gino that perhaps Stellina now being part of the mayor's family could arrange the release of Peppino. However if she couldn't Gino was to see him.

When every one had left and Stellina had finished with the cleaning up, Biachio and Stellina left for the north wing of the mayor's house where they were to live. They were both very nervous. They really didn't know what to expect. Biachio showed her around the quarters. It had an outside entrance. Just inside the entrance there was a small landing. To the right of the landing was a large sitting room. It had a fireplace and seemed very comfortable. Behind the sitting room was a large dinning room. To the left of the dinning room was a beautiful kitchen. Stellina had the impression that the wing. which was originally the living quarters of the chief servant, would be a small two room apartment. She was awed at the grandeur of the rooms. Next, he took her through the kitchen to a rather quaint windowed area he called the breakfast area. It was a little kitchenette. A hall way that came off of the kitchen area led to the bedrooms. Two bedrooms were a nice size. One was set up as an office.

"I hope you don't mind, but I set up one of the bedrooms as my home office. I want to be as near to you as often as I can." Stellina couldn't answer. She was still dazed at what she saw. Next was the main bedroom. It's elegance left Stellina breathless. It was as large as the whole area where she was born including the courtyard. Off of the bedroom was a terrace that was as private as and more beautiful than the courtyard she was used to. The bedroom also had a private bathroom. She had no idea how it worked. There also was a large clothes closet built into the wall. Out in the hallway was another bathroom. At the end of the hallway was what Biachio called the music room. It had a piano and a mandolin in the corner with about ten chairs around the piano. The door on the left of the room led back to the entrance landing. Stellina was shocked into being speechless.

"Well what do you think?" asked Biachio.

"I think I could live here," she said hiding her excitement. "The truth is that it is much more than I expected. I'm breathless at its elegance."

"I'm so glad you approve. It's getting late we should probably go to bed."

"Biachio," she said getting red in the face. "Because now I am officially your wife are you going to renege on your promises? Technically you are the head of the family."

"I will keep my word till death. I will keep my promises." "Then where will I sleep?"

"I have one request to make of you. Since these quarters will be serviced by servants and will be opened to my parents it would be very embarrassing for them to see two beds that have been slept in. No one knows of our agreements."

"What are you asking?" she asked being suspicious of his intentions.

"I promised I would not touch you until you want me to. We can sleep with our backs to each other."

"You want me to sleep in the same bed with you? That wasn't part of the deal. Besides we don't need any servants."

"Please grant me this request. You are my wife. You have to start to trust me some time. Besides, I am providing a servant as a companion for you during the day when I'm not here. She will be here tomorrow morning. I will introduce you before I leave."

"I don't need a servant. I will take care of the quarters and do all the cooking. That's the way I want it."

"You're the boss. She will help you where you want her help. If you don't need her help she will sit and keep you company. I even thought one servant wasn't enough. Do you realize the work require to keep this place clean and livable."

"Who is this servant to be? She isn't one of your mistresses is she?"

"Oh Stellina," he said getting small tears in his eyes. "Why are you hurting me so, especially on our wedding day?"

"Biachio, I'm so sorry. Please forgive me. I am so nervous I don't know what I'm saying. Please forgive me."

"Please share the same bed with me."

"Okay," she finally agreed. "We can try it for awhile. That night they slept back to back to each other. Biachio kept his promises.

The next morning Stellina woke up and found she was alone in bed. The bed was a thousand times more comfortable than anything she had ever slept in. She hated to get up. She heard a bell ring so she put on her robe and went to the front entrance to see who it was. Biachio was there to let in a young and very pretty woman.

"Stellina honey," he said. "I want you to meet your helper and companion. This is Anna Maria Cradoni. We all call her Anna. Anna this is my new wife Stellina."

"How are you Anna," said Stellina. "I'm so happy to meet you." Stellina's mind raced through all her knowledge. She finally realized that this was Gino's girlfriend. The one he was crazy about. God really knows what he is doing. She was so thrilled in this latest development.

"I'm so happy to meet you," said Anna.

"Well you two get acquainted. I have to go to work. I will be home about five."

After he left, Stellina turned to Anna.

"Anna, you are the girl friend of Gino's, aren't you?" Anna looked frightened. "Oh don't worry I'm on your side. I think of Gino as my little brother. I won't give you away."

"If they find out that I am involved with an outsider they will kill me.

It isn't allowed."

"That is the most ridiculous thing I have ever heard of," said Stellina. "I'm so glad that it is you that they sent. We are going to be great friends. God knows I need one here."

"May I ask you a question," asked Anna. "Of course, what do you want to know?"

"You just got married yesterday. Why aren't you on a honeymoon?" She had some of the story she got piecemeal from Gino, but she was not aware of the special deal that they had made.

"That's a long story. You will learn about it in time. Right now, let's make the bed and then go out to the grocery store. I want to make a special dinner for my new husband." They tidied the apartment as Stellina preferred to call it and they went shopping. That evening, after Stellina finished cooking, Anna left for her own home. She had to cook for her elderly mother. When Biachio got home he surprised

Stellina by bringing her a beautiful bouquet of flowers. Stellina served him the fantastic dinner she had prepared. "I never thought you could out do the lunch you made for me the last time you cooked for me but you have done it. It is fantastic.

Don't you know you are setting up a problem for yourself? I mean you will spoil me and I will expect it all the time"

"It's the least I can do for denying you the other privileges of marriage."

"Don't you understand? Just being with you is the most wonderful thing that has ever happened to me." The rest of the evening they sat in the parlor and talked. Biachio related to Stellina all the stupid things he did with Pietro. Several times he made Stellina laugh hysterically. In a small way they were both happy.

Biachio brought Stellina flowers every evening. Stellina tried to out do her previous night's dinners each day. Soon she had to repeat her menu. Biachio was happy with what she cooked and never forgot to praise her. Stellina and Anna became great friends. They invited Stellina's father, Maria, and Gina, the Wednesday before her fathers wedding. Stellina made her best dinner according to Biachio who suggested it. The guests all agreed with him. They seemed to accept Biachio, especially since Stellina seemed to be happy. Salvatore and Maria were married that next Saturday. It was a very joyful day for all. Gino was the best man standing in for Peppino. Gina was the maid of honor. Biachio blended in with the crowd and even Gino spoke with him about the weather. Stellina and Gina spent a lot of the time together during the reception.

"Listen Gina," said Stellina. "You saw my apartment. It is more than I need."

"Are you kidding? It is fantastic," responded Gina.

"What I'm trying to say is, I want you to sell your house and move into the house Tano and I had. It is empty and you will have the use of the courtyard. You will also be near to mama and papa but not to near to disrupt their romancing."

"Are you serious?" said Gina. "I would love to live there. Are you sure? You expect to stay with Biachio?"

"I married him in good faith," said Stellina. I made vows before God. I will do all in my power to keep my marriage together. I intend to spend the rest of my life with him."

Gina was surprised at what Stellina said. Even Stellina was surprised at what she said. It was the truth, but she had not kept the vows she made. He was her husband, but she has not been his wife. Her deep thoughts were noticed by Gina.

"What are you thinking?" she asked.

"I was just thinking that I have really changed my attitude towards him. He has changed. He is trying so hard to be the man I want. He is very thoughtful and fulfills every desire I have. I don't think I love him but I have a lot of respect for him. Anyway, I would love for you to live in the house I lived in. I hope I will never need it. Besides as you can imagine I am spoiled." At that they both laughed. Gina and Stellina hugged each other.

"I love you, sis," said Gina. "I love you too."

The festivities ended around one o'clock in the morning. Stellina and Biachio went home. They didn't speak all the way home. When they got there, Biachio questioned Stellina.

"Honey, is everything all right?" he asked. "Yes why do you ask?" "You seem to be especially quiet."

"I'm tired. I'm not used to being up so late." Stellina knew it wasn't that she was tired. She was wondering if she could ever be a real wife to him. After all, she believed that he was involved in the death of her first husband. Stellina felt guilty. Was she betraying Tano? She was starting to forget the time they had together. She could hardly remember what he looked like. Her silence scared Biachio.

"Honey what is it?" Did I do or say something at the church or reception that annoyed you?"

"Oh no, Biachio. You were a perfect gentleman. I was so proud of you." She was taken back when she saw a small tear appear in his eyes. He really loved her.

"The wedding of my father and Maria brought memories back about my own life."

"You are missing Tano?"

"No it's not that. If anything, I feel guilty because he is slowly fading from my memory. No it's more like I see them so happy and then I look at my life."

"Don't I make you happy just a little?"

"Oh Biachio, It's not you, it's me. I feel bad that I can't be a wife to you. You deserve better than me."

"You are a wife to me. I am deliriously happy. Please don't worry about that."

"I do worry about that. I made vows to God. I should love you with all my heart."

"I'm working on that," he said with a smile.

"I know you have and you have been a perfect husband. I couldn't ask you for more."

"Let go to bed," he said. Things will look better in the morning. Believe me I have no complaints." Stellina went into the bathroom to change into her night gown. When she came out Biachio wasn't there. She got into bed and wondered were he was. He showed up a few minutes later.

"Where did you go?" she asked.

"I had to get things ready for a meeting I have Monday." He then sat on the end of the bed and started to undress. After he had gotten down to his shorts and tee shirt he looked at her.

"Please turn around and close your eyes," he asked of her. "Why," she asked.

"Because I'm bashful, all right. Now you know." "You're too bashful to take off you tee shirt?" "Yes,"

"Were you this bashful with all the other girls that you have made love to?"

"I have never known a girl." He said being very bashful at the confession.

"You have never made love to a girl? Are you saying that you are virgin?"

"So I never thought of girls before I met you. It's not that I'm so holy or anything it's just that the occasion never came up. Pietro and I were having fun just being boys.

"You don't like boys more than girls do you?"

"Dear God, no. I have the desires like any other man. Don't you understand why I have not made a pass at you? I wouldn't know what to do. I have a great desire for you. I hurt in my private place when I think of you. Now go to sleep and stop embarrassing me." "I'm sorry," said Stellina with a silly grin. She turned on her side away from him. He put on his pajamas and got into bed.

"Now you can turn around so I can see you." She did and she was still smiling.

"Go to sleep," he ordered.

The months slipped by like they were days. Nothing really changed between Stellina and Biachio. He never failed to bring her flowers. He never failed to tell her how much he loved her and how happy she made him. He was always very romantic in his actions and his words to her. Stellina was beginning to soften towards him. They saw her family often and it seemed that they had come to accept him completely. Stellina began to notice his smile; it was a very lovely smile she thought. And he was sort of handsome. He had gorgeous eyes. Every once in a while he would fall asleep before she did and she would stare at his face. She liked it. It was a soft and kind face. He also had juicy lips. She wondered what it would be like to kiss them. This happen more often every day. Still things remained the same.

It was on a Friday evening in early winter when Stellina and Biachio were sitting in their parlor when Biachio started to question Stellina about the bible.

"Stella, he asked. You know a lot about the bible don't you?" "I used to read it every day before we got married."

"Doesn't the bible say that a person who has accepted Jesus as his savior and obeys his commandments is born again and becomes a new man?"

"Yes that is right," she said wondering where all of this was coming from.

"Doesn't it also say that after you are saved that God forgives and forgets all your sins?"

"Yes, where is this all coming from?"

"Doesn't it say in Ephesians 5:22 that a wife should submit herself to her husband?"

"I submit to your authority," said Stellina in her defense. "Doesn't the bible in Corinthians 7:4 say that the wife has no power over her own body and it's the same with the husband?" Yes, what are you getting at?"

Doesn't the bible in many places say that we should be fruitful and multiply?"

"Biachio, what do you want?" said Stellina being confused at his knowledge of the bible.

"I think that I deserve a kiss when I leave in the morning and when I come home in the evening. Is that too much for a husband to ask his wife? Don't I deserve that much?"

"You think you're so smart, don't you? You're so sneaky." said Stellina with a condescending smile. "I suppose I owe you that much. Are you slowly trying to sneak up on me?"

"I'll never tell," he said his face showing the joy of having won the first round. Stellina found herself looking forward to the kiss. She had already been dreaming of kissing the lips she had learned to admire. She changed the subject and they finally went to bed. She got to bed first. When Biachio sat down to change, she was still awake looking at him.

"Do we have to go through this again?" he asked.

"Okay you won one now it's my turn to win one. I want you to take off you undershirt and let me see your chest. You can keep your shorts on."

"Do I have to?" he pleaded, his face turning red.

"You quoted the bible to me about your body being mine and my body being yours so what goes for me also goes for you."

"But I didn't ask you to show me your body."

"But I agreed to what you asked for. Besides when we got married you promised to give me what ever I asked for to make me happy. I'm asking you to strip from the waist up. I don't see what a big deal that is. I've seen many men working with their shirts off." "Yes, but not in front of the woman that they are crazy in love with." With a red face he removed his undershirt. He quickly put on his pajama top. Then with his back to her, he slipped off his shorts and slipped on his pajama bottoms. He slipped into bed besides her.

"There, are you happy now?"

"I don't see what the fuss was all about. You have a very beautiful chest. It's very manly and muscular. You should be very proud of your shape."

"Go to sleep," he said still red faced. "You have had your fun for today." Stellina moved closer to Biachio so that their faces were almost touching.

"Wait until tomorrow when you leave for work. I will give you the kiss of your life," said Stellina lovingly. Biachio smiled with love in his eyes. "I love you so much," he said as he fell asleep.

The next morning when Stellina awoke Biachio was not in bed.

She quickly dressed and found him in the kitchen. "Good morning," she said "What are you doing?"

"I'm making breakfast for us. It's the least I could do after the great dinners you have prepared for me." He described the three different breakfasts he was good at cooking and told her of his plan. "I will call you when breakfast is ready. I always get up earlier than you so I thought, why don't I make breakfast for us." What do you think of that?"

"I'm so sorry, Biachio. I was always up before my father and should get up early for you. Forgive me. I'll get up earlier tomorrow. It's just that the bed is so comfortable I can't resist it."

"No, you don't understand," said Biachio. "I'm not criticizing you. I like it when you are happy. Besides I like doing something for you. By all means, stay in bed as long as you want. You're not at your father's house. You are in a brand new life. We will form our own habits as we go along."

"Are you serious?"

"Yes, my darling. Let me do this for you, please."

Well then let me set the table and pack your lunch. I like the idea that we do things together. I made a special Sausage bun yesterday for your lunch today. I know you will love it. It is my best luncheon receipt."

"Sounds perfect to me. Our life is shaping up wonderfully." "It's not too bad. I have a feeling it will get better." She added. "I'm not even going to ask," said Biachio. As Biachio was ready to leave Anna showed up.

"You guys are all up early," she said.

"Get used to it because this is the pace we are going to set," said Stellina.

"Well I'll be going," said Biachio waiting to see if Stellina would follow up on her promise.

"Biachio, have a wonderful day," she said and then she put her arms around his neck and kissed him on his lips. She held it for awhile. His lips were so warm and soft she felt something new inside. She didn't want to let go.

"Wow," said Biachio. "You are a woman of your word." He said and left for work.

"Anna I have a special plan for today. I'm going to try and see my brother."

"Do you need me to go with you?"

"No you had better not. They may retaliate. I expect to get nasty." You can stay here and clean what ever you think needs it. I don't think you should go home. The powers to be may not like it."

"Should I check Biachio's office?"

"No, he wouldn't like anyone to go in his office. That is the only thing he is strict about. I'll check it before I leave." After getting ready Stellina went into Biachio's office. It was very tidy. She was about to leave when she spotted something on his desk. A closer look revealed that it was a bible.

"Anna, do you know what I found in his room?" "I haven't the slightest idea,"

"The dear man has been reading the bible," she said with a very surprised tone.

"It looks like we have greatly misjudged the man," said Anna.

"I think rather he is really trying to change. I'll be leaving now." "Can I make some lunch? You never let me cook. You should be back before lunch."

"We don't have much food. I was thinking of going shopping when I get back. Well you can get enough for lunch if you want."

"I can get everything you need if you tell me which of your receipt you intend to use."

"I thought I would make lasagna for tonight we haven't had that for along time."

"I'll get everything and get it started."

"That would be fine Anna, thanks. I'll see you later."

When Stellina got to the jail, the jailer in charge was tying up another convict and told Stellina to wait. It took everything in her to just sit, but she knew that if she got impatient, things would be worse for Peppino. It was definitely one of the longest hours of her life.

"What do you want?" the jailer growled. Stellina ignored his gruff tone and insolent attitude. She resisted wrinkling her nose at the foul smell coming from him, or perhaps it was his clothes, she thought.

"I want to see Peppino Casolini," she answered.

"No one is allowed to see him," he said in the same nasty voice as he walked to the small desk on the side of the room..

"Do you know who I am?" asked Stellina getting upset with his attitude.

"You could be the son of God but you're not going to see him today." Stellina knew this guy could not be scared. She left with her tail between her legs. When she got back home she told Anna what had happened.

I know him," said Anna. "They use him as an extra when their regular guard is on another task. Let's go Wednesday. I know the guy who is there then. I'll go with you. I don't have to go in the cell area but I can be a witness if you need one." Stellina understood what Anna was saying. She was smarter than anyone had given her credit for. She could see why Gino was crazy about her.

That Wednesday, Stellina and Anna arrived at the jail about ten in the morning. They walked up to the guard who was sitting at the entrance to the jail cells.

"Ciao," said Stellina. "I've come to visit with my brother, Peppino Casolini."

"No one is allowed to see the prisoners," he said.

"I've been here before with my husband. The guard at that time let us in with no trouble. Why are you so difficult?"

"I was told not to let any one in." he insisted. "Do you know who I am?" asked Stellina. "No," he said simply.

"I am Mrs. Biachio DiVincenso. My husband is the mayor's son. I don't think you want him angry with you."

"I can't let you in," he insisted. After much pleading with him and getting the same answer, she decided to play her trump card.

"Look, I'm not going home without seeing my brother. So if you don't let me in the cell area in the next two minutes I'm going to tear my dress and claim that you tried to rape me. I have a witness. Didn't you see the whole thing, Anna?"

"Yes," said Anna. It was so horrible. He tore at your dress and I started to cry and yell till you let her go and we ran all the way home to tell Biachio what happened. We were so scared."

"You girls aren't serious are you?" he asked sounding serious himself.

"Were you born yesterday?" asked Stellina. "Don't you know what happens to people who cross the DiVincenso family? And you are making me very cross right now."

"Why are you putting me in the middle? When they find out I let you in I'll be dead anyway." He said sounding scared to death.

"I'll give you a chance. I'll make a deal with you. You let us in and no one will know we were here. What do you think Anna?"

"We were never here. Why would we come here?"

"You girls will be the death of me," he said sounding like he was about to relent.

"We certainly will be if you don't do as I ask," said Stellina pushing as hard as she could.

"If I let you in will you promise that the next time you will get a note from the mayor?"

"He is such a busy man, but all right" He opened the main door that led to the cell area.

"His cell is the last one on the left," said the guard.

"I'll wait here for you," said Anna. "I'll keep this nice man company." Stellina nodded her head in agreement and after shutting the door she walked to the last cell.

"How are you, Peppi?" she said to Peppino.

"I'm doing a lot better now. You know that Gino has been feeding me every night. The guard has also been feeding me twice a day instead of once and they are sometimes bringing me some olives or a fruit. The other day they brought me a large piece of cheese."

"How did you ever find such a great friend like Gino?"

"I'm lucky I guess. How have you been, sis? How is Biachio treating you?"

"Peppi you wouldn't believe how he caters to my every wish. He spoils me worse than you did. He isn't as bad as we assumed. He was just unlucky to be born to a rotten family. Did you know he is reading the bible? I think he reads it every morning."

"He is a strange man," said Peppino. "Did you know that every once in a while he stops in just for a second to see if I'm all right?" "He does?" said Stellina. "No, he never told me about that. He is doing everything he can to make me happy. He wants me to love him so badly."

"Is he succeeding?"

"I really don't know. I have a lot more respect for him then I did before."

"How are papa and our new mother?"

"They are the sweetest couple you ever saw. Their love is so obvious. They can't keep from hugging and kissing, even in front of Gina and me."

"Well at least they are happy."

"Peppi, I want to assure you of one thing. I am not unhappy. I am much happier then I ever dreamed I would be with him. He is a lot of fun to be around."

"Have you been his wife completely?"

"No, and I feel guilty about that. I married him willingly. I made vows in church in front of God. Peppi, what do you think my duty as a wife should be?"

"I guess you agreed to marry him for life. You should enjoy it as much as any married person. A marriage under God should be consummated. Do you have desires toward him?"

"I feel guilty of depriving him of his rights as a married man. I also desire his affections if you know what I mean."

"Do you feel any love for him?"

"When he tells me how much he loves me I feel like jumping into his arms and then I remember that he may have been involved in the death of Tano. I'm very confused."

"If he is reading the bible and is trying to become a Christian, then God will forgive him. You should also. Make sure he is dependable to your satisfaction. If you are sure he is really changed then let him consummate the marriage. I assume he has never known a woman."

"What makes you say that?"

"Well if he had any experience he wouldn't have been able to resist this long. I don't think he knows what to do."

"I had better be going. I'll try to see you more often. I'm so glad to have spoken to you. I think my marriage is going to be much better from now on."

"Good for you sis. The agreement you made is for life. You may as well enjoy it."

"Ciao Peppi, I love you."

"Ciao Sis, I love you too." Stellina left and met Anna in the outer lobby.

"Let's go," said Stellina to Anna. "I had a very good visit. Thank you guard. I don't know your name."

"I didn't tell you it," said the guard.

"I understand," said Stellina. "Thanks anyway." They left the area and when they made it outside Stellina was all smiles.

"Okay," said Anna seeing her happy face. "What happened?" "Peppino is doing much better. They are feeding him better and Gino has been giving him food every night. What a sweet heart Gino is."

"Where do we go from here?" asked Anna. "Let's go to see my parents."

"Your father won't be home will he?"

"I don't think so but Mama Maria should be. And Gina should be there to. She will be interested in how Peppino is doing." They arrived at the Casolini house at about eleven-thirty.

"I just come from visiting Peppino. I thought you would want to hear how he is." said Stellina to Maria.

"Ciao sweetheart," said Maria. "How are you? And it is so nice to see you Anna."

"Ciao, Dona Maria. It is nice to see you too."

"You girls are just in time for some lunch with me. I don't like to eat alone."

"Why, where is Gina?" asked Stellina.

"She went with Gino. Gino decided to farm our land. He plowed his land to keep its soil rich and is helping to harvest our crop. Your father, with his helpers, is harvesting his land. We thought we could use the extra income. Gina is helping Gino harvest our land of the summer grain" Gino will seed his land for the winter crop if he has time, also depending on the weather. Gina will help him then." Maria made some pasta and three pieces of fish which she had ready to cook.

"Did you know we were coming," said Stellina surprised that she had the fish ready.

"I bought the fish yesterday but your father and Gina came home late and were too tired to eat, so I had left over fish. I have to cook it today, because as you know, fish doesn't stay fresh long…We will each have a piece and I won't have to worry about it lasting."

"As long as we aren't taking food from the workers we will love to stay." While Maria was cooking Stellina brought her up to date on the condition of Peppino. Maria was so happy to hear he was being feed sufficiently. "Your father will be so happy to hear the news. He will be happy to know you have seen him."

"We can visit after we eat. I'll make some coffee," said Maria. "You aren't in a hurry are you?"

"No, I'm not," responded Stellina. She looked at Anna. Anna shook her head indicating no.. Stellina and Anna stayed most of the afternoon. Maria enjoyed the time they spent together. Stellina loved Maria like her own mother. About three-thirty they decided they had to leave so they could cook for Biachio.

"I have never in the year we have been married, missed serving him a good dinner. I don't intend to miss today."

"That's right," said Maria. "I almost forgot. Tomorrow is your anniversary. How are you two getting along? It seems to me that you are pretty happy."

"I am, Mama Maria. I never even dreamed I could be this happy. Biachio has treated me like a queen. In the entire year he has never come home with out bringing me flowers."

"Well then Happy Anniversary" they hugged each other and Stellina and Anna left for home. When they got there Stellina was hesitant to prepare dinner.

"I would like to prepare something special tomorrow since it's my anniversary. So what should I make tonight?"

"I beg to differ with you but weren't you married on September 16 of last year?"

"Yes, so what, today is the 15th"

"No today is the 16th. You lost a day somewhere."

"Oh my Lord!" said Stellina getting hysterical. I can't miss my anniversary." They ran around to all the grocery stores looking for something special. They found a small standing rib in a little meat store.

"I know how to cook it," said Anna. "I have cooked it on special occasions for Biachio's uncle, the police chief. I don't think that Biachio has ever tasted it. It tastes out of this world." They bought it and Anna helped cook it. The aroma that filled the room was enough to make anyone hungry. Biachio came home around six as usual. The flowers he presented her were twice the size he usually brought and included some very exotic types.

"Welcome home, dear husband. How was your day?"

"It was full of longing for you," he said as he moved in for his welcome home kiss. The kiss was more passionate then it had ever been before. He found her tongue was forcing its way into his mouth. His tongue automatically caressed hers.

"Wow," he said. "That was the best welcome home kiss you have ever given me. What's up?"

"You know what's up. You know what day this is. It's the anniversary of our wedding."

"Has it been that long?"

"Don't be silly," she said "Your flowers gave you away. I have made a special dinner to celebrate."

"I didn't think that you considered it a day to celebrate."

"Now you are fishing. I'll not bite on that one," said Stellina with a pixie smile.

"Can't blame a guy for trying. Actually, I am very pleased that you want to celebrate."

"Wait until you get the special present I got you for our anniversary."

"I can hardly wait, although I smelled it the moment I walked in the door." She then brought out the standing rib. She sliced a one inch slice and placed it on his dish. She then sliced a piece for herself. Next she placed a large spoon full of mashed potatoes and a large portion of spinach on his dish. The wine was on the table and a large bowl of salad was next to it.

"Honey, as head of the family, please say grace." Biachio broke out in a very happy grin. "What's so funny? Did I say something wrong?"

"No it's just that you called me, honey. It's the first time you said something affectionate to me. It thrilled me down to my heart."

"Will you stop and say grace?" teased Stellina.

Biachio folded his hands, "Dear Lord," started Biachio. "We thank you for all the blessings you have given us. We thank you for our health and safety and the health and safety of all our loved ones. On this special day, our one year anniversary, I thank you for Stellina. Lord I pray you will guide me to be a better husband to her. Lord, we thank you for the food you have placed before us. We pray that you bless it and the hands that prepared it. In Jesus' name we pray, amen."

"Dig in, Honey," she said stretching the words out as sweetly as she could, kidding him with the honey she had addressed him with. Biachio smiled a loving smile and began eating. He didn't look up until his dish was empty.

"Stella, that was the greatest dinner I have ever had and I can't see how it can ever be topped. I've never tasted anything so good. Words can not say how satisfied I feel."

"Glad you enjoyed it. I must confess I had a lot of help from Anna. She is very valuable to me." "Is this my anniversary gift?"

"Only part of it. The rest you will get later tonight. Did you bring me a gift besides the flowers?"

"Yes, but I will give it to you after you have given me mine." Biachio went into his office while Stellina cleaned the kitchen and washed the utensils and dishes. Afterwards they sat together and reviewed the past year. Many things that they brought up, they reviewed in a humorous way which caused them to laugh through most of the evening. Soon it was time to call it a night. Stellina went to bed before Biachio came into the room. She was still awake when Biachio came in and put on his pajama bottoms and then the top.

"Please don't put on the top," requested Stellina. "Why," he asked.

"My gift requires that you are bare above the waist." "What?" he asked, caught by surprise.

"Trust me," she said.

"I trust you with my life, but I'm very confused."

"Just climb in bed and it will all come clear to you." He climbed into bed keeping the bed covers high near his neck. "Are you still bashful?" she asked with a soft laughter.

"Now what?" he asked ignoring her.

"Part of your present is you can now kiss me good night after we get into bed and good morning just before getting out of bed." "That is the best present I have ever had," he said joyfully. "I'm thrilled. Do we start right now?" She didn't answer. She just pulled him to her and softly kissed him. Her tongue reached out for his. This time his tongue was ready to fondle hers. Next she placed his hand on her stomach and pulled his body tight against hers. He suddenly realized she was entirely nude.

"What is going on?" he asked, stupefied by her actions.

"I was thinking about what you said the other day," she started. "I went into the marriage with my eyes wide open. I made a vow before God to be your wife. The agreement we made is in reality not binding. We can not put a condition to God's law. What I'm saying is I want to be your wife completely. My body is yours and your body is mine" She saw little tears coming into his eyes. She let her hands wonder around his chest as she kissed him passionately. His hand began an exploration of its own. Stellina raised her foot until it caught the top of his pajamas bottoms. Will a little effort she managed to pull them down to his feet. He instantly kicked them off. She could tell that his passion and excitement had reached a peak paralleling her own. He started to kiss her neck and slowly worked down. Because of the long and passionate foreplay the pleasure reached a height she had never achieved before. Not even with Tano. After they had consummated the marriage, Biachio rolled over on his back to take a deep breath. After a few seconds, he rolled on his side and pulled her against him so her body and his seemed like one.

"It's like a miracle," he said after he had kissed her several times. "You liked it that much?" she asked gleefully.

"Oh it was fantastic. It was more than I even had imagined it could be like. You're in trouble now. It will easily become a habit. No, that is not what I was feeling. Although I do think what we just had was miraculous, I was thinking if you had asked me before how much I loved you I would have said that it would be impossible to love you more. Yet I find that at this moment I love you a thousand times more. I feel like I'm going to bust." They laid there looking at each other. Stellina was wondering what it was she was feeling. Was she madly in love with the man she had hated just a year ago? Or was what she was feeling just an after affect of the activity they had just experienced. She had to admit to herself it was better then what she had experienced with Tano. With Tano there wasn't as much foreplay. She thought she would wait until morning when her excitement had subsided. Then she would be in a better mental position to evaluate her feelings. They finally fell asleep nude in each others arms, his lips never far from hers.

In the morning, Stellina woke up with the strange feeling that something was on her face. When she was fully awake she realized that her husband was kissing her all over her face.

"I'm sorry sweetheart. I didn't want to wake you but I love you so much. I want you very badly."

"I'm glad you woke me. I want you too, very badly." She kissed him and pressed her body against his. He knew what to do this time. When it was over Stellina took a deep breath. She couldn't believe it was better this morning then it was last night, perhaps because they were more relaxed.

"Why don't you get dressed and I will go and prepare breakfast." She said finally. She put on her robe and went into the kitchen.

He came out clean shaven with only his pants and shirt on. They ate breakfast and afterwards he went into the bedroom to finish dressing. Stellina found she was over the excitement and felt calm. Now she will be able to tell how she really felt about him. When he came out fully dressed and ready to go to work, she looked at him in awe. As he stood there she suddenly realized he was the most handsome man she had ever seen. She didn't want him to leave. She felt a pressure in her stomach. Her heart started to beat in tune with the lump in her throat. Like a lightening bolt the realization hit her that she was madly in love with him. It took her by surprise.

"Honey, do you have to leave yet?" she asked. "Why are you feeling lonely?"

"Yes, I miss you already and you haven't even left yet."

"Okay what do you have in mind?" She was trying to think of a way to detain him, when she realized she had given him his anniversary present but he had forgotten to give her his.

"You promised that after I had given you your anniversary present you would give me mine. You didn't give me it."

"Oh my," he said suddenly remembering. "I completely forgot. Your present was so fantastic that it made me forget everything." He reached into his inner jacket pocket and pulled out an envelope. "This is all I could manage, my love. It is not enough. Tell me, how I can make it up to you?" Stellina ignored his statement and opened the envelope. It was a letter to the jail administrator. Stellina read it out loud.

"This is an order from the mayor of Barrafranca. I am directing you to allow Stellina DiVincenso to visit her brother Giuseppe Casolini. She can bring with her one other visitor. This order is only good for once a week. It is signed by Mayor Mario DiVincenso. Oh Biachio this is the greatest present you could give me."

"I wish I could get him released. I don't think this is equal to your gift."

"Okay," she said with that pixie look on her face.. "There is something you could do that would make me very happy."

"What is it? I will do anything you ask. Tell me and it's yours." "I would like a week or two on a honeymoon with my husband." "You're going to kill me with joy and happiness. I'll see what I can do. We may have to wait for a slow time at the office. This is harvest time. This is when we collect the taxes, but as soon as that is completed I'll ask for time off. Now I'd better go. It wouldn't be nice to get fired by my own father."

"Ciao, come back quickly," she requested.

"Wait a minute," he complained. "I can't leave with out my good-bye kiss. It is the only thing that will keep me going until I come home." Stellina kissed him a kiss he could never forget. As he left she stood there watching him disappear through the door.

"She felt a burning in her bosom for him. Her love for him had blossomed into a beautiful flower.

Chapter 8

BLACK THURSDAY

Biachio and Stellina did go on their honeymoon after the first harvest was over. They visited Rome, Florence, Pisa and Milano. They spent a week in Capri. They had gotten tired of traveling and sight seeing. They wanted to spend more time alone together. They did take one day to see the blue grotto. The rest of the week they spent together. The first day they never bothered to dress. But the next morning they found they were pretty hungry. The days after that were pretty much identical. In the morning after they awoke they made love. They went out for breakfast and came back and made love. At noon they had lunch and came back to their room and made love. At evening they went out for a fine dinner and after they got back to the room they made love. Before they went to sleep they made love. Stellina found that she loved him with all of her heart. She didn't tell him however. She thought she would tell him on a special occasion when he may need a lift. Things were going too nicely now and a declaration of love may change things. For her everything was going perfect.

When they got home, Biachio was floating on air. It thrilled Stellina to see how happy he was. It took a couple of days before things settled back to normal, although that was difficult to define since their life was far from what was normal before their honeymoon. Stellina didn't do things for Biachio to impress him or to try to be a good wife. She did it now because she loved him and wanted to please him. They settled down to a comfortable routine. A few days after they got back

Stellina and Biachio went to her parent's house. It was late in the evening when Stellina was sure that her father was home. They all hugged each other upon their arrival "Papa, how are you doing on the farm?" Stellina asked her father. "All the grain is in and the field is ready to plow."

"Can you take a day off?"

"Why do you want me to take a day off?"

"Can't a daughter have a day alone with her father? I miss you. You have two men to help you. Surely you could take a day off to be with me."

"First of all I only have one helper, and secondly I need to plow the field."

"Why do you only have one helper?" asked Biachio" "One was called back to work for your family."

"They can't do that," said Biachio getting very disturbed. "Those two men are my men. I'll see about that. When did they take him back?"

"It was when you two were out of town," answered Salvatore. "That's all right; I don't really need him now that I'm back to normal. Don't make a fuss. I don't want you to get in trouble with your family. I will take a day off tomorrow if that is what you want, Stella."

"Good," said Stellina. "I'll be here early in the morning. We can have breakfast together." The rest of the evening Stellina and Biachio told them about their experience traveling through Italy. They described in detail what they saw in Rome and Pisa. They told them of beautiful Capri. They went home late that night. After they had gone to bed before Stellina kissed Biachio he held back her advancement.

"Honey, sweet heart, before you start kissing me and I lose all senses, could you tell me what you have in mind about tomorrow." "I have a special place I want to take my father. Thanks to you, I can do it now. I want to take them all one at a time to see Peppino."

"Oh I wish I could be with you. I would love to see the joy he experiences."

"Why don't you come?"

"No, that should be a private and personal meeting."

"You are such a sweet and thoughtful person do you know that. Now shut up and kiss me." He complied with her request but he didn't stop there.

The next morning Stellina was at her family's house at eight in the morning. They had waited for her to have breakfast.

"Your father has been up since six this morning. He has been so excited to spend the day with you. I don't think he was this excited at our wedding."

"That is nonsense. I was there remember."

"Well maybe he was a little more excited at our wedding. He was so excited I was worried he was going to have a heart attack." Just then Salvatore walked in from the stable.

"What are you girls up too," he asked.

"I was wondering where Gina was," said Stellina.

"She went with Gino to help him," he said "You know we should get help for poor Gino. He is trying to farm three farms. People are starting to talk about Gina."

"What is that all about?" asked Stellina.

"Well Gina and Gino are always together. They work together and we have him here for dinner every night. People think they are having an affair. The rumor is being spread that she is a lose woman."

"What does Gina think about that?" asked Stellina.

"She said they could go to...hades, Well that isn't exactly the word she used, but you know what I mean."

"Well I can spread a rumor also," said Stellina. "I'll have Biachio spread the rumor that anyone caught even saying Gina's name will be jailed as a trouble maker."

"Well what do you want to do today," asked her father. "I want you to come with me. I have a surprise for you." "Why, it's not my birthday?"

"Never mind the smart remarks. Come with me." "Can I come along too," asked Maria.

"I'm sorry Mama Maria. I have to do this alone. I will take you next Wednesday." They got into the buggy Stellina had come in, and rode to the other end of town.

"Where are we going and when are we going to get there?" asked her father.

"We are almost there. I have to stop and deliver a message at the jail first," said Stellina trying to keep their destination a secret as long as she could. When they got to the jail Stella started in and suggested he come in for a minute.

"Why do I want to come in there? Are you trying to put me in jail?" he said in jest.

"I may be awhile," she answered. "You can come in and sit and rest for a minute. I have to do some business for my husband." "Well I want to tell you that so far this has not been any fun." "Trust me, Papa. You will understand in just a little while." She grabbed him by the hand and pulled him inside. When they came to the guard she gave him an order.

"Open the door we are going to visit a prisoner." The guard having seen the note from the mayor opened the door without saying a word. Salvatore's face turned white. He started to stumble and as soon as he realized what was happening tears appeared in his eyes. He had a lump in his throat so he couldn't speak. Stellina led him toward the last cell where Peppino saw them coming and began to cry.

"Papa, is that you?"

"Peppi," was all he could say. As he got to the cell he reached through the bars and they hugged each other as best they could. Peppino and his father talked for about an hour. They talked of all early days they spent together. Peppino wanted to know all about the marriage and the days his father spent with his new wife. Was he happy?

"How can I be happy with you behind bars for something you didn't do," he answered. "Maria is a very sweet and a wonderful person. You would love her. If you were home life would be absolutely perfect."

"Papa, I want you to be happy with Maria. I am so happy for you. Don't worry about me."

"Fellows," said Stellina. "I hate to be a party pooper, but the guard is getting nervous. We are allowed only an hour. We are over that now. I will bring Papa back again. I am allowed one hour once a week."

"You take care of yourself," said Salvatore. "Don't do anything to get them upset. We are going to get you out of here somehow if it's the last thing I do." After they got back in the buggy, Stellina's father started to weep.

"Papa what is wrong? Why are you so sad?"

"Honey I'm crying because I'm so happy. This has been the best present anyone has given me. I'm crying because I thought I would never ever see him again,"

"Papa, I promise you that I will bring you here again.""Sweetheart, can't you and Biachio do anything to get him out?""Biachio would give his right arm to get him out, especially since he blames himself for Peppino being there. We have to be patient." "It's hard," When they got home Salvatore explained excitingly where Stellina had taken him. He couldn't stop talking about his hour with Peppino. Every one was excited.

The next week went by with little excitement. Stellina and Biachio led happy lives, each trying to please the other. Stellina was still surprised that she loved Biachio so much. However she had not told him as yet. She wanted to declare it at a special occasion. That Wednesday Stellina brought Maria to see Peppino. Gina and Maria flipped a coin to see who goes. Gina lost. Peppino was thrilled to see Maria. He treated her as if she was his biological mother. He had always loved her even before she met Salvatore. The next week Gina went to see Peppino. They both cried most of the hour. Stellina left them alone for a while so they could exchange their words of love and kiss through the bars.

"No matter what happens I will always love you," declared Gina. "Gina you must move on. It is not likely I will ever get out of here alive.

"Even if it was necessary for me to move on you will still own my heart. I will always be yours in my heart." Peppino didn't really understand what Gina was telling him. She knew that Peppino would never get out and that God may have other plans for her. It was what she feared most of all. Gina left still holding on to his hand until she was too distant to hold on.

"I love you," she said as she went through the door "I love you too," said Peppino. But the door had closed and Peppino wasn't sure she heard him.

Several weeks went by. Stellina and Biachio were happier than they had ever been. He still brought her flowers every night. They kissed more every day then they did the day before. The only disturbing thing was that Salvatore was more disturbed and unhappy every time he left the jail after seeing Peppino. Stellina was afraid that his attitude would affect his life with Maria, but didn't know what she could do. She talked to Maria about it one morning after her father had left.

"Mama Maria," said Stellina. "I'm worried about papa. Every time we leave the jail he seems more depressed. How is he at home?" "He has changing moods. Sometimes he's the happy loving man I married. Sometimes he is moody and talks about trying to fine find a way to free Peppino. I try to talk him out of talking that way but you know how stubborn your father is."

"What does he think of doing?"

"He doesn't say. He just says that there has to be a way." "Please try to talk him out of trying something stupid. Tell him that Biachio and I have a plan that we are working on. He would be out of jail now if it wasn't for Biachio's mother. We had his father convinced. She pulled the rug out from under us. The problem is that she hates me with a passion because I'm a peasant girl and she wanted him to marry in their class. I can't believe she would hate me for that alone."

"Believe it, my dear. Those people look at us as we look at cattle. They believe we are here only to serve them, the blue blood. To her, Biachio marrying you is like Peppino marrying a cow." They both thought about it for a moment and then they both bust out laughing. Little did they know there was more truth to that statement then they both believed.

It was three weeks later. Stellina and Anna were having coffee together. Biachio had left for the office about an hour before. They were talking about Gino and what a blessing he was to them all when there was a knock on the door.

"Who could that be?" said Stellina. "I'm not expecting any one." "I'll get the door," said Anna. "Could it be one of your in-laws?" "They would never knock," said Stellina. "They own this place."

Anna opened the door. Standing at the threshold, stood a man about forty years of age.

"What can I do for you," asked Anna.

"I would like to talk with Dona Stellina please," he said. Stellina had walked to the door to see who it was.

"I'm Stellina. What do you want?"

"Dona Stellina please excuse me for intruding, but Don Biachio told me if anything unusual happens that I should report directly to you."

"Well what has happened?"

"My name is Giovanni. I was ordered by Don Biachio to help your father on his farm. We used to meet at your father's house and we went to the field together. Your father requested I not go to his house. He said he wanted us to meet at the field. We have done that for a long time now, but this morning your father didn't show up. I went to his house and he wasn't there. Dona Maria said that he left very early this morning to go to the field. That is why I came here." "You did the right thing," said Stellina beginning to worry. "Thank you. Please go back to the field and finish what you were ordered to do." After the man left Stellina ordered the buggy and she and Anna went to her father's house. When they got there Stellina heard the wailing inside and began to cry. She knew immediately that something terrible had happened.

"Mama," Stellina yelled. "What has happened? Where is father?" Maria ran and hugged Stellina. For several minutes, she couldn't talk. Then finally she sputtered it out.

"Oh lord, Stella, we lost him." After a few more mournful wailings she continued. "A policeman came and told me they found him on the road to Enna. They said he had been robbed and killed. But it was them. They killed him. The monsters killed him."

"What was he doing way out there?" asked Stellina between her own wailing.

"I think he was going to Enna to try and free Peppino." Stellina broke down completely after hearing that. She should have done something to stop him. Anna tried to comfort her. She loved Stellina.

She hugged her and wept with her. After about an hour they became quiet. Stellina recovered first.

"Maria, will you be all right? I must go and find Biachio. He will be feeling very bad. I know he will be blaming himself. He had promised to protect him." The truth was she also needed comfort from the man she loved. Maria didn't answer. They waited seeing that she didn't answer. They figured she didn't want them to go. Unexpectedly Gina came rushing into the house. Full of tears she threw her self in her mother's arms.

"Mama, I'm so sorry. Are you all right?"

"I'm all right," she said between tears. "Stella why don't you go do what you wanted to do. Gina's here now to comfort me." Stellina and Anna both kissed her and Gina and left. On the way Stellina recovered enough to start thinking of what had to be done.

"Listen Anna," she said tearfully. "Would you do something for me?"

"There isn't anything I wouldn't do for you," she said through tears of her own. "Just ask me."

"Would you take care of the food needed to take care of the people that will come to visit? I have no idea of what or how many. I'm not thinking too straight right now."

"Don't worry about it. I will take care of everything. I have experience in this sort of thing. I don't even need money. You can take care of the costs later. I will be very happy to be able to help."

"What would I do without you," said Stellina with gratitude.

"I hope you will never find out," said Anna. She regretted saying it as soon as she finished. It was no time for humor. However, it had the opposite affect. Stellina managed a weak smile and squeezed Anna's hand. "Drop me off at your place. I'll handle everything from there. You go find your husband." Stellina dropped Anna off in front of the house and proceeded to her husband's office.

Biachio arrived at Maria's house minutes after Stellina had left. He had found out about what happened from a police friend. He quickly ran out to find Maria and Stellina. He presumed she would be there with Mama Maria. He ran in and found Maria sitting in a chair in the rear of the room. Gina was lying on the bed. He immediately fell on his knees before her and hid his face in her lap. "Mama Maria, I'm so sorry," he said crying loudly. "It's all my fault. I promised Stellina I would protect her father. I have failed everyone. Please forgive me."

"Biachio," she said surprised at his sorrow. "The one thing I'm sure of is you had nothing to do with it."

"It was my family, I know it. If I would have left Stellina alone with Tano everyone would now be happy. I can't bear to think of what Stellina will do. It will kill her. I had promised her. She will never forgive me."

"Stellina has been here," informed Maria. "She is very broken up but she is very strong. She will be all right. Biachio honey, why don't you go to her? She needs you now more then ever."

"She won't want to see me. I let her down. I promised to protect her family. I can't even do that right."

"Trust your heart," said Maria starting to cry again.

"Mama Maria will you let me make the funeral arrangements. Would you let me pick the coffin? It will be all on me. I'll take care of everything. I'll pick the best of everything. It may be the last thing I do as a member of this family."

"Why do you expect to leave us?"

"Stellina will not want to stay with me. Please let me do this. It will make me feel like I have done a small part in helping the only real loving family I have ever had."

"All right," said Maria. "If it will make you feel better. We do need someone to make the arrangements. None of us are thinking straight enough to take care of it. But dear Biachio, It seems like you are as sorrowful as the rest of us."

"I'm a man. That makes a difference." "Go find Stellina first."

Biachio left but afraid to face Stellina. He knew how much she loved her father. She would be in very deep emotional depression. His first duty was to her. He had to go home no matter what the consequences were. Stellina had looked for Biachio and not finding him returned to her home hoping he would come home as usual. When

Biachio got home he found her sitting in their living room just staring at the wall. She couldn't believe what was happening. It was like a bad dream. She needed Biachio very badly. Biachio started crying as soon as he saw her. He ran to her and fell on his knees before her.

"Stellina I'm so sorry. Please forgive me. I know that I have not kept my promise. I was too negligent. I never believed this would happen. I didn't know anything about it. Please Stellina, I can't live without you. Please forgive me. Please don't leave me."

"Biachio, I went looking for you. I couldn't find you. Where were you?"

"Please don't leave me. I'll die without you."

"Get up and sit here besides me. What makes you think I will leave you?"

"Our deal was that I was to protect your father. I failed to keep my side of the deal. I never even dreamed that my family would do this." "Don't worry, Biachio. Forget the deal. That was finished when you made love to me."

"You won't leave me?" asked Biachio holding his breath.

"There are three reasons why I won't leave you. First, I know beyond any doubt that you had nothing to do with my father's death. Secondly, we are married and I love you with all my heart. Don't you know that?"

"You never said that before," said Biachio starting to breathe again. "I thought you were just hungry for sex. I was satisfied with that if that was all I could get. But to have you love me was more than I would dare to dream."

"I do love you very much with all my body and soul. I need you now more then ever. I need you to comfort me. I loved my father very much. I will miss him terribly." She pulled him to her. "Please hold me and love me," Biachio held her very tight. He was sad and happy at the same time. He kissed her on the cheek.

"I will never leave your side. I will hold you throughout this hour of sadness." He thought for a while then it came to him. "Sweet heart, you said that there were three reasons you would never leave me. What was the third reason?"

"I didn't want to tell you like this," she said. "I suppose you should know so you can be as protective as husbands usually are."

"What are you talking about?"

"Biachio, love of my life," she said being shy. "I'm pregnant."
"What?" said Biachio. He almost fell of the couch he was sitting on with her. "I can't believe it. You tell me that you love me with all of your heart and now you tell me that I'm going to be a father. The news is more wonderful than I can take. I'm the happiest man in the world." He started to kiss her all over her face. He kissed her eyes and her nose and her cheeks. Then he remembered why he was there. "I'm so sorry sweet heart. I almost forgot about your loss. I have gone from the lowest moment of my life to the highest point of my life. An hour ago, I thought I had lost you and now I find I not only have you but I also will be a father. I'm sorry. I can't hold down the joy."

"That's all right. I need your joy. It gives me a great lift. By the way, where were you? I went to the office to find you and no one was there."

"I almost forgot. I told your mother Maria that I would take care of all the funeral arrangements, including getting the best coffin." "Go Honey," she said. "Go do what you have to do. I trust you. I will go to be with Mama Maria."

"I just promised you I will not leave your side and the first thing I do is leave you."

"You will be in my heart," she said "I'll take the buggy. I'll be all right. Go do what has to be done." Biachio left and made all the necessary arrangements. He found the best coffin in town and ordered it to be delivered immediately. It had brass handles and brass carvings of Jesus in front and angels along both sides.

Biachio followed the wagon carrying the casket to Maria's house. They had just lowered the casket from the wagon when the police wagon arrived with Salvatore's body. Stellina was already there being comforted by Gina. Maria got out Salvatore's good suit. They brought the body and the Casket in the empty room on the left of the courtyard. Because Maria broke down Biachio and Gino, who had just arrived, offered to dress him. After they dressed him, the people who delivered the casket placed the body in the casket and set it in the middle of the main room in the house. They set chairs that Biachio had brought, all around the casket. Stellina, Maria and Gina sat there and began crying. Biachio and Gino stood outside. "We are going to need pall bearers," said Biachio. "Who else can we get besides you and me?"

"I think we will need at least four and six would be better," responded Gino. "I think I can get Tano's cousin Nino and probably Tano's younger brother Alex."

"That makes four of us. Is there any one else in the family?" asked Biachio. "I don't think I should ask any of my relatives." Then thinking it over he said, "sure as if they would come."

"We could ask Tano's father, Don Luigi, and his uncle, Don Michele. They all came to the wedding. I'm sure they will come to the funeral." As they talked Don Michele DiFranco, his wife Antonietta and their son, Nino, arrived. Before they entered the house, Gino asked Don Michele and Nino if they would be willing to be pall bearers. They said they would. They entered the house, approached the family, gave their condolences, and sat down around the casket. Later that afternoon Don Luigi DiFranco, his wife Lina, and their son Alex arrived. Gino asked Don Luigi and Alex if they would be pall bearers. They said they would. They entered and also greeted the family with their condolences. Don Luigi sat next to his brother. His wife sat next to him. Alex and Nino sat together away from the others. They whispered salutations to each other. Anna showed up later in the evening.

The night went by very slowly. Maria, Stellina, and Gina stayed up all night sitting and watching their beloved. A few of the friends stayed until the wee hours of the morning. Most of the time there was silence. Once in a while an outbreak of wailing could be heard which followed with silence again. When one started to cry the rest followed. It went this way all night. Gino left after midnight to get some sleep and returned early in the morning. Biachio stayed near his wife until early morning and only left for a short time to dress for the procession. All the guests of the previous night were assembled by the casket by nine the next morning. At ten, a priest came and gave a short sermon and a prayer. At ten-thirty a church deacon came and after a short prayer asked every one to walk by the casket, say goodbye to Salvatore and wait out in the courtyard. The immediate family went last. Stellina wanted to crawl into the casket with her father. Biachio restrained her, begging her to stay with him. When everyone had passed by and said their goodbyes the deacon closed and sealed the casket. The pallbearers were called and the procession began. He was walked by the church he had attended on the way to the cemetery. At the cemetery, the priest gave a condensed version of Salvatore's life. He emphasized how every one who met him loved him. He explained that because of his love of family he would never be forgotten. He was placed in the family Mausoleum next to his first wife. The mausoleum contained eight places. Salvatore's mother and father occupied the first two positions. Salvatore and his first wife Marianna occupied the next two places. Biachio wondered who would occupy the other four places. The walk back was a very somber one. No one spoke. When they got back to the house, a caterer had a beautiful spread on a table set up in the courtyard. By two in the afternoon everyone was gone except the family and the caterers who were cleaning up. Biachio would see that the family was taken care of until the food ran out. After that he would see to their needs as required. That eve they had a small dinner. Stellina didn't want to eat. Biachio reminded her she had to eat for two. With a little urging she ate a little. No one in their sorrow understood what Biachio had said. Stellina wanted it that way for the present. They got home late that night and went to bed immediately. Stellina had not slept at all last night. When they got in bed Stellina hugged her husband.

"Make love to me," she asked Biachio as she kissed him. "I need you to make love to me."

"Are you sure," he asked knowing how tired she must be. He was also worried about the baby. He kissed her and pulled her nude body close to his. She nestled her face in his neck. Before Biachio could make another move he noticed that she had fallen asleep. She just needed his loving embrace to put her to sleep.

The next morning Stellina woke up suddenly as if out of a bad dream. She looked at Biachio to see if he was awake.

"Honey, are you awake?" she asked, her voice almost a whisper. "Yes, what is the matter? Did you have a bad dream?"

"No, it came to me that we almost forgot about Peppino. I'm wondering if he knows what has happened."

"Do you want me to go to him?"

"No, thanks Biachio, I think one of the immediate family should go. I don't mean that you are not part of the immediate family. I mean, I, as his sister, should go."

"I understand, to him I may not be accepted as family yet."

"I think he knows how much I love you. For that reason I'm sure he accepts you as family. What I should have said is that I am closer to him than anyone."

"Sweetheart, you only have to tell me what you want and I will climb mountains to do it for you."

"I'll go later this morning and spend an hour with him alone. We could cry on each other's shoulders."

"Please be careful. I don't want anything to happen to you and especially with the baby. Do you want me to stay here and wait for you?"

"No, why don't you go to work and try to find out who did this." They got dressed ate a little and after kissing her he left. As he was walking out the door Anna came in. They greeted each other.

"Anna, take care of Stellina and go with her. I want you to be with her every minute of the day. You can only leave her when she is in jail talking with her brother. Don't let her talk you out of anything else or you will hear from me. Do you understand?"

"Yes sir," she responded with a surprised look on her face. "What's with him?" she asked after he had left.

"Oh he is being over protective," answered Stellina. "I guess you should know; I haven't told any one except Biachio."

"What are you talking about?" asked Anna.

From the big smile on Anna's face, Stellina suspected Anna knew what she was about to tell her.

"We are going to have a child," said Stellina like a proud hen. "Oh my God," yelled Anna hugging her. "What wonderful news."

"It would have been better news if my father were alive. He would have been so proud." Stellina started to cry. Anna hugged her again. They cried together.

172

Later that morning Stellina went to the jail. The jailer let her in to visit in spite of the fact it wasn't Wednesday. Because of this, she suspected the word had gotten around. She went to her brother's cell. As soon as she entered the cell area she knew that Peppino had heard. He started crying as soon as he saw her.

"Stellina, we lost our father," he said crying louder. Stellina hated to see her big brother cry. She remembered how strong he was. This was not in character for him, but years in jail could break anyone's spirit.

"I know," was all that she could say. They hugged through the bars and cried together for a while.

"Tell me the details of what happened," asked Peppino gaining his composure.

"I really don't know all the facts yet. I suspect that Papa was trying to sneak out and report to Enna what was going on here. He must have thought that since I was happy with Biachio they wouldn't be watching him. Apparently he was wrong. He was very depressed since he first saw you here in jail. He was determined to get you out. He was killed on the road to Enna when he wanted to report to the Provincial government."

"What does Biachio have to say about this?"

"Oh Peppi, he was devastated. He cried in my lap for an hour. He felt he had let me down. It took a lot of talking to get him to believe I didn't blame him. He was afraid I would leave him. He had promised me that he would protect you and father."

"What did you tell him to convince him?"

"I told him that I was pregnant." She answered with that proud look that followed a weak smile.

"Are you?"

"Yes,"

"Oh dear Lord, how wonderful. Did Papa know?"

"No," said Stellina starting to cry again. "I didn't get a chance. He would have been so happy."

"I'm happy for you enough for both of us." "Thanks." "Do you have any idea as to who did this thing?"

"No, but Biachio promised he would find out." Stellina held his hand and kissed it. When the guard come in and told her that her time was up, she kissed him and promised to come again soon.

Biachio arrived at work an hour later than usual. His father wasn't there. He asked around and finally decided to go to the police office and ask questions. The answer he got was that his father took care of it personally. The police had stopped Salvatore but the mayor took care of everything else. When he got back to the office his father was there.

"Papa, I understand that you took care of Salvatore Casolini yourself. Why did you do it? Why didn't you just scold him or beat him and send him home?"

"Are you questioning my judgment?"

"I want to know. What did he do to you that you had to do it personally?"

"First he had a daughter that has caused a break up of our happy home. Your mother hardly talks with me. She hardly talks with you. Listen, I couldn't let him get away with it. Can you imagine how many of these peasants would try to escape if they though that they would not be punished by death? I couldn't let that happen. I think they got the message."

"You are a monster, do you know that?" said Biachio in anger.

"I know your wife has probably made life miserable for you so I will pretend I didn't hear that. One more word and you are out of here."

"My wife is the most wonderful person alive. She has brought me more happiness than I deserve." He walked to his office and said no more. He prayed to God to forgive him for hating his father. He recalled that the bible says you should honor your mother and father. That was going to be a very hard commandment for him to follow. When he got home that evening he told Stellina what he had found out that day.

"That's all right, sweetheart," said Stellina. "As long as you don't do any of the things they do, God will understand."

"How did I ever deserve you?" said Biachio with tears in his eyes. "God is really so good."

"I thank him every moment of the day. We need his protection. I don't think we know what danger we are in. Both of your parents hate me and they are angry with you. That can't be very healthy."

"They wouldn't dare hurt you. Maybe we should leave here and settle in Italy somewhere."

"Do you think they would let us leave?" said Stellina. "And if we did, what would you do?"

"I could get work in some business as an accountant or as a laborer if necessary."

For the next two months, Stellina and Biachio lived a very happy life together. Biachio had approached both his parents hinting about leaving the area. Both responded with the same comments. "You're not going anywhere." Apparently they were not going anywhere. Stellina was beginning to show her pregnancy. One Wednesday, as she always did she went to the home of Maria and Gina, to take one of them to see Peppino.

"How are you doing?" asked Stellina of Maria.

"I still miss your father as much as ever. The pain doesn't seem to go away."

"I know. I miss him too."

"Besides, the mayor has taken the helper away. It is only Gino now to take care of three farms. He can't do it. Not only that, but people are still talking. We had to ask Gino to stay away from our house."

"I'll talk with Biachio," said Stellina, "but I can't promise anything. Biachio and his parents are not getting along very well. Where is Gino working at present?"

"He is working our land and we will give him a portion of the harvest to keep him supplied with food and the necessary things. Presently he is seeding. Gina is going to help him tomorrow. His land is plowed but he will not have time to seed it."

"Maybe I could go with Anna and help them. That way he could seed his land."

"In your condition? Forget it."

"I'm only a little over three months. Our grandmother used to help in the field until the baby came. I'm pretty strong. I could help a little. You are still my family you know."

"It's because you are part of our family that we won't let you do it. Forget it," said Maria, strongly against it. Stellina said no more. She would do what she had to do. After breakfast Stellina took Maria to see Peppino. Stellina had not missed one Wednesday since her father died. She alternated who she took to see him when ever it was possible. Presently Gina was busy helping with the seeding so it didn't matter. She wouldn't be able to go anyway. The first thing that Maria did when she arrived at Peppino's cell was to related to Peppino the notion that Stellina had in helping do the seeding.

"Sister dear," said Peppino. "You have to be careful. I don't want to lose my nephew before I get to know him. I certainly don't want to lose you. You and I are the only members of the Casolini family."

"What am I?" said Maria in jest, "A cucumber?

"You know what I mean," said Peppino. "I'm talking of our original family. You and Gina are very dear to us. We are so lucky to have you as part of our family."

"Don't explain," said Maria smiling. "I was just kidding you." "I'm barely showing and it doesn't hold me back in anything as yet. I will only help for a while. I'm not stupid. If I feel tired I will stop and rest or go home."

"Let's talk about getting me out of here," said Peppino.

"Biachio is doing everything he can," said Stellina. "He even has his parents angry with him. We will not stop trying. Father was stopped because he wanted to free you. We don't want to make that mistake again."

"Have you found out anything yet as to who did this to Papa?" "Biachio thinks it was his father," answered Stellina. "His father wanted to set an example to any one else who might think of escaping. Biachio asked him why he just didn't stop him and send him home. He told Biachio he couldn't let any one think they could try and live. Then all would try and one might succeed."

"Sounds like the way they think," said Peppino. "You have to watch out for them Stellina. You can't trust any of them."

"I trust Biachio," said Stellina defending her husband. "He will not let anything happen to me."

"I believe that," said Maria. "But his influence is very limited. It sounds like he is on the verge of being disinherited."

After the hour was over, they kissed Peppino and left. Stellina dropped Maria off and went home.

When Maria entered her house she found Gina at home. "Gina," what are you doing home?" asked Maria "I finished most of the seeding and got tired. It's no fun working alone.

"I'm glad you brought it up. I need to talk to you." "What about mama?"

"Listen, with Salvator dead, and Biachio out of vavor with his parent we will not have any one to help on the farm."said Maria with a sad voice. "And I know that you don't want to hear it, but Peppino is as good as dead. He will never get out of jail alive. Gina we need some one to work the land."

"What are you suggesting mama?"

"You know what I am suggesting. You have to get married some time. We need a man if we are to survive."

"I know mama. There is no one that I want to spend my life with. I'll think about it. I suppose we don't have anyother choice." "What are we having for lunch?" Stellina asked Anna when she home.

"How are you? We are having French toast.."

"The French toast sounds delicious." After eating Stellina laid down and took an afternoon nap. She woke up about five o'clock.

"Oh my," she exclaimed out loud. "I have to get something for Biachio. I refuse to let my marriage slide into common every day ho hum relationship."

"What are you talking about," asked Anna. "Are you talking to yourself or are you talking to me?"

"Both, I guess. I need to get dinner ready for my husband."

"I hope you don't mind, but I didn't want to wake you so I took it upon myself to start dinner."

"What are you making and what can I do?"

"I'm making a beef roast. I found a nice piece of beef at the butcher. It used to be one of Biachio's favorites. You can make the side dishes and the salad. I bought some Swiss chard and some carrots. You can boil them and make the salad with the lettuce and the other stuff

I bought. It will be ready in time. I would like to leave early if I may. I want to eat with my mother. She isn't feeling too good so I want to cook something for her."

"Of course, go now. I can take over from here." "Are you sure?" "Yes, you need to be with your mother. But before you leave I want to tell you that tomorrow I would like us to go to Gino's farm and help him seed his land. So be thinking about it and be ready. Dress accordingly."

"Are you sure in your condition?"

"Not you too?" said Stellina looking angry.

Later that evening Biachio came home later than usual. However, he didn't forget to bring her flowers. He gave her the flowers and hugged her and kissed her several times.

"What have you done now that you are so considerate? Do you have another girl you are seeing?"

"Who would want me? I'm too much in love with my wife. The most painful thing I did today is miss you terribly." He then kissed her again. "For some reason I missed you more than usual. I had this terrible fearful feeling that you wouldn't be here."

"Only God can take me away from you," promised Stellina. "Listen Biachio, I have something to tell you."

"What is the problem?" he asked beginning to worry.

"Since you have not been able to restore the help to my family, they are having trouble making the necessary planting requirements. They are presently in the process of seeding. I would like to take Anna with me and help them."

"Stella, sweetheart, I will never be dictatorial to you. I will not order you to do anything. But I ask you please don't do this. I will not rest worrying about you and our child. I beg you, do not put yourself and our child in danger."

"Biachio, I am not a child. I will not put myself and our child in danger. I will be careful. I promise you I will come right home if I even feel a slight bit tired."

"My response is I would rather that you didn't go."

"I will think about it," said Stellina getting romantic. "Right now I want you to make love to me. Soon you will not be able to." It was very strange that evening. Perhaps because Stellina was thinking of going out to the farm and it scared both of them, but their love that evening was as if they were just married and on their honeymoon. Their love was never stronger.

The next morning Stellina woke up first. She lay there for a while. An unexplained fear griped her. She couldn't explain it. She became afraid she would never carry the child to full birth. What was it that was happening? Was it some kind of morning sickness? She didn't want to scare Biachio but she needed his love now more than ever. She finally decided to wake him.

"Biachio," she said. "I need your love this morning more than ever."

"What's wrong?" he exclaimed being frightened with her action. "I just feel more romantic then I have ever felt toward you. It must be the fact that I'm pregnant. Love me like you have never loved me before." He didn't have to be asked twice. He loved her that morning like he would never make love to her again.

After he had dressed and eaten breakfast he prepared to leave. He found it very hard to leave her especially since their love making last night and this morning. He wanted so badly to spend the rest of the day with her. However he didn't want to aggravate his father any further. He hardly talks to him now.

"Honey," he said very romantically "I don't want to leave you this morning." He kissed her as if it was the first time he had ever kissed her.

"Wow," she whispered and kissed him with the same passion. "I wish you could stay home too." She kissed him again. They would have continued kissing if it hadn't been for the arrival of Anna.

"Goodbye, sweet Stella. I can't wait until I come home tonight." "I'll wait breathlessly," she answered with another kiss. After Biachio left, Anna looked at Stellina with a wondering look on her face.

"What was that all about?" she asked. "Having a baby makes us more romantic."

"I'll bet," said Anna with a big smile. "What is on our agenda for today?"

"Well, I would like you and me to go to the farm and see if we could help with the seeding. They have been in trouble since Biachio's parents pulled back the helpers that Biachio had obtained for my family. Do you have any problem with that?"

"No, I insist I go with you. I'm not going to let you hurt yourself." "You're such a good and sweet friend," said Stellina. "Let's pack a lunch and pack up the horses to go as soon as we can. I still want to get home in time to cook my husband dinner." They packed everything they would need and were ready to go when Stellina became aware that they did not have everything they needed.

"Anna," said Stellina as she was about to mount her horse. "We forgot the water. Will you go back in the house and fill two small bottles of water we can take with us."

"That's right," said Anna. "We almost forgot the water. I'll run in and fetch two bottles of water." She no sooner disappeared from the stable when the mayor's wife, Lucia and her nephews Roberto and Cianni walked into the stable.

"Ciao Mama Lucia," said Stellina. "What are you doing here this early?"

"I come to balance the score," she said. "And don't call me Mama. You could never be worthy to be a daughter of mine."

"I don't understand," said Stellina. "Have I done something to displease you?"

"Yes," she answered. "First you married my son and then you became pregnant."

"You came to my house and requested my hand for your son. Also, I thought you would be please to have a grandson or granddaughter." Stellina had no idea as to what was happening. Stellina attempted to mount her horse when her mother-in-law yelled to her nephews.

"Pull her down from her horse. Don't let her mount." As soon as she said that, the two boys pulled her down and brought her to Lucia. "Tie her hands behind her." Stellina struggled but they were to strong for her.

"What are you doing?" yelled Stellina becoming very frightened. "Please let me go. What are you going to do to me?" Realizing that Anna had to be back by now, Stellina reasoned she was hiding. She hoped she could hear everything. "Biachio will hear of this and come and stop you from doing what ever you have in mind." When Ann came back with the water she heard voices, and hid by the doorway and listened to the conversation. She heard what Lucia had in mind so she quietly sneaked out the back door and ran to get Biachio.

"How is he going to hear?" said Lucia. "He is at work. Nothing is going to save you."

"Why are you doing this?" asked Stellina starting to get panicky. "You don't intend to kill me do you?"

"How did you guess? Do you think this is a joke?"

"Why are you doing this? If you hurt me you will lose your son and your only grandson or granddaughter." said Stellina getting frantic. "Please don't hurt my child. I beg you. Please have mercy. It's your only hope of having a grandchild." Stellina was very confused. She couldn't believe what was happening. Was this a bad dream?

"You want to know why I'm doing this. It's because I can't allow your children to dilute the royal blood. I will not allow half-breeds to infest our family." She went into the house and got a chair. Stellina was now crying loudly. Then Lucia, pointing to her nephews, ordered them to stand her on the chair. They did as she requested. She then threw a rope over the stable beam.

"What are you doing?" said Stellina now crying abundantly without restraint. "You're not going to hang me? Please wait and talk this over with your son! Please!"

Lucia's answer was to put the rope over her head. "Please don't hurt my baby."

"Don't waste the little time you have left begging. Pray to this God you believe in. I would like to see him save you." She started to laugh.

Stellina knew her only hope was to delay Lucia until Biachio came to rescue her. Stellina pulled all the strength she had to put her mind to think of ways to delay her.

"Do you realize what this is going to do to your son? Give us time to say goodbye. You're the queen in these parts. You can do this anytime."

"Why should I wait? What's wrong with now? You should be happy. I am sending you to be with your God in heaven."

"What will your son think? You are taking me away from him and sending me to heaven to be with Tano my first husband. I guess I should thank you."

"You're welcome," said Lucia as she kicked the chair from under Stellina. The rope tightened around her throat. She couldn't breathe. She tried desperately to bring her hands up to her throat to pull on the rope but her hands were tied tightly. With her last breath she yelled out, "Biachio!"

Chapter 9

THE LAST OF THE CASOLINI

Anna ran as fast as she could to the office where Biachio worked. Fortunately the mayor wasn't there. Anna wasn't worried that she was crossing the mayor's family. She would gladly die for Stellina. When she got to Biachio she was so out of wind she could hardly talk.

"Biachio," she managed to yell. "Stellina...trouble," she stumbled breathlessly. "Your mother... killing her."

"Where are they?"

"In the stable... hanging her."

Biachio had heard enough. He raced out the door and jumped on his horse and was out of sight before Anna could reach the door. Anna tried to follow with the little breath she had but she couldn't keep running any longer. She just fell on her knees and prayed that Biachio would reach her on time. When Biachio got to the stable every one was gone except Stellina hanging from the rafter. Biachio yelled from the top of his voice.

"No," he yelled so every one in town could have heard him. He picked up the chair and jumping on it taking out his knife he cut her down and loosen the rope around her neck..

"Stellina," he cried. He couldn't say more because he was giving her mouth to mouth recitation. He pushed on her heart trying to get it started again. He continued to give her mouth to mouth. He blew into her lungs as hard as he could. He repeated it and repeated it. As he worked to save her he kept repeating to himself, "Stellina please don't leave me, Please. Oh God please don't take her from me. Oh God! I'll never ask for anything the rest of my life. Please don't take her," he promised. These thought kept repeating in his mind over and over again while he worked. He was not going to give up. After a few minutes, Anna came into the stable.

"Please Anna," said Biachio pleadingly. "Please go get Dr. Bonavista" Anna mounted the closest horse and galloped to the doctor's office. Soon Dr. Bonavista and Anna arrived. The doctor quickly went to Stellina's side. He checked her pulse but found none. He quickly started pumping on her chest to get the heart started. After about five minutes he gave up.

"I'm sorry Biachio. It's too late. She has no pulse and her body feels cold."

"Please Doctor, don't give up," said Biachio crying as his heart was breaking. "I can't lose her."

"I'm sorry. There is nothing else I can do." Biachio couldn't hear him. He was yelling at the top of his voice. "No, Dear God, no! It took several minutes before they could calm him down. He fell to the floor his wailing slowly diminishing to a heavy sobbing. His complete body was shaking from the pain in his heart.

"Biachio, please," said Anna crying sorrowfully. "Stellina would want us to be strong."

"Please Anna will you make the arrangements. I want her to be buried with her father. Please Anna see that I am buried with her." "Biachio, I'll do anything you ask. Please remember that I and Peppino need you. Without you, we will both be killed. Stellina would want you to protect her brother."

"Who is going to tell Peppino?" said Biachio breaking down to another burst of crying. It's all my fault. God is punishing me."

"If you have accepted Jesus then he has forgiven you. You must not lose faith." Anna now was harkening to her own words. "Biachio, do you want me to make all the arrangements, like picking a coffin and all the other things as needed?"

"Please," he answered.

"There is nothing I can do here," said the doctor. "Anna, I am writing a prescription for Biachio. It will calm his nerves for awhile.

Give him one every six hours." After giving Anna the prescription the doctor left. Anna helped Biachio, who now was in a stupor, go into the house and lay down for a while. He followed her looking back and yelling Stellina's name over and over again. Anna made him comfortable and left to get someone to stay with him. She went to Maria. Maria sent one of the neighbors to fetch Gino and Gina. Afterwards she went to Biachio to be with him until Gino and Gina arrived. Anna went about making arrangements. Gino found her as she came out of the pharmacy.

"Anna," said Gino sadly. "How can I help?" "Where is Gina?" she asked.

"She is with her mother staying with Biachio."

"Good, then I would like you to accompany me. I need to make all the arrangements for the funeral and I could use the company." By early afternoon Gino and Anna had completed the final arrangement. With the help of the church deacons they obtained Stellina's body and placed it in Maria's house. A few friends came by and gave their condolences. Maria and Gina cried for a while but soon became silently depressed. They were cried out from losing Salvatore and now Stellina. They didn't think they could take any more pain. They loved Stellina so much. Anna and Gino were the most focal of the grieving. Biachio sat besides Stellina's casket and cried silently. He was in a state of denial and sat as a zombie. In the late afternoon they had the procession to the graveyard. Biachio walked along the side of the casket in a state of spiritless stupor. He never heard the preacher or the comments of condolences said to him. They laid her in the crypt above her father and mother. The preacher gave his last remarks and everyone began to leave.

"Where is Biachio?" asked Anna. "Someone should be with him. He isn't yet completely aware of what has happened."

"I don't know," said Gino. "He was here a minute ago. "We better look for him. You can't tell what he will do in his present state. Gina have you seen Biachio?" Gino turned to ask Gina.

"No, he just disappeared. The poor fellow is out of his mind. Why don't you two go look for him? I have to take care of my mother."

"I'll go look at his home although I can't imagine him going there.

It will remind him of Stellina too much," said Anna.

"I'll go look for him in town and his office. But I can't imagine his going there." Anna went to his home. He didn't show up all night. Anna felt the worse of all. Not only did she lose her best friend but now she wondered what would happen to her. Besides all this pain she was also worried about her mother who was very ill. Gino didn't find him either. At midnight Gino gave up and went to feed Peppino.

Early the next morning Biachio, looking like he had been trampled by a herd of horses, arrived at the jail. The jailer saw him and wondered how he could still stand up.

"Biachio," he exclaimed. "What are you doing here?" "I come to see Peppino Casolini."

"I'm not sure he is still alive," said the Jailer. "Why what has happened?"

"Yesterday evening Pietro, the son of the chief of police came here and talked to Peppino. He told him that his sister was dead. He told him she had hanged herself from a rafter in the stable. I thought he was going to destroy the cell. His yelling must have wakened the dead. He battered himself against the walls and the cell bars. He was bleeding from every inch of his body. I think he was trying to kill himself. I should have called a doctor but I didn't"

"Let me in to see him," ordered Biachio.

"What happened to you," asked the jailer. "You look terrible." "Never mind, just let me in." He was let in and Biachio walked to Peppino's cell. Peppino looked worse then he did. Biachio walked up to the cell and put his face through the bars as far as he could.

"Kill me Peppino. It's my fault that Stellina is dead. Put your hands through the bars and choke me." Peppino ignored him. He had recovered from his grieving although they were both crying like babies.

"Pietro said that Stellina hanged herself. I don't believe it. She was too much of a Christian to kill herself."

"She didn't hang herself. My mother hung her from the rafter in the stable."

"How could she do that? She isn't strong enough."

"It was my cousins Roberto and Cianni that tied her up and put her on the chair. My mother kicked the chair from under her. I got there as soon as I found out. I cut her down and tried to save her. I tried with all the breath I had within me. I couldn't save her. My own mother killed my wife and she also killed me. I can't live with out Stellina. You don't know how much I loved her. But I didn't love her enough. If I had really loved her unselfishly I would have let her live happily with Tano and then Maria could have been happy with your father and you would marry Gina and every one would have been happy. I wanted to kill my mother…How can I kill my own mother?

"Biachio, listen to me. What you are saying is hindsight. If you knew what was going to happen you would have done everything differently. Besides, Stellina told me that you accepted Christ as your savior. Therefore you are forgiven of all your sins. It isn't your fault."

"You don't know what I have done. I need to be punished.""What are you talking about?"

"After the funeral yesterday I went to a bar and got drunk. I couldn't handle being without Stellina. I was so drunk I didn't know what I was doing. I went looking for my mother. The witch hid herself. I found one of the servant girls and I raped her and beat her to death. I was taking out my hatred of my mother on her. So you see. I am as bad as my family. I don't deserve to live."

"Tell me what you did to that servant girl."

"I don't really know," said Biachio. "All I know is that I raped her. I didn't enjoy it. She was screaming and struggling. Then I passed out. When I awoke I was on top of her and she was out. Her face was swollen and covered with blood. I must have beaten her."

"Are you sure she was dead. Did you check later or this morning?" "No, I didn't spend the night there."

"Where were you all night?"

"I spent it with Stellina. I spent all night at the base of her crypt." "Then Biachio, you don't know if she is really dead."

"She was in very bad shape. I can't see how she survived.""What is important is how repentant are you of what you did last night?"

"I would give anything to undo what I did to that poor girl. I have been bad all my life except the three years I spent with Stellina."

"You were forgiven of your sins you committed before you accepted Jesus. For the sins you committed after you have but only to confess to God and you will be forgiven. I recommend that you go to the church and ask Jesus to forgive you. Talk to God. He will hear your prayer."

"Do you forgive all I have done?" asked Biachio wanting Peppino's forgiveness more then anything.

"If God can forgive you who am I to hold a grudge." "Thank you Peppino," said Biachio his spirit being lifted.

"Before you leave please tell me everything you know of all the murders."

"Tano was killed by Pietro," confessed Biachio. "Roberto and Gianni helped. My father killed your father to make him an example. My mother hung Stellina to punish me."

"Thanks for being truthful," said Peppino as gently as he could, although fire was burning inside of him.

After leaving Peppino, Biachio went directly to the church he and Stellina visited every Sunday. He was feeling very badly, not just because of the loss his beloved wife, but because he felt so unworthy. Not only what he had been as a kid, but what he had done to that poor woman at his parent's home. The front doors of the church were locked but he found a side door open. No one seemed to be in the church. He went directly to the altar and knelt down in front of the crucifix. He started praying softly.

"Dear father, please forgive me for the way I have lived and wasted my life. Lord I am not worthy of your love. I have been selfish, inconsiderate, thinking only of my self. The three years I was married to Stellina are the only decent years I've had. She made me believe in you. Stellina gave me a conscience. Oh heavenly father please forgive me for what I did to that poor woman. Lord if you never answer another of my prayers please answer this one. I only ask that the woman survived and will be back to normal. Lord I confess all of my sins. If you do not need me on this earth please take me home. I don't see what I can do here. I will never have any influence with my parents. There is nothing on this earth that has any meaning to me. I have no interest in anything on this earth except to help people. And you know Lord that my family will never let me do anything now that my strength is gone. Stellina was my strength and my guide to do good."

Unknown to Biachio, a shadowy figure was slowly and silently creeping up behind him. Biachio bent his head down toward his praying hands, praying silently. He never heard the loud blasting sound of the pistol. The bullet entered high on the back of his neck and came out of his forehead. Biachio fell forward on his face. He was dead before he hit the floor. God had answered his prayer.

The morning after Stellina's funeral Gino went to the Casolini house to get instructions from Maria and to bring them water. He had spent the night looking for Biachio, never dreaming he had spent the night by the gravesite. He finally visited Peppino, gave him some food, and went to bed. That morning Maria and Gina were still up mourning the loss of Stellina.

"How are you Dona Maria?" asked Gino trying to be sensitive to her sorrow.

"I'll survive," said Maria.

"What can I do this morning to help," he asked. "I'll go get the water for you and then if you wish I can go to your farm and do what has to be done."

"Please do get the water," she answered. "But after you get through please go looking for Biachio. He is so broken up. I worry about him." Gino went for water and after dropping the water off he went looking for Biachio. He went to the cemetery first to see if by any chance he went there. One of the grave caretakers told him that Biachio spent all night by Stellina's gravesite. Gino next went to his home to see if he went back there. He quickly snuck around the back so the mayor's wife wouldn't see him. He knew the mayor would be at his office so he wasn't worried about him. The mayor, however, had guards watching the house. He went into the building thinking security wasn't very good. Inside he heard a noise and hid behind a door. It was Anna Maria.

"Anna," he said softly not to scare her. It didn't work. She jumped nearly out of her skin. "I'm sorry Anna. I didn't mean to scare you. I didn't know it was you I heard."

"Don't do that. I almost had a heart attack. What are you doing here?"

"I'm looking for Biachio."

"He hasn't been here all night. I'm worried about him too. He was so broken up."

"I know that he slept by the gravesite all night. I don't know were he went after that. I looked for him at the cemetery but he wasn't there."

"You had better go," said Anna. "If they catch us we will both be in trouble." Gino suddenly and unexpectedly, completely surprising Anna, kissed her and then disappeared out the rear door. Gino headed toward Biachio's office. He couldn't imagine he would go there but he had run out of places to look. On the way, he met Pietro.

"Ciao Pietro," said Gino trying to be friendly though he hated the man and everything he stood for.

"Ciao, Gino," he responded. "Why aren't you with Peppino's girl?" Gino ignored his comment.

"I'm looking for Biachio. Would you know where he is?"

"Sure I know where he is. He's in church. He is dead. Shot through the head."

"Did he commit suicide?"

"Not unless he has a six foot arm. He was shot through the back of his head. Maybe you peasants want his body. After all, it was you people that made a peasant out of him. The priests don't know what to do with the body. The mayor and his wife have disowned him. They don't want the body."

Gino returned quickly to the Casolini house. "Maria," he said with tears in his eyes. It wasn't that he particularly cared that much for Biachio. It was because of all the turmoil the last few days and he felt sorry for Maria and Gina. The loss of Stellina was also constantly on his mind. "Biachio is dead," he said. "Someone shot him through the back of his head." Maria stood there in a complete state of shock.

"When did this happen?" she finally managed to ask.

"It happened some time this morning. He was praying in church when some one snuck up behind him and shot him as he knelt at the alter. The worse part of it is his parents don't want anything to do with him. The priests don't know what to do with the body."

"We will have to take care of it. I hear him say yesterday that he wanted to be buried with Stellina. I think we should honor that request." Gina walked in just as Maria made that comment.

"What should we honor?" she asked. Gino explained everything to Gina. She was just as shocked as her mother was. She broke down in tears.

"The whole family was destroyed in two days," is all she could say.

"Gino," said Maria getting control of her emotions and beginning to think logically. "Could you do another thing? Could you go and order another casket exactly like the one Stellina is in and have it delivered to the church? We will meet you there. We will have the funeral from there. There will not be enough people there to have a procession. I will borrow a wagon and we will carry him to the grave yard and place him next to Stellina."

"I'll do that right away," said Gino being glad to be able to help. He left and was back within a half hour. He had taken care of all he thought should be done.

"Are you back already?" said Maria to Gino.

"I got a coffin and had it delivered to the church. They said they will put the body in the casket and let us use the wagon to deliver it to the cemetery. I contacted the cemetery people and told them the body was coming and it should be placed next to Stellina's body. Is that all right with you?"

"That is a great job," said Maria. "What would we do without you?"

Maria, Gina, and Gino, walked silently and sorrowfully to the church. No one said anything along the way. When they got there, everything was ready. Biachio was in the casket and the casket was closed. It was in the wagon. As soon as they got there a deacon and a church volunteer walked the horse pulling the wagon slowly toward the cemetery. A priest led the way. There were only the six of them following the body. At the cemetery, the priest said a few words. The casket with Biachio then was laid next to the casket that held Stellina. Biachio's parent didn't show up. Neither his uncle nor any of his cousins were there. Maria said a few prayers. After she made the sign of the cross the others did too and the three left for home. Gino saw them safely home and then left for his own place. He wondered how this was going to affect Peppino's chances for survival.

That evening at midnight, Gino went to the jail to communicate with Peppino and to bring him some food. As usual he lowered a note telling him about the death of Biachio. He then expected a signal that it was all right to send down the food. Gino didn't get any signal from Peppino. He tried again with no results. After the third try with no response he became worried that either he was dead, sick, or they had moved him. He quietly left the jail area and decided to go to see what Anna knew about what may have happened. It was past twelve-thirty when he arrived at Anna's house. He knocked on the door as silently as he could. At first there was no answer. After the third knock Anna opened the door. She was in her night gown.

"Gino what are you doing here?"

"Anna I'm sorry to come so late but I'm worried about Peppino. Do you know anything about what could have happened to him?" Anna grabbed him and hurried him inside and started to cry. "Anna honey, what is wrong?"

"Every thing is wrong," she said trying to stifle her crying. "Tell me what is wrong please," insisted Gino.

"My mother had a stroke last night. The doctor gives her two days at the most. I can't handle this and all the other things that are going on."

"Like what else?" asked Gino.

"Donna DiVincenso told me to report to the cook who I worked for before. She also said that after my mother dies I will have to move into the servant's quarters. I will never see you again."

"We will have to trust God. I will never love anyone else. We will find a way."

"They will never let me go," she said starting to cry again. Gino hugged her and tried to comfort her.

"We just have to pray that the officials at Enna will eventually find out what is going on here. What will happen to Rose if your mother dies and you leave?"

"Rose is gone already" said Anna. "She came home last night. She was bloody all over her face. I could hardly recognize her. It looked like she was badly beaten. She was limping badly. She packed what little clothes she had and left."

"What did she say?"

"She didn't say much. She just said she had to go hide or they will kill her. I was hoping that Biachio would come home so I could comfort him. I am more worried about him than I am of Rose. He loved Stellina so much. He said he couldn't live without her. I loved her too. She was my dearest friend. She made me feel like life was worth living. I don't know what I am going to do without her. I wonder where Biachio spent the night."

"Biachio spent the night at the feet of Stellina's coffin."

"Oh the sweet dear man," said Anna beginning to cry again. "Is he still there?"

"Oh Anna," said Gino starting to cry. "He is still there and he will be there forever."

"Oh no, did he kill himself?" she asked crying with increased sadness.

"No he was in church praying when someone shot him in the back of his head. His parents didn't even come to the funeral. Maria and Gina buried him this morning next to Stellina."

Anna hugged Gino and cried on his shoulder. They stood there for a few minutes in each others arms.

"What I am most sad about is that I will not be able to see you and give you any information."

"Do you have any information about Peppino?" asked Gino after they had both reduced their crying to a sob. "I went to the jail as I have every night but this time he didn't respond."

"I overheard Donna Lucia ask her husband why they are keeping Peppino alive. He answered that he would take care of it."

"I have to go now. I'll be back to help you with arrangements for your mother."

"No, Gino, please don't come here. I don't want you at the funeral or the cemetery. If they saw us together or find out that you even know me, we would both be killed. Before you leave come and give me a hug and kiss me like it will be the last kiss for a long time." Gino with renewed tears wrapped his arms around her and kissed her passionately. Their lips would not part. Their tongues had their joyful moments before it was over. Gino gave her one last hug and kiss and turning left quickly.

Gino's heart was aching. He was loosing hope. He had hoped he had gotten better news from Anna. He was out of options. The only hope he had were Mr. Michele DiFranco's words he had spoken to him at Stellina's funeral. He had said if Gino ran into trouble getting Peppino released to come and see him. He had no idea what he meant. He had to find out. It was his last hope of saving Peppino. Gino rode his horse to the DiFranco home. He was told that Mr. DiFranco was at the orchard. Gino galloped his horse to the orchard as fast as he could. When he got there he asked one of the workers where Mr. DiFranco was.

"He is at the north side of the orchard," responded the Man.

Gino rode to the spot he was told. When he found him, he dismounted his horse and approached him.

"Gino," he said "how are you? What brings you out here?"

"I have a problem," he said. "I tried to communicate with Peppino as I have for the past year or so. I didn't get a response."

"How did you communicate with him?"

"I went to the jail late at night and standing on my horse I lowered him paper and pencil through his cell window. After he responded by jerking the rope three times. He would then send up a note and I would lower him some food. They had not been feeding him well."

"How do you know he wasn't asleep or sick or had some other reason for not responding?"

"Because, I talked to a friend who is a worker at the mayor's house. I was told that the mayor's wife asked her husband why they were keeping Peppino alive. He said he would take care of it."

"Dear Lord. I think Peppino is in trouble," said Michele. "Get on your horse and follow me." They both mounted their horses and Gino followed Michele until they were away from the orchard into a large open field. Michele dismounted and asked Gino to dismount also.

"I don't think anyone can hear us out here. I'm not sure I can help.

Anyway I don't want anyone to hear what I have to tell you. "I understand," said Gino.

"First you must promise me two things. One, no one must know what I am going to tell you. Secondly, you must promise that you will think of a way to hide how you got Peppino out of jail. Do you understand?"

"I don't completely understand but I promise you I'll do what ever you ask."

"You will understand as I explain to you what I have done. I was contracted to build the jail. Knowing that my life was always in danger from these criminals I looked for a way to build a secret passage to escape in the case I was jailed. The opportunity came when they asked me to build a lower level dungeon. It was to be a single room located below the main jail cells. It's was to have a secret entrance at the end of the cell corridor behind the stone wall at the far end. The stone wall was to have a secret latch which when pressed would cause the wall to move so one could enter and proceed down a set of stairs to the dungeon cell. They wanted this so they could make men disappear without a trace. They would put one down there at night and starve him or her to death. They could remove the bones or what was left of the body months later at their leisure."

"So what has this to do with Peppino?" asked Gino.

"Listen and I will explain. As the builder, I went in at night and build a tunnel from this cell to the side of the cliff. There is a loose stone just under the front end of the bed. The bed is cemented in so the loose stone is not noticeable. It has metal stops which limits the inter travel of the stone. On the outside of the stone are two 'U' shaped iron handles which are cemented in and have two ropes tied to them. To close the tunnel you pull on the ropes until the stone hits the stops. To get in you push the stone so it goes under the bed allowing you to enter the cell."

"I understand the first promise. I don't understand the second requirement," said Gino.

"I'm not sure they took Peppino down there. If you go there and Peppino is not there you have to come back out leaving everything like you found it. There should be no evidence that you were there. If Peppino is there and you save him you have to make it look like Peppino never escaped."

"How do I do that?" asked Gino.

"That's your problem. Don't you see? If they go down there and Peppino is gone they will search every where to find out how he escaped. They will eventually find the loose stone and the tunnel. That will have two devastating effects. First we loose an avenue of escape should we need one. Secondly they will come after me because I built the jail. That would put my complete family in jeopardy."

"I see what you mean," said Gino. "What I have to do then is substitute Peppino with a body that is his height and weight."

"Now you get the picture," said Michele. "Do you have any friends in the cemetery?"

"I have to think about this," said Gino. "Money will buy many friends. The problem is to find a friend you can trust." Gino thought for a while. Then another question came to his mind. "How do I find the tunnel?"

"Behind the jail cells on the left, the cliff is very close to the building. At the edge of the cliff at that point you will see two great rocks at the edge of the cliff. If you dig between them you will find a metal hook. Tie a rope to it and lower yourself down to the lower end of the two large rocks. There will be an opening between them. This is the entrance to the tunnel. It is about six feet below the edge of the cliff." Gino shook his hand, kissed him in both of his cheeks. "Thank you so much, Don Michele. I will not let you down. I will do what ever I have to do and I promise to protect you." "Don't wait to long. You probably have about a week at the most if indeed he is down there and still alive." Gino mounted his horse and headed for home. He had a lot of planning to do in a very short time.

That evening about midnight Gino tried to communicate with Peppino. He tried three times with the same results. Peppino just wasn't in his cell. Gino went home and started to think where was he going to start looking for a body? While deep in thought he fell asleep. When he awoke it was morning. He had decided that he would talk to the doctor. He had to be careful as to how he would ask the questions. He didn't think he could trust the doctor. What was he going to give as the reason he asked. He came up with the idea of being interested in a new business. After all he had a lot of experience handling funeral arrangements. He had his hand in Salvatore's, Stellina's, and Biachio's funeral arrangements.

He found the doctor just coming into his office.

"Doctor Bonavista, can I ask you a question?" "Ciao, Gino. What is your problem?"

"Doctor I am tired of working the land. It gets pretty lonely. I was thinking of possibly going into the business of arranging funerals. I have done it very successfully for three friends."

"How can I help you?"

"Well doctor can you tell me about how many deaths have occurred in the last month. Is there anyone who has passed away recently?"

"I am not in the position to know this. Not all deaths come through me. Deaths caused by our government are all buried in the unknown graveyard. They would not need funeral arrangements any-way. I don't think I can help you. Perhaps the church will be in a better position to help you. Anyway, I don't think there is enough income from that to live on."

"Thank you, doctor. It was just a wild idea." Gino left and was happy because the doctor had given him a lead without knowing it. He had informed Gino of the unknown grave yard. He knew what he had to do. Late that evening after the sun set and it was too late to have a burial, he went to the cemetery. There he met the graveyard guard.

"Ciao," he said to the guard. "My name is Gino. I was just taking a walk and saw you here by yourself."

"My name is Bruno. Do you always go walking through cemeteries?"

"Both of my parents are gone. I'm alone. I have walked every-where else, why not here. I thought you would be lonely and we could keep each other company."

"Well I certainly appreciate the company," said Bruno. They talked about the weather and recent funerals. Bruno told him of an eight year old girl that died of a mysterious disease.

"You know," said Gino. "I used to have a few drinks at the bar with a fellow. I don't remember his name. I'm told he passed away. Would you know about him? He was about in his mid twenties very slim but very tall. He must have been over six foot. You couldn't miss him."

"Do you mean Antonio," said Bruno. "He was about six foot. There aren't too many that tall."

"That sounds like him, said Gino. What became of him?" "He died from an overdose of whisky. He liked to drink a lot. This time he went too far."

"Did his family bury him here in this cemetery?" asked Gino hoping to use him as the replacement body.

"No, he didn't have any family. He was the only son and his parents died in a fire several years ago. He used to do odd jobs for the mayor's people. That's how he lived. When he died they brought him to me to bury."

"Did they put him in a pine box?" asked Gino.

"What pine box? They wrapped his body in a tablecloth and I buried him in the unknown grave section. That's where all the mayor's victims are buried."

"Can you tell who is where? Just in case someone wanted to give him a decent burial. Could you find him again?"

"Yes, I have my own system. I put a number on a rock as the head stone. Antonio is under rock sixty-three."

"How can you remember the number? Do you remember the number of everyone who is buried there?"

"Well Antonio was just buried the day before yesterday. I don't remember all of them. I do have a list of names and their number just in case someone needs to know. I would only give the number to a member of the mayor's people." That was funny thought Gino. He had just given him a number.

At almost midnight Gino said ciao to Bruno and prepared to leave.

"God willing I will see you tomorrow. What do you like to drink? Maybe I'll bring something we could sip on while we whittle away the evening."

"There is nothing like a good bottle of red wine," said Bruno. "You got it," said Gino as he left to go to Anna's house. When he got there he knocked at the door and was surprised that Anna answered immediately.

"Gino, it's so good to see you. I thought I would never see you again."

"Anna, how are you. How are you holding up? Is your mother doing better?"

"No, mama's breathing is very shallow. I don't think she will last through the night. I sent for the doctor and a priest. They will be here soon. So you can't stay long. What do you want?"

"First I want another last kiss," said Gino. Anna gave a very forced smile but her eyes showed love. She hugged Gino and he got his passionate kiss.

"Anna, do you still have some of those pills the doctor gave your mother to make her sleep?"

"Yes there is a half bottle full. Do you want them?"

"Yes please. I need them in the effort to free us all. God willing I will explain it all to you later. I'm not giving you up without a fight." "I love you, Gino," she said with love in her heart "I have another piece of information for you. I don't know if it will help but I heard Donna Lucia say that a guy named Paulo had to be paid for giving information of Salvatore Casolini's escape attempt."

"Thanks Anna," said Gino as he kissed her one last time and left before anyone showed up. Gino went home and had a good nights sleep. He now knew what he had to do.

The next day Gino went out to the Fanucci farm. He was so far behind he almost felt the effort was wasted. About an hour after he started to work, Gina showed up.

"Gina what are you doing here?"

"I can't let you do all the work. I have to find a way out of our problems. Until then I will do what ever I have to do to help."

"It's close to a losing battle," said Gino. "I feel bad like I have let you down."

"Gino, you have been an absolute angel. Now let's get to work and see if we can get us out of trouble." They worked until noon, ate a lunch that Gina had brought for both of them, and went back to work. They did not quit until it got too dark to work. Gino saw Gina home and then went and bought two small bottles of wine. He took them home and made a small hole in the cork of one of the bottles. He dissolved several of the sleeping pills and slowly poured the liquid into the bottle. He forced the cork down the neck a little further so that it sealed the hole in the cork. In the dark, Bruno would not be able to see the hole. He loaded his horse with digging tools and on his way to the cemetery he stopped at Gina's house. They were all in bed. It didn't matter. This was an emergency. Gina finally answered the door.

"Gino, what in the world are you doing here this late in the evening?"

"I need a pair of Peppino's pants, a shirt, socks and a pair of shoes. Don't ask any questions. Please hurry." A few minutes later, she brought what Gino asked for. He thanked her and left her wondering what was going on. Gino stopped just short of the cemetery. He tied his horse near by out of sight of Bruno.

"Ciao Bruno," he said acting as if he had been drinking. "How are we to night?"

"We are fine," he said with a smirk on his face. "I was beginning to think you weren't coming."

"I had to work at the farm. We have to get the seed in." "Isn't it a little late to plant now?"

"I have no other choice. The worse that could happen is we will have to do with what we have saved. Here I brought you the best wine I could get. It's from the grapes from three seasons ago when we had the best grape weather in years."

"Thanks," said Bruno. Gino gave him the bottle that had been doctored. They talked for awhile and within fifteen minutes Bruno was fast asleep. Gino went back and got his horse and found grave sixty-three. He dug up the body. Fortunately, it wasn't buried very deep. In fact, it was more like it was covered with dirt. The actual hole wasn't more then a foot deep. He loaded the body on his horse and silently made his way to the jail. He dug between the two large rocks as Michele told him and found the hooks. He tied one rope to it and lowered himself over the side. Sure enough, there was the small slit of an opening. By kicking against the cliff he was able to swing wide enough to gain the entrance. After getting a good foothold he tied a knot on the rope about the distance to the center of the opening. He climbed back up and measuring the distance from the edge to the knot, he was able to tie the body so it would hang where Gino could get it and pull it into the tunnel. He tied a second rope to the body so he could pull it through. With little effort he had the body in the tunnel. He then crawled down the tunnel until he got to the end. He found the stone with the hooks and the ropes and planting his feet against it he pushed it into the room under the bed. Gino crawled through the opening and since it was pitch black in the cell, he lit a candle he had brought with him. He was shocked to see Peppino hugging the door at the other end of the room wondering what kind of a creature was entering his cell. It was so unexpected that Gino broke out laughing.

"Now that is a sight," said Gino still laughing. "What did you think was coming after you a serpent?" Peppino stared at Gino with his mouth open.

"Where did you come from? Am I hallucinating?" Gino stood up and extended his arms toward Peppino.

"Come here and give your buddy a big hug, you big bear." Peppino not only hugged him but picked him up in the air and spun him around with great joy. "We don't have time to waste. I'm getting you out of here, buddy. Wait here, I'll be right back" Gino set the candle where it would not fall and entered the tunnel. A few minutes later he came back with Antonio's body.

"What is that?" asked Peppino still being in a state of shock over what was happening.

"This is your body, friend. Now help me take him out of the cloth he is wrapped in and undress him. Then put your clothes on him. It's got to look like it is you who died in here."

"What do we do with his clothes?"

"We take them with us. Never mind," said Gino after unwrapping him. "He doesn't have any clothes on. They wouldn't even let him keep his clothes. What animals."

"What am I going to wear?" said Peppino as he started to undress.

"I brought you some clothes. I just couldn't carry everything. They are on my horse up above." They dressed Antonio with Peppino's clothes.

"Go into the tunnel and wait for me at the other end. I have to stay behind to make sure there is no trace of my being here." Gino put the body on the bed and taking the candle he entered the tunnel. He pulled the stone so that it pulled in snuggly against the stops. He then made his way to the other end of the tunnel.

"Peppi, climb up the rope and before you go over the edge make sure no one is around. If it is safe go to my horse. In the saddlebags you will find your clothes. I didn't bring you any underwear. You can get those later. I'll be right behind you." A few minutes later, they were both safely in Gino's house. Peppino would be safe there at least for the time being.

"Well where do we go from here?" asked Peppino still thinking he was dreaming.

"I think we will have to find you a home on Monte Uno. We can't have people seeing you around here."

"Before we go there I want to get some guns and some ammunition. Also before we go I want to see Gina."

"We can do this tomorrow night. You will have to stay hidden here till then. In the meantime I'll check out the armory. For now let's get something to eat and get some rest. It's been a long day." After getting a bite to eat, they both went to sleep.

The next morning Gino left early to case the Armory before he went to the farm. He decided to walk innocently past the armory to see how things were. He was surprised that there were two guards on each end of the entrance way. As he walked by he stopped to talk to the guard.

"What's going on?" said Gino trying to act as a disinterested party. "I never saw guards here before."

"Where have you been?" said the first guard. "The armory was robbed a few days ago."

"Did they get very much?" asked Gino, surprised at his comments. "They got two rifles, two pistols and a basket of ammunition." "Who would want all that armament?" said Gino, honestly interested.

"I think it is the robber that has shown up lately. He probably uses most of it to kill animals for his own food. The police department doesn't really care about the small rancher, but this guy has robbed the

Duke. He is too powerful to ignore. He has more men than the city police."

"What was robbed from the Duke?"

"That's the funny part about it. He steals a lamb, slaughters it, cleans it, and only takes a small part of it and returns the rest to the Duke."Gino watched as he walked away looking for ways to separate them. He noticed that there was a chair along side of the building. Gino surmised that at night one would hide or sleep hidden on the north side of the building. This gave him something to think about. When he got back to his house Peppino was sleeping on Gino's bed. He hadn't had a decent bed for over three years. Gino went out and bought enough food for the next three days. Peppino woke up about five in the afternoon. He was starving. After they ate, Peppino started asking questions.

"Gino tell me what has been going on while I was in jail."

"I have been trying to help at the Fanucci farm. Gina has been coming out to help me but we are loosing the battle. I haven't even plowed my land. We are presently trying to seed the Fanucci farm but it is almost too late now. I imagine that Gina is there now wondering where I am. Anna has been a big help. It has been because of her that I was able to feed you and now help you escape. We are in love but there is no hope for us. Her mother is dying and after she goes, Anna has to move to the mayor's servant's quarters with the other servants. She will not be allowed to go outdoors again."

"Doesn't another girl live with Anna, a girl named Rosina I think?" "Yes but Rose, as we call her, came home one evening one breath from death. She had been raped and beaten to an inch of her life. She packed up and left for places unknown."

"Dear Lord," said Peppino putting two and two together. "I think I know what happened to her. The last time I saw Biachio he was grieving uncontrollably over the death of Stellina. He said that he got drunk and killed a maid at his house that night taking out his hatred for his mother. You know that his mother actually hanged Stellina. By the way, do you know where Biachio is? Is he all right?"

"He is beside Stellina," said Gino. "Someone shot him while he was praying in church."

"I sent him to pray in church," said Peppino. "The poor guy was torn in half. God finally gave him rest."

"We all have to trust God. And we will need His help if we are to get through this night. We should first try to rob the armory. If we succeed we will see Gina. The robbery will not be discovered until morning. By then we will be far away in the country. Now is the time to explore the Monte Uno caves." It was around midnight when they went to the armory. Peppino snuck around the building and jumped the guard on the side of the building. He wasn't doing a good job because he didn't expect to be attacked. Overconfidence is always a disadvantage. Since Peppino's man was out, he came up behind the other guard who turned to defend himself from Peppino when Gino knocked him out with a blow to the head. They found the key to the armory in his pocket. They dragged the men inside, tied them and helped themselves to what they wanted. Ten minutes later after stashing their loot behind the city dump they were at Gina's door. Gino ran the bell. Peppino hid in the darkness against the wall. Gino rang three times before he got an answer.

"Who is it," asked Gina from the courtyard. It's late come tomorrow."

"It's Gino. It's very important that I talk to you tonight" "What is so important that can't wait until tomorrow," she said as she opened the door. Gino pushed the door open and he and Peppino slipped into the dark courtyard. Gino quickly closed the door behind him.

"Don't talk," he whispered. "We'll talk inside." He then pulled her into the house and after Peppino slipped in, he shut the door. "Light a lantern. It is very important."

"Who did you bring with you? Who is this guy?" she asked as she lit the lantern. As soon as she saw that it was Peppino she jumped into his arms. When she let go he kissed her passionately. When his tongue reached for hers she pulled away.

"Peppi, I can't. How did you get out? What are you doing here? What has happened?"

"Gino broke me out of jail and I had to come and see you." "Oh Peppi, I have dreamed about having your arms around me.

But how did you get out. Won't they be looking for you?"

"We got out. That is all you need to know. To tell you more would endanger others. As for anyone looking for me, they don't know I'm missing yet."

"It's so good to see you. Gino have you gotten yourself in trouble over this?" asked Gina now beginning to worry about Gino's safety. "No, they will never know I had anything to do with it. It will be a while before they even know that Peppino is missing."

"I'm glad you're here Peppi," said Gina sounding very serious. "I need to talk with you."

"I know," said Peppino anticipating her question. "I'm not in the position to offer you anything."

"Peppino, listen to me please. You know that as long as I live my heart will always be yours. I love you more than my life. You are my first real love and the last. I'll never love anyone the way I love you. You will always be in my heart, in my thoughts and in my dreams." "I hear a 'but' in there some where," said Peppino beginning to get suspicious that she was going to tell him something he didn't want to hear.

"Sweetheart, I have been grieving for you since you were jailed. To me you died with Tano. You've been a dead man since you were jailed. I knew that you couldn't survive. It was a matter of time."

"But I'm not dead and I am out of jail," said Peppino wondering what she was trying to say.

"You are just having a few hours, perhaps days, but you are a dead man. You will soon have an army after you. You can't fight them all forever. Besides I know you. You are like a part of my body. You will always be a part of me. I can hear your thoughts in my head.

I know that you could sneak past the guards and flee this area. But I know you too well. You are going to revenge your family aren't you? If I thought you would leave the area....but love of my heart, it wouldn't make any difference. I could never leave my mother. She needs me now more than ever. I would never forgive myself. I have to think of her first before myself. But it doesn't matter. You wouldn't even consider leaving."

"Gina honey, what are you trying to tell me?" "Do you know Nicolo Nicci?" asked Gina.

"Yes I remember him from school. He was about five years older than me. He's a very nice fellow as I remember. He was very kind and gentle. What about him?"

"He's nine years older than me," said Gina trying to side step his question as long as she could.

"That's nice so what? What are you trying to say? Stop dancing around the question"

"He and his parents came to visit the other day. They asked mama for my hand in marriage to their son Nicolo."

"What did you tell them?" said Peppino tears starting to roll down his face.

"Peppi, I have no choice. We don't have anyone to work the land. We need some one or we will starve to death. I owe my mother that much. It is the only way."

"What you are telling me is that you said 'yes.'"

"I told him about you. I told him I could never forget you. He said that even if you had my heart he would be happy to have the rest of me. He understands that my heart belongs to you. Please, Peppino. I trust you completely. Tell me I am wrong. Give me an option. How can I help my mother? Tell me you will not let it happen."

"I wish you hadn't put it that way. I don't have an answer to your problem. I understand too well what it's like to want to help your parents. I understand and it will not change the way I feel about you. I will always love you. You will always be mine in my heart and my dreams," said Peppino tears now running freely. The fact that I understand doesn't mean that I have to like it. It is breaking my heart."

"My heart has been breaking for nearly four years," said Gina now crying more than Peppino. Peppino grabbed her and hugged her tight.

"Give me one last good-bye kiss," said Peppino as he searched for her lips. She gave him a final kiss. Peppino turned and headed for the door where Gino was waiting.

"I will always love you and constantly pray for your safety," said Gina as they slipped out the door and out of her life probably forever.

Peppino and Gino walked back to the city dump where they had left their horses, the guns and ammunition and headed towards Monte Uno.

"Tell me, Gino," asked Peppino. "Where did you get this horse for me?"

"I bought it with the money I got from my uncle's land. I guess I didn't tell you that I sold it."

"I'm glad you didn't steal it," said Peppino trying to forget his sorrow at losing Gina. They rode for a while in silence. Peppino couldn't get his mind off of Gina.

"How are you doing, old friend?" asked Gino seeing that he was too silent.

"You know, Gino, a thought came to my mind. My father is dead. I have no brothers or sisters and now Gina is out of my life. I am an outlaw and not likely to have any children. Do you know what that means?"

"No, what does that mean?"

"It means that I am the last of the Casolini."

Chapter 10

THE OUTLAW

It was around two in the morning when Peppino and Gino got to the foothills of Monte Uno. It was too dark for them to find the entrance of the cave. The weather was warm so it would be pleasant sleeping under the stars. They rolled out the blankets Gino had thought of bringing with them and soon they were fast asleep. Peppino woke up a few hours later. It was still dark. He immediately started to think of Gina. The thought of someone else making love to her started the pain all over again. He pushed her out of his mind. He had to think of what he was going to do next. He prayed for guidance from God. He decided he had to build a home in the mountain. He needed wood and carpenter's tools. He also needs some sort of mattress. He would need some cooking utensils and a way to cook the food. He had to practice shooting the guns he stole. He had gone hunting with his father and he was pretty good, but he had to be better because to do what he had to do he had to be perfect. He would only get one chance. The sun started to come up before Gino woke up.

"Hey sleepy head, you must like the open sky. You have been sleeping like a baby."

"I was very tired. Yesterday was a very long day for me," said Gino getting up. "We don't have anything for breakfast, do we?"

"I haven't eaten breakfast for almost four years. I don't remember what breakfast was like," responded Peppino. "Listen, why don't you go to work on your land? We are going to need the grain. No one will be looking for you."

"Unless the guard at the armory saw me in the dark and remembers me," said Gino. "Anyway before I go lets look for the cave. I'll go up the East Slope and you go up the North Slope. Yell out if you find anything."

"If I remember correctly, the cave is on the ground level," said Peppino.

"Well then, check the ground level as you go up," suggested Gino. They both started their search. It was about ten minutes later when Gino yelled out to Peppino.

"Did you find anything?" asked Peppino.

"No, but look out there towards town, what do you see?"

"I see a cloud of dust followed by what looks like three clouds of dust. It looks like someone is being chased by three people. What do you think it is?"

"Remember that I told you someone had robbed the armory before us? The guard at the armory told me when I was casing it, that there has been a rash of robberies lately. That must be the outlaw that apparently is about to be caught."

"Let's ride around the west side of the mountain. We can get there before them and lend a hand to a fellow outlaw."

"I'm with you. We can stay high on the mountain and be shooting from above them." As they got to the south side they noticed that the fellow had jumped from his horse and was defending himself from behind a rock. The three pursuers where also behind rocks, shooting back at him. Peppino and Gino dismounted, tied their horses at a safe distance and crawled down behind rocks. They started to shoot at the three men they recognized as policemen. The outlaw wounded one man and Peppino hit one of the other men. The police retreated pulling his comrades with him. He realized he was now out numbered. He threw the wounded man and the dead man across their horses and retreated back to town.

"That was an interesting adventure," said Peppino. "Let's go see who it was that we helped."

"That is going to be difficult," said Gino. "Why?" asked Peppino. "Because he isn't there anymore. He is gone. You would think he would have stayed long enough to wave at us in gratitude."

"Let's go down there and see if we can find a trace of him." They both rode down and searched the whole area with no success. They went back to the North side of the mountain and after searching for an hour they found the cave where Peppino had guessed it would be. It was hard to find because of the over growth of shrubs that blocked the entrance. They went in and found it to be very large inside. It was a perfect place to hide.

"I'm going to the Fanucci farm to see if I can help Gina. Then I will go to my farm. I will see you tonight. I will try to bring us some food. What are your plans?"

"I'm going to go to my land. My father had a lot of tools in the shed. I know he had a saw and a hammer and nails. The lumber yard is over by the Dukes ranch isn't it?"

"That's right; it is just east of the ranch. Be careful. They will have a guard there after six. How are you going to get into your shed? It was pretty sturdy and had a heavy locked door."

"My father was always worried that he would lose the key. So we devised a nice hiding place for it near the shed. I remember where it is. That will not be any problem." Gino left and Peppino went to the shed. There he not only found the tools he needed but he also found two sacks of grain and a lantern with a can of kerosene for it. He also found a spyglass. It was an expanding type telescope. He returned to the cave and decided to explore while he waited for dark and Gino. Using the lantern, he walked slowly down the cave toward the center of the mountain. He found several tunnels that lead either straight down or at an upward angle. He continued down the main tunnel. He was very careful because of the stories he had heard about people who disappeared and were never seen again. He suspected they fell into a hole in the tunnel. And he was correct. He found at least two fissures that looked like they had no bottom. Peppino almost stepped into one, and soon came to a place that looked like men had at one time been digging a side tunnel. It was a dead end. Peppino traced back and continued down the main tunnel. Suddenly the lantern was not as bright as it was before. It kept getting dimmer and dimmer. For a while, he became alarmed that maybe the stories he had heard were true. But then his superior intelligence figured it out. The reason the light seemed dim was because the walls were very dark and no longer reflected the light. Peppino suspected it was some kind of coal that lined the walls or perhaps it was iron ore. Whatever it was didn't reflect the light and it was difficult to see where you were going. A hole now could mean death. He was about to turn around and go back when he felt a strong chill like he usually felt in the middle of winter. He also heard a noise he couldn't identify. Curiosity got the best of him and he proceeded down the tunnel. About a hundred feet deeper, the walls started to reflect light again and he found what was making the noise; an underground stream. Carefully he worked his way down and around the many sharp rocks that surrounded the area. At the edge of the stream, he bent over and stuck his hand in the water. He pulled it out immediately. The water was ice cold. Carefully, he cupped his hands and scooped a hand full of water and drank it. It was as pure as the spring water he was used to drinking. All he needed now was some glasses. He promised himself he would get some. He found his way back to the entrance to the cave and sat on a rock outside. He contemplated what he had discovered and how it could be useful. Obviously, it was good for cooking and drinking water, but it dawned on him that it would also serve as a preservative. He could tie a piece of meat or even a complete deer and submerge it in the water and the meat could last for a week or more. Things were beginning to look up. This could be a perfect home. Gino wouldn't probably come until after dark. Peppino decided while he waited to practice shooting. He found a large clump of dirt which he set upon a rock. He moved about three hundred yards away, then taking one of the rifles and lying prone on the ground, he started to practice shooting at the target. It wasn't long before he had to replace the target. He found a piece of heavy paper in one of the saddlebags. Using a dried olive he found in the food package Gino had brought he marked a target on the paper. Folding the one side of the paper he hung it on a small ledge above the cave. He set two small rocks on each corner of the folded section of the paper so it would hang over the ledge. He then backed away from the cave until he could barely see it. From there he became familiar with the rifle and its particular sights. He learned how to aim it and to softly pull the trigger as the small movement of the rifle passed the target. Moving back every few minutes, shooting from behind different rooks, he learned to allow for windage, the inaccuracies of the rifle, and the bullet's loss of altitude due to gravity at the different ranges. It was dark when Gino showed up. He had two broken chairs on his cuffinas along with several old wooded chair legs.

"What are these?" asked Peppino amazed to see what Gino had brought.

"These are chairs," he said being sarcastic. "Did you expect new ones? I found these at the city dump. Someone threw them away. You can fix them can't you?"

"Well if I can't we will set them on a flat rock," said Peppino being sarcastic also.

"What have you been up to all day?" asked Gino.

"I've been practicing shooting. What did you find out is going on in town?"

"First I don't have to worry about the guard at the armory. I guess I hit him too hard. He died. I was relieved however to find out that he was an old bachelor."

"Did you help Gina," asked Peppino.

"No, she had a fellow helping her. His name is Nicolo."

"What else did you find out in town?" asked Peppino not wanting to hear any more about Gina's helper.

"I also found out that there has been a series of robberies in town. They have police watching everything. Must be the work of the outlaw friend we helped."

"This would be a good time to steal what we need that is out of town," said Peppino. He was correct. They had no problem stealing the wood he needed and on the way home they killed one of the Duke's lambs and brought it with them. Peppino showed Gino the stream he had found, always being cautious of the holes. They cleaned and skinned the lamb, took what they needed for that evening, and tied the remaining lamb by a foot and set it in the ice cold stream. They made a fire from the brush they could find plus some of the small tree branches they gathered and cooked the lamb. They saved whatever fat they could from the lamb. They could burn it for cooking at a later time.

They spent the next few days building a table, fixing the two broken chairs, and with the wood they had stolen, the extra legs Gino had brought they end up with fourchairs. Some how a table did'nt look right with out four chairs. This made the cave livable. Gino went back and forth to town to bring back news and anything he thought could be useful. One evening he brought back two single bed mattresses. He found them in his uncle's old house which had been closed since his death. Gino didn't know what to do with them. Peppino made two low bed frames to hold the mattresses off the ground.

During the next few evenings after dark, they would sneak into town and steal meat from the butcher and other food from the grocery store. One day when Gino reported that the main stores were heavily watched, they stole some fish from the fish market. Because of the heavy guards, some days they had to live on animals they got hunting; mostly rabbit. They stayed away from town for a few days. The outlaw also stayed away. That gave Peppino the opportunity he had waited for. Since all the police and guards were in town around the main stores, this was a time for Peppino to do what he felt God saved him for. The first target was to pay Paulo a visit. He had betrayed his father and sold him out to the mayor for money. Later that night he snuck into town just before dawn. He painted a target on Paulo's door. He waited across the road in the darkness. Paulo came out to go to his land and saw the markings on the wall.

"What is this?" he said. It was the last thing he would ever say.

Peppino's bullet hit him in the back of his head. He fell forward against the door dead. The shot was heard all over town through the silence of the early morning. Peppino ran down the street to his horse and fled towards his mountain hideaway. Several horses tried to follow him but couldn't in the dark. Peppino got back to the mountain as Gino was getting up.

"Where have you been?" asked Gino still somewhat groggy.

"I went to take care of personal business," said Peppino. "I had a message for an old neighbor called Paulo."

"The next time let me know. We should be together to protect each other's back."

"Okay," agreed Peppino. "This was a small job. If you want to help, case the area around the city hall. I have some business with the mayor."

"Going after the big one next are you?"

"Yes, but I need some information. Find a place we could hide, do our job, and have a good escape route."

"I'll see what I can do. What will you do in the mean time?"

"I think I'll ride down toward Piazza Armerina. There are a lot of woods down there. My father and his friend used to hunt deer in those woods. I'll see if I can bring home some meat for us."

"Be careful they don't think you are going to Enna."

"I don't think they will be that far east. I'm sure they will only be checking the roads that lead to Enna." Gino left for work on his farm.

That evening when Gino got back Peppino was there waiting for him.

"What did you find out in town," asked Peppino.

I found a place where we could climb up on the roof of a building about four buildings down from the city hall. Since they are all connected, we could make our way to a building one building away from the city hall. There is a good view of the city hall from there. I picked that building instead of the building across from the city hall because it has a low wall all around the flat roof. We could hide there for days if necessary."

"Good work," said Peppino. "We will go tomorrow night and stay there all night. We can catch the mayor as he goes to work the next morning. We will bring blankets with us so we could cover ourselves, not only to sleep but also to hide if we have to stay the next day."

"By the way, there is something else I want to tell you. I went home to my house to see how things were and to be seen by my neighbors. I found an envelope under my door. It had a note and a key in it. The note said that it was Anna's house key and that she will not be using it for a while. It is a very nice place, small, but has the advantage of being on a corner where it is hard for any one to see what is going on in the house. It is close to town and we could use it to hide our horses"

"That sounds perfect," said Peppino. "I guess we are ready." "How did you make out today in the woods?" asked a very hungry Gino.

"I got a deer. I dressed it, took what we need for tonight and got the rest in the water to keep cold."

The next evening came quickly. They ate some of the deer meat that Peppino had prepared. After enjoying some small talk about the days of their youth, they prepared their horses for the trip into town... They arrived a little after one-thirty in the morning. They silently hide their horses in Anna's stable and worked their way to the roof top Gino had recommended. It was perfect. They placed the blankets on the roof next to the brick wall that gave them cover and folded it so it covered them. Peppino was by the south wall and Gino was by the north wall. After a few minutes, Gino feel asleep. Peppino was too excited to sleep. He closed his eyes and thought of his father and of his sister Stellina, whom he loved so dearly. He promised that he would avenge their deaths. Morning came slowly. Gino woke up to the noise of the early workers going about their business. The mayor wouldn't go to work until probably ten. They would have to wait.

"Don't shoot unless you have to," whispered Peppino to Gino.

"We don't want to hurt innocent people." It was about nine-thirty when Peppino saw the mayor tie his horse in front of city hall and head for the door. Peppino had his rifles sights aimed at the front door. As soon as the mayor stepped in front of the door, someone called him. He turned as Peppino fired. The bullet pierced his heart. Peppino's father was avenged. Peppino was glad he didn't shoot him in the back. Somehow, it made a difference. They both covered themselves with their blankets and prepared to wait.

It was just beginning to get dark that evening, when they allowed themselves to move. All day they heard the yelling and running around of a dozen police. The police searched every house in the area for information. The activity didn't seem to diminish as time went by but seemed to increase as discouragement set in the mayor's people. Peppino's knees, his belly, and his elbows hurt as he lay there on his stomach. Gino was even worse since he had not had the hard jail experience that Peppino had. They had been there on the roof for almost twenty-four hours before the activity on the ground was reduced to silence. Peppino and Gino worked their way back to the last building and as quietly as they could they climbed down and hid in Anna's house. In the early hours of the morning, Peppino made his way back to the cave. Gino left about five minutes later and went to his land. No one was the wiser. It was late in the evening when Gino and Peppino met again. Gino, after working on his land, had gone back to his house where he got the latest information. He then left for the cave.

"Ciao Gino," said Peppino as he arrived. "How are you doing after the day's activities?"

"I'm very hungry," said Gino. "What do we have for dinner?" "We are having something special and unusual," said Peppino kidding Gino and acting like it was very yummy. "We are having deer stew."

"Oh boy," said Gino with a sour look on his face. "Deer stew." "Forget your stomach and tell me what the news is in town." "Give me some food and I'll tell you while we eat." Peppino spooned some of the deer stew into Gino's dish and some into his own. Gino began eating immediately. Peppino didn't stop him but he said grace before he ate. "If you remember" continued Gino,, "I didn't even get a glass of water all day yesterday."

"Well there is plenty of food today. You can eat for two days. Now tell me what's going on in town. I have spent all day over a hot stove to feed you and you keep me waiting for the news I'm dying to hear." "Well, the mayor got shot yesterday," said Gino with a very innocent look on his face. "He died. The paper says that the police think it was one of the peasants who was unhappy with something the mayor did. The mayor's wife, Donna Lucia, being a Malavista, will take over as temporary mayor. Lucia's brother, Vittorio Malavista, is really the next in line to take over. However, the family is considering that perhaps his son Giovanni should reign seeing that his father is getting up in age. Vittorio doesn't think his son is ready and he should be mayor even if it was for a little while. He could then train his son."

"Is this the fellow we know as Gianni?"

"Yes, that's him," said Gino. "He is the guy who helped Donna Lucia kill your sister."

"He is the next on my list," said Peppino getting angry. "He, his brother, and his father are all on my list. Also on my list is Donna Lucia. First come, first served." "What does that mean?"

"It means that who ever I can get to first will be my next target." They decided to hold off for a while to allow things to settle down. Gino went to work on his land. Two weeks went by without any action. Peppino was getting restless. Gino finally showed up after almost two days since the last time Peppino had seen him. "Well, ciao old friend," said Peppino. "I thought you had forgotten about me. I haven't seen you in two days. What have you been up too?"

"I've had personal business in town."

Peppino knew Gino too well. He sensed that Gino was holding something back. "Gino, dear friend, this is me, remember. We grew up together. I know you better then you know yourself. What are you holding back? Where have you been?"

"I'm sorry, Peppino. You have to understand that Gina is like a sister to me. I love her like the sister I never had. I have tried to help her and her mother since you went to jail. I couldn't desert them any more then I could desert you."

"What are you babbling about?" asked Peppino with no idea of what his friend was saying.

"I'm telling you that I attended Gina and Nicolo's wedding. I'm sorry. I know how this will hurt you. I had to go."

"Of course you did," is all that Peppino could say. The sadness showed in his face.

"I have seen Gina several times and she and her mother have never failed to ask about you. When I danced with her at the reception she asked about you and asked me to tell you that she will always love you."

"I want to get even with the people that caused me this heartache. Are you still with me?"

"You know that I will die for you. What do you want me to do? I have told you all I know. I spent most of today casing some possibilities. The only other information that I have is that Roberto is going to join the police force. He is going to Catania to a police academy."

"Is he going alone? I don't suppose his brother Gianni is accompanying him. We could kill the two together."

"I'm afraid not. Gianni is going to work with his father in city hall.

He is in training to someday be mayor." "When is he leaving?" "Tomorrow morning."

"He will have to pass by Monte Mangone. The land there gets pretty rugged. There is only one road that you can use to get through the mountain pass. We can set up an ambush there at the pass. We should start late tonight and sleep on the slope of the mountain."

"We will take out the old blankets again and sleep on the ground," said Gino not sounding too happy with the thought.

"Gino dear friend, you don't have to come if you are too tired." "Don't mind me. I wouldn't miss it for the world." They got some sleep and left very early in the morning.

It was about eleven in the morning when Gino spotted two riders coming down the road towards the pass. Peppino got out his spyglass and checked them out. This was the fifth riders that they had checked.

"It's them," said Peppino getting very excited. It's Roberto and a policeman to guard him." They hid behind a rock and waited for them to come into range.

"I'll get Roberto. If the policeman runs let him go. We don't want to hurt him if he is not going to fight." When they got into firing range Peppino set his rifle on the rock to steady it and took careful aim. Gino took aim at the police ready to shot should he offer resistance. As they got closer, Peppino noticed that the policeman took out his rifle and was ready to shoot. He was aware that they had reached a place that could leave them wide open to attack. Peppino took aim at Roberto's heart. "Remember Stellina," he said to himself, as he pulled the trigger. Roberto fell over dead. The police guard jumped off his horse and landed behind a large rock, shooting at Peppino the entire time. His bullet hit the rock just inches from Peppino.

"Looks like he wants to fight," said Gino.

"Hold your fire. Maybe he will give up and go home, said Peppino. He was wrong. The officer shot where he thought the attacker was and moved to a closer rock. His bullet again hit near Peppino.

"Stay low and keep out of sight. He doesn't know there are two of us. Move carefully and try to get him from the left. We will get him in a cross fire." Gino moved to a rock farther from Peppino. The police officer had keen eyes. He noticed that something had moved and shot at it. It missed Gino by inches. Peppino trained his rifle at the point the police officer had popped up to shot at Gino "Hey, that guy is good," said Gino. "Protect me will you." "Move one last time," said Peppino. Just as he suspected, his movement was detected and the police came up to shoot. He never got the chance. Peppino's bullet hit him square in the forehead. Peppino and Gino didn't waste anytime. They quickly packed their horses and were on their way home.

"You know, Gino," said Peppino after they returned to the cave,. "They never did figure that we shot the mayor from the roof top. I wonder if we could use that place again one last time."

"I think the risk will be much more a second time than it was the first time. They now know where the bullet didn't come from. They don't have to be very smart to figure the other possibilities. Well you figure it out. I have to go to my land and do some work. I haven't been there for three days now. I'm sure the seed has germinated by now."

Three weeks later when Gino came to the cave home, Peppino had a rabbit cooked and ready to eat. It was cooked in a tomato sauce and had boiled potato in an olive oil based dressing.

"Is this my last meal you are serving tonight," said Gino suspicious that Peppino wanted something. "What do I have to do for this meal?"

"I want to go to the roof across from the city hall one last time." "It's too dangerous. They will surely figure out where the shot came from. You can fool them once but not twice."

"You're right," said Peppino. "I don't have any right to put your life in danger. You don't have an ax to grind. You don't have to come. I can probably get away faster by myself."

"Don't do this Peppino. You know I will never let you go alone. I'm worried about you. Let's figure some other way."

"You know that the roof is the safest place to hide while waiting. They will not be able to see it coming. After the shooting, we will have to be smart to get away. This time after the shooting we will immediately run down the roofs and slip into Anna's house. They can't follow us from the ground. Then when it is clear, we leave from there. Let's bring a set of clothes that are detectably different"

"I think it is too risky. But you're the head of this outfit so tell me what to do." They left at about one and followed the same procedure they did when Peppino shot the mayor. They both hated the waiting. In the morning the new future mayor Vittorio arrived first. After a few minutes Giovanni came tied his horse in front and headed to the door. He never made it. Peppino's bullet struck him in the back and through his heart. Peppino and Gino started to run down the roofs to get to the end roof where they could come down. Two police officers on the ground were yelling. "They are on the roof! Get help. Don't let them escape." They were following them running along the buildings. They had more obstacles to fight on the ground then Peppino and Gino had so they were being left behind. Peppino and Gino ran to the other side of the roofs. The officers ran to an ally and crossed to the other side. Peppino and Gino meanwhile came back to the original side. They jumped down from the last roof and ran to Anna's house. They changed their clothes and looking out they found that several police were searching each house.

"We have to make a run for it," said Peppino.

"Let's go," said Gino getting on his horse and both rode out of the stable at full gallop. They were almost out of town when they noticed that several police following them at full gallop.

"They are after us," said Peppino. "We could stop and play innocent."

"No way," said Gino. "They would recognize you and it would all be over. We have to get to the mountain and fight it out. We have a chance on the mountain." Peppino hoped that the police were far enough behind them that they would not recognize them. He hoped that they only knew they had flushed out two fellows on horseback.

They shot at them to get them to stop. They were too far out of range to do any harm. Peppino and Gino arrived at the cave. They ducked their horses in the cave and climbed above the cave and settled behind some rocks. When the police arrived they dismounted their horses and ducked behind some rocks. The shooting started and soon was very heavy. There were five police. They soon had Peppino and Gino pinned down. It was a matter of time before they would be flushed out. Three police stayed to pin them down while the other two moved closer. The two started to separate to get Peppino and Gino in a cross fire and eventually come up on both sides and catch them like sitting ducks. Peppino thought it was over. There wasn't anything he could do. As the police on his right was about to shoot, a shot rang out from above them. The police on the right fell. Peppino turned and shot the other policeman coming up on his left. He was hit in the forehead. As Peppino looked out for the other three, another shot from behind him hit the officer in the middle. The other two retrieved their comrades and fled. Peppino looked up to see who had helped them but he was gone.

"Did you see who that was?" asked Peppino.

"I didn't even see his rifle. I presume it was the fellow we helped the other day."

"I wish we could thank him."

"I'm hungry," said Gino. "Why don't you cook us something and I will go up to where he was and see if I can pick up his trail."

"You are always hungry."

"Better cook it inside," suggested Gino. "We don't want some smoke to tell them where we are. They may be coming back with help."

"Don't you think that they already know where we are?" "All they know is that we took a stand here."

While Peppino was cooking Gino climbed up the side of the mountain looking for some evidence that could tell him who the mysterious outlaw was. As he looked around he noticed a strange smoke coming out of the mountain. He followed the smoke and was surprised to find that it came out from behind a rock. Thinking it might have been the outlaw he lowered himself to the rock. He was amazed at what he found. On the far side of the rock, hidden by the rock formation, there was a very large opening. He would never have found it if not for the smoke. From the ground, it could not be seen because the cliff below it jutted out enough to hide the opening. Gino went inside. It was a very large cave. He followed the smoke down a small tunnel that suddenly veered left for a few feet and then went straight down. Stopping, he went back outside, got his horse, traveled about two hundred feet past the cliff, and rode his horse up the side of the mountain to the top of the cliff where the opening was. Gino brought his horse inside He got a rope he had on his horse and tying it to a rock let himself down, dropping down inside the cave they were living in. He walked toward the opening and walked up behind Peppino.

"Where did you come from? I thought you were outside looking for clues."

"I was. But I found something better!"

"We had better eat and get out of here. I'm sure the police are rounding up an army to come after us. We have to hide what we can."

"That's what I found," said Gino. Gino then slipped outside, brought Peppino's horse to the upper cave and a few minutes later let himself down again into the cave where Peppino was.

"How did you get past me again," said Peppino seeing Gino come from inside the cave. What kind of games are you playing?" "Just grab a mattress and follow me. Trust me," said Gino.

Peppino grabbed his mattress and followed Gino out of the cave. "Where are the horses?" said Peppino getting excited.

"Don't worry. I hid them."

"Where in the world did you hide them? I don't see anywhere you could hide them. I searched every inch of the mountain side." Peppino followed Gino up the side of the mountain and they entered the cave where the horses were. "Dear Lord, how did you find this place?"

"I followed your smoke. There is a connection between the lower cave and this one. I saw your smoke coming out of the mountain side and followed it here. We have to block that hole whenever we cook down there." Gino then took Peppino through the tunnel to the hole.

"Go down the rope and hand me all the tools you want to hide. The mattresses were too big to bring up this way but everything else can be brought through here. Tie what you want up here on the rope and I will haul it up." They brought everything they owned to the upper cave except the table and chairs. For the time being they would still have to eat in the lower cave, since the water and food were down there. When they had finished eating they went up the east side of the mountain were they could see if anyone was coming. It was just before dusk when they saw a cloud of dusk coming their way. Peppino checked looking through his spyglass.

"It's a lone rider," he informed Gino. "There is no one following him. It looks like he is headed toward the south side of the mountain. Let's get our horses and ride to where we last saw the outlaw. I think that is him." They got to the point where they had aided the outlaw and staying hidden they watch where he went. There were two small trees and a large bush where he entered the mountain. They quietly made their way down to where the outlaw had disappeared and searched around the base of the mountain. Sure enough, behind a large shrub was an opening. They were about to enter when they heard a sound behind them.

"Put your hands behind your head and don't move if you want to live," said a female voice. Gino who was in front of Peppino turned around as he was putting his hands over his head. The outlaw recognized Gino.

"Gino," she yelled as she dropped her rifle and threw her arms around him. "It's so good to see you." Gino, recovering from the initial shock, pulled his head back so he could look directly into her face.

"Rosina," he exclaimed. "Is it really you? What are you doing here?" She ignored his questions and looked at Peppino who had just lowered his hands. She pulled them inside her cave were she felt safer. "You look like Peppino Casolini," she said as if she was talking to herself. "How did you get here? I was sure that you were dead or at the least in jail."

"I'm neither," said Peppino being very impressed with what he saw. "I'm here as you can see. Was it you that saved us earlier today?" "I was just returning the favor," she said with a beautiful smile on her face. While Gino and Rosina chatted over passed times Peppino studied this girl outlaw that had outsmarted them. She was a very beautiful woman. Her skin was very fair and her hair was a dark brown. Peppino found himself comparing her to Gina. He found that Rosina was a little shorter than Gina but still taller than Gino. She was a little fuller than Gina. He found her to be very attractive. Suddenly he felt like he was betraying Gina. For a moment, he forgot that Gina had married someone else.

"You guys are making things tough on me," said Rosina. "I don't feel safe here any more. I just come back from town. I need some food. The town is in an uproar. Police are everywhere. I couldn't steal anything."

"If you're hungry we can feed you," said Peppino. "You had better come with us anyway. You're not safe here any longer. We expect an army of police to come here either later or tomorrow morning. They will search the whole mountain. I see that you have a small mattress, a kerosene lamp, and a small stove. Let's load everything we can carry and get going to the cave." Rosina obeyed without question. She had heard of Peppino's authoritative stature and leadership qualities, now she could see first hand how they compelled confidence, respect and obedience. They moved all that Rosina had to the new hideout without incident. Rosina was amazed at the undetectable entrance to the cave. They set it up so that the horses were located at the right side of the cave. Peppino and Gino's mattresses were located on the left side. They put Rosina's mattress at the far end of the cave next to the tunnel that went down to the main cave. After they were settled, Peppino took Rosina down to the main cave and served her some of the deer meat that was left over. After she had eaten, he took her down the tunnel to the stream and showed her how they kept their meat in the ice cold water. When they came back up Gino was watering and feeding the horses.

"I think that we need someone up top keeping an eye on the road from town. We don't want any one sneaking up on us, Peppino." "Why don't we all go up for now?" asked Rosina. "I would like to get to know you guys a little better. We can take turns later. I'm guessing we don't need a guard after we go to sleep."

"That's right," said Peppino. "When we are asleep they will not be able to detect us as long as we stay in the upper cave." When they got to a good position on the east side of the mountain they sat on smooth rocks and began getting to know each other. Peppino kept checking the town road using the spyglass.

"Tell me what has been happening in town?" asked Rosina. "Do you guys get any information? The last time I was in town I escaped after Biachio tried to rape me and when not successful beat me almost to death."

"I thought that was you," said Peppino. "The day after Stellina was killed poor Biachio came into the jail to visit with me. He wanted me to kill him. It wasn't so much that he couldn't live without Stellina, but because he felt so bad about killing a poor woman in his parent's house. He felt that he didn't deserve to live."

"Did he tell you why he did that to me?"

"Yes, when he found out that Stellina was dead he went out and got very drunk. He was looking for his mother who had hanged Stellina. His mother apparently hid from him so he took his hatred out on whoever got in his way. Believe me; I have never seen anyone who was sorrier for what he had done than Biachio. That's why I sent him to church to ask forgiveness from God."

"I kind of feel very bad for him too. He must have really loved Stellina," said Rosina looking like she wanted to cry.

"Why should you feel bad for him?" asked Peppino, surprised at her statement.

"I feel bad because I'm the one who shot him while he was praying in church. I didn't know about his love for Stellina. I only heard how he forced Stellina to marry him."

"The reason Biachio's mother was angry with Stellina was because Biachio loved her so much and treated her so well that Stellina fell madly in love with him. Do you know that he brought her flowers every day from the time they got married till the day she died? Then when she got pregnant she hated the idea of half breeds running around her house," said Peppino showing no shock at what he had heard "And I take it you feel it is your job to even the score?" asked Rosina.

"That is the only purpose for living I have left," said Peppino. "My whole family is gone, and I have even lost my fiancée."

"Do you think they will let you get close to the mayor, or his wife?" "You don't know me very well. Or should I say you don't know what all the fuss is about in town." She could not have been aware of his previous success.

"I suspect they are angry with your robberies," said Rosina "Did you know that Mayor Mario DiVincenso personally killed my father? Did you know that Biachio's cousins, Roberto and Giovanni, both tied my sister Stellina and placed her on a chair with a noose around her neck so that Donna Lucia could personally kick the chair and hang my sister?"

"No, and I'm sorry I asked," said Rosina

"Did you know," continued Peppino, that mayor Mario, Roberto, and his brother Giovanni are all dead?"

Rosina looked at Gino. Gino nodded his head in a yes gesture. "I don't think they are coming tonight," said Gino changing the subject. I generally go to my farm during the day. However, in view of the situation we are in I had better stay here until they come.""You are welcome to stay," said Peppino. "But it isn't necessary.

We are not going to fight them. My hope is that they will come here and search the area, find the cave and find only trace evidence that we have been here. They hopefully will figure that we moved or left the area. They should have no reason to come back here. We would be fools to come back to an area they had discovered and knew about."

"You really know how they think, don't you?" said Rosina. "You're amazing…I wonder how soon they will regret not getting rid of you while they had the chance."

"Believe it or not, I owe it all to Biachio. He fought to keep me alive to fulfill a promise he made to Stellina."

"Gino, have you seen Anna lately," asked Rosina. "You know that she is crazy about you."

"I saw her right after you packed and left. Did you know that her mother died and the mayor's wife directed her to move into the servant's quarters with the rest of the servants? She is not allowed to go out of the house any longer."

"There is no one left in the house we lived in?"

"We used it as a hideout when we took care of the mayor and one of his young nephews."

"Who is mayor now?" asked Rosina.

"It's a battle of the sexes," said Gino. "Donna Lucia has assumed power for now. The family was grooming Giovanni as the next mayor.

His father, Don Vittorio, has moved into the mayor's office and is doing all the paper work. The only ones left in the family are Donna Lucia's brother who is the police chief and his son, Pietro." "It is getting too dark now for them to come after us," said Peppino. "Let's go to the ground level and relax. We should go to bed early. We have no idea when they will come. I would guess just at dawn."

"Well we have another hand to help us now. Things are looking up," said Gino.

"And she is an excellent shot," added Peppino.

"We have solved another problem," said Gino. "We now know who the outlaw is."

Chapter 11

NOTORIOUS CASOLINI

Morning came too soon. They got up and decided to take turns watching from their look out spot on the mountain. Peppino offered to take the first watch. After he left Gino and Rosina came down the rope to the main cave.

"You fellows don't eat any breakfast do you," complained Rosina. "We don't have anything to eat. We don't have access to eggs which is what I am used to eating for breakfast."

"I noticed a couple of bags of grain in the upper level,' said Rosina starting to laugh.

"Why are you laughing?" asked Gino, also starting to laugh. Rosina's laugh was very catching.

"It's just something dumb. I started to say that I saw bags of grain upstairs. There are no stairs," she said starting to laugh louder. They both stood there for several minutes just laughing.

"Why are we laughing?" asked Rosina. "It's kind of stupid."

"I guess it's a release of tension. We don't know what is going to happen." Rosina grabbed a bowl and got some of the grain from the bags in the upper level and using a round stone she found she started to grind the grain to powder.

"Would you get me some water," asked Rosina. "Sure," said Gino. "What are you doing?"

"I'm going to bake some bread."

"Do you have all the ingredients you need?"

"I've been baking bread in my cave every week. I have obtained all the ingredients I need from the friendly grocery store in town. I have everything I need here in the bag that you helped bring over here." Without another word, Gino went and got fresh water from the stream. Rosina started to roll mix the dough.

"Listen Rosina," said Gino. "We have to talk." "What is it, Gino?"

"I noticed from the way you look at Peppino that you have very strong feelings for him."

"I have very strong feelings for you too, so what?"

"Rosina, don't play games with me. I think you are falling in love with him. I don't blame you. He is a very wonderful, loyal person. He has very high ideals."

"All right, So, I'm falling for him. Why does that bother you?" "I don't want you to get hurt. Peppino has loved Gina Fanucci since he was seventeen. She was thirteen. They were engaged before he was jail on the false charge of killing Gaetano."

"Then why haven't I seen her here and why hasn't he gone to see her?"

"Gina's father died years ago. Gina depended on Peppino to take over working the land. She loves her mother very much. She was thinking of her when she accepted the proposal of Nicolo. They were married a few weeks ago. He will never stop loving her. I just though you should know."

"Thanks for telling me. I now will know what to expect. It will not change anything. I am still going to try." She had finished the bread dough and set it aside to rise.

"Gino, Rosina," yelled Peppino from the upper tunnel. "I think someone is coming. Get up here and bring everything with you that you can. We want it to look like we have been gone for a long time." Gino and Rosina cleaned up as fast as they could and sent everything they could up the cave hole. She brought up the bread dough with her. Gino stayed behind to blow a little dust on the table and chairs to make it look like no one had been there for a long time. He then climbed up the rope and settled in his bed.

Rosina stayed at the end of the tunnel so she could hear if some one came into the cave. Peppino stayed on top watching with his spyglass until the police were almost there. He then came into the upper cave.

"There are about eight of them, too many to fight. Where is Rosina?"

"She is at the end of the tunnel at the mouth of the hole to listen to any one who might enter the lower cave."

"That is a good idea. The hole is not detectable from below. I think I will join her." Peppino then crawled through the tunnel to the mouth of the hole where Rosina was.

"Hear anything yet, Rose?" he asked as he forced himself next to her. The tunnel at that end was very narrow and Peppino's body couldn't help being tight against Rosina's.

"Nothing yet," she said. "I see you call me Rose. I haven't been called Rose for a long time. My father used to call me Rose. It brings back fond memories."

"Do mind my calling you Rose?"

"No, I rather like it." To make more room Rosina turned sideways facing Peppino. She noticed that Peppino adjusted himself so that he was sideways facing her. There was more room that way though their bodies were still against each other. Rosina was thrilled almost beyond her ability to control herself. She wondered if Peppino felt the same way. After all he was a man and she was a woman. When ever either one moved their bodies would rub against each other.

"Are you okay?" asked Peppino. "I mean, are you comfortable or should I move back away from the hole."

"I'm fine. You won't be able to hear if you move back," she said hoping that he wouldn't move. She was enjoying being close to him. She didn't care what Gino told her. She was in love with Peppino and she couldn't do anything about it. She didn't care if he would not love her back. Loving him was wonderful in itself. Beside, he was here with her and not with Gina. It was about an hour before they heard some yelling.

"I found the main cave here behind this shrub," said one of the men. Soon several men entered the cave.

"It looks like they were here at one time," said one of the men. "But I think they are long gone from here."

"What makes you think that, Don Vittorio," said the other man. "It is the new hopeful mayor," whispered Peppino into Rosina's ear. Rosina nodded.

"Well because there is a table and two chairs here and they are all covered with dust.

"Do you think they are still around the mountain here?" asked the other man.

"Probably not," responded Don Vittorio. "They are probably somewhere near Monte Mangone. That's where they found my son Roberto. But since we are here let's check this mountain out completely. These outlaws are pretty smart. I wouldn't put anything past them." There was indication that two men set up a post there in the mouth of the cave out of the hot sun. Peppino and Rosina didn't dare move. Two hours passed. Rosina had rolled slightly towards Peppino so that she was partly on top of him. She put her head on his shoulder and fell asleep. Peppino slipped his right arm around her and with both arms around her he positioned her so that she would be more comfortable in his arms. Peppino loved the feel of her in his arms. It felt so natural. He was growing very fond of Rosina. Not only did he think she was beautiful but he respected her intelligence and ability to survive. She was very soft and feminine and yet a very strong person in every other way. If he didn't love Gina so much he could love Rosina.

"Don Vittorio," said a new voice as he entered the cave. "We found another cave that looked like someone has lived in. It is completely on the other side of the mountain."

"Is there any evidence that they are still around," asked Don Vittorio.

"No, the only evidence that some one was there is the burned wood that is in a hole in the rock inside the cave. It looked like at some time it served as an oven. It could have been a thousand years ago."

"All right, mark it down on the map so that we have a record of all the caves in this mountain. No one will be able to hide from us in this mountain."

"Don Vittorio," said the first voice they had heard with the man. "We have two more men that have come to join us in the search. One wants to talk with you."

"Send him in." Peppino and Rosina tried to adjust their position. They were getting stiff being in the same position for several hours. They tried to rotate so that they would lie on their other side but it caused too much dust so they remained still. They didn't want to provide any signs that they were there.

"Ciao uncle Vittorio," said the new voice. "I came to help you hunt the criminals that killed my cousins. I know this mountain like the back of my hand."

"I'm glad you came, Pietro. We could use all the help we could get." Pietro left and two other men were called in.

"Listen fellows. Grab a lantern and both of you go search down the tunnel. We want to make sure no one is hiding down the tunnel waiting for us to leave."

"Don Vittorio, isn't there a legend alleging that whoever goes in the tunnel will not come out alive?"

"It's just an old wives tale. I understand that some miners started that rumor to keep people away from their diggings. Go explore the tunnel." Peppino and Rosina kept very still as the two men walked past them below. It seemed like an hour when they heard a scream coming from deep in the cave. A few minutes later, one of the men came running out of the tunnel into the area where Don Vittorio was. He was babbling something that was unintelligible. Two other men who had apparently stood outside came in and helped settle down the screaming man. After a few minutes, he was able to talk. "Antonio and I were exploring deep inside the cave. Suddenly the lanterns light got very dim. We could hardly see where we were going, then Antonio screamed and disappeared. I heard his screams as his voice diminished as if he was being transported into a distant world. You may fire me but I'm going home. I won't stay here another moment." They apparently let him go. No one else agreed to go and find out what had happened to Antonio.

"Keep looking for other caves. I think however this is a waste of time. The culprits are miles away." They stayed there until eight in the evening. Peppino and his friends were starving to death.

"When are they going home?" whispered Rosina to Peppino. Peppino shrugged his shoulders. He put his hands up in front of her face as he pulled his head back as far as he could. He made a twirling motion with his hands. Rosina understood perfectly. She nodded her head in an affirmative motion. Peppino grabbed her by the shoulder and pulled her on top of him and then sliding over he pulled her to his left side. He wrapped his arms around her and softly and gently placed her head on his left shoulder. She looked up at him with loving eyes and then gently settled her face in his neck. She acted like she was going to sleep. She was not sleepy at all. She realized that in spite of the danger they were in, she had never been happier in her whole life. With his arms around her she was in heaven. She was enjoying the moment immensely. Her only worry was that it would end too soon.

"Uncle Vittorio," said a voice that Peppino recognized as Pietro's. "I found a fabulous cave around the west side of the mountain. I found it quite by accident. There are two large rocks that are part of the mountain. They fit perfectly as part of the foothill of the mountain. No matter how you search the area, you would never find this cave. The reason I found it was because I followed a rabbit I thought would be a good meal. It went behind the rock and when I followed him I found that the area behind the rock was hollow. An elephant could slip into the cave. Inside it is as large as a standard house."

"Did you find any one there?" asked Don Vittorio.

"No, it doesn't even look like any one had ever been there."

"It is getting pretty dark outside. I don't think that any one is coming back here tonight. Let's pack up and go home. "Sergeant," he yelled out. "We're leaving. Just to be sure leave a few men here just in case they should return here." A mumbling sound was heard outside. Apparently, the sergeant was instructing men to stay behind all night. It wasn't long afterwards that the sound of horses hoofs was heard as they left. They could hear two men enter in the cave and make themselves comfortable...It sounded like two men were outside while two men were inside...The two men who came inside were discussing their experiences while setting up their blankets to sleep. Their discussions caused Rosina to shake and her mouth opened in horror. Peppino became filled with anger. One of the men was telling the other how he enjoyed killing a seventeen-year-old girl he was ordered to make disappear. He described in detail how he stripped her naked and tortured her; how he cut off her fingers and carved out her navel and her nipples. He excitedly explained how he got sexually excited as he watched her naked body tremble and shake while she screamed at the top of her voice in pain.

"I got such a pleasure watching her die. Her body continued shaking after her eyes got glassy and settled into a death stare."

"You're so lucky," said the other man. "I've only gotten men to take care of. Not only that I was only allowed one young man to do what I wanted with. I fixed him so if he had lived he would never be able to do any monkey business." They both busted out laughing. "Go to sleep you guys in there," yelled one of the men guarding outside. A low giggle was all that was heard as a result.

It was about eleven when all grew silent except for the snoring of the men inside the cave. Peppino whispered in Rose's ear to go get Gino. She understood and slowly and as quietly as she could, she backed out of the tunnel and sent Gino to Peppino. Gino went down and came back up a few minutes later.

"Peppino wants you to stay up here where you will be safe. We are going down to reduce the odds. Peppino told me what you guys heard. We will get something to eat when we get back. Gino went back down the tunnel to the hole. Peppino lowered the rope and they both quietly descended to the ground of the main tunnel. Peppino took on the bigger fellow. He put his hand over his mouth and grabbing him by the chin, he gave his head an immense twist. He heard the neck bones crack. The man struggled for a moment and then was motionless. At the same time, Gino put his hand over the other man's mouth and with his other hand holding the knife stabbed him in the heart. He didn't struggle long. They dragged the bodies to the rope. Peppino motioned to Gino to climb up the rope. Gino obeyed not understanding what Peppino was thinking. Peppino got all the gear and blankets that the men had brought into the cave and one at a time transferred them to Gino who laid them in the tunnel. Gino then came back down bringing a lantern. They both dragged the dead men down the tunnel to the holes. They searched the bodies for anything they could use. What they found mostly was money. They took the money and threw the bodies down the hole.

"Let's go see if our lamb meat is still there. I think we are all hungry. Perhaps we should sneak out and cook the lamb elsewhere," said Peppino. They continued down the tunnel. They had to move slower because they didn't want to make any unnecessary noise. When they got to the place the lamb had been they found that the lamb was gone. Only the rope remained.

"What happened to our lamb?" asked Gino.

"I don't know," said Peppino. "Maybe it broke loose with a strong water flow and is further down." They continued down the tunnel being very careful since they were now exploring unknown territory. About fifteen minutes later they came to the end of the tunnel.

"It ends here," said Gino. "We can't go any farther. The stream seems to go underground here."

"You're right, and look there against the near wall. There is our lamb." Peppino worked his way down to the edge of the steam to retrieve the lamb. He suddenly stopped in his tracks. "Look Gino," said Peppino. "Aim your light at the other side of the stream. Do you see it?"

"It looks like a body," exclaimed Gino.

"It looks like three bodies," said Peppino, just as surprised as Gino. "Look, there is a small ledge at the center of the wall above the area where the stream goes under ground. If you set down the lantern and hold my hand to steady me I think I can get to the other side."

"Why do you want to go to the other side?" asked Gino. "We had better go back. Rosina is probably frantic by now."

"I want to see if two of those men are the two that we just took out. That would prove that those holes lead to the water." Gino did as Peppino asked. Peppino stepped on the ledge and holding on to Gino, he reached a protruding edge on the other side. As he let go of Gino's hand he faltered and stepped on one of the bodies before he got his balance. The little push that Peppino gave to the body caused the stream undertow to suck it under the ledge and then disappear. Peppino pulled the other two bodies out of the water and searched them. One was the body that Gino had stabbed. They other body was the man who had disappeared while exploring the deeper end of the cave. He had a bundle of money on him. Peppino confiscated the money and after careful consideration put the bodies back in the water and with a little push they were sucked under the cliff and disappeared. Gino grabbed the lamb and pulled it ashore. He then lent a hand to Peppino to bring him back to his side of the stream.

"That was one of the fellows we killed. That means that we could set up a bucket and get water closer to the entrance and no longer risk of falling into one of the holes. The two men that I checked were very badly torn up. Apparently there are very sharp rocks underground which means no one could survive the trip." They started to work their way back to the rope. It was pretty close to the time the men outside would change positions with the men who were inside; they had been gone about two-and-a-half hours. After climbing back up the rope, they pulled the rope up so that the hole would not be detected.

"We will see what the remaining guys do," said Peppino. "If they decide to stay we will have to eliminate them. We out number them, three to two."

"Say, where is Rosina?" asked Gino. "She isn't in her bed."

"We have to trust that she will take care of herself," said Peppino. "We have to go down to the edge of the tunnel to see what the other two guys do."

"You go, Peppi," said Gino. "I will stay here and wait for Rosina." "Whatever you do, I don't want you to go outside looking for her. Trust her." Without another word, Peppino went down to the edge of the hole and waited for the other men to come inside the cave. It wasn't long before Peppino heard one of the men call out to the other.

"Rudi, they are gone. There is nothing left of them." The other man came running in.

"What happened to them?" he yelled. "Where are their blankets and their other stuff?"

"I don't know. Could they have packed up and left?" "Impossible, I haven't left the cave opening and I certainly didn't fall asleep."

"I don't know what happened to them and I'm not hanging around to find out." Peppino heard the rustling of their gear and in a few minutes he heard the sound of the horses galloping away. "They're gone," said Peppino going back up to the upper cave.

"We can now go out and look for Rosina."

"Where do you intend to look," said a voice coming from the entrance way.

"Rosina," said Peppino with worry in his voice.

"I thought after taking care of business you boys would be hungry," said Rosina. "How would you like a slice of hot bread soaked in olive oil with pepper and salt?"

"You're an angel from heaven," said Gino. "I have never been hungrier."

"That's great, Rose," said Peppino. "Please don't do that again without telling us."

"Did you miss me? Were you worried about me?"

"Maybe he wasn't worried about you but I was," said Gino. "Why do you say he wasn't worried?" asked Rosina.

"Because he told me that you could take care of yourself and that I should trust you. That's what he said. But his voice and face said something else."

"Were you worried about me Peppi," asked Rosina with a smirking smile on her face.

"Where did you bake that bread," asked Peppino side stepping the question. "Did you bake it in your old hangout?"

"You guessed it," she answered handing him a slice of hot tasty bread. The three of them ate the bread with great enjoyment.

"Gino," said Peppino. "I would like you to take all the money we got from those barbarous and bloodthirsty police and go work your land. Get established as an innocent farm boy. We will need you to get information for us. Don't come here unless you have important news for us."

"I don't like the idea of leaving you alone," said Gino. "I want to help you."

"Gino dearest friend," said Peppino. "I could never repay you for the help you have already provided. Don't look at this as if I was sending you away. I need you to be my eyes and ears in town. Do you realize that we are wanted men after all the people we have eliminated? They are going to get more vicious as more of them are hurt by us. If you find out that they are going to mount an all out attack on us you can come and fight with us."

"Okay, if you think that is the best way for me to help."

"You can check up on us every once in a while to find out if there is some thing we need. We need to know what is happening in town. Also don't forget to be seen at the fountain getting water." "I will do it on one condition. If you decide to eliminate anyone else you let me in on it."

"That is one of the things I want you to do. After things settle down I would like you to find a safe way to get the last four brutal pigs one at a time. Come up with a plan and we will discus it when we get together. Don't neglect your land. We will need grain and vegetables if you decide to plant some."

"Okay I will leave early in the morning."

Donna Lucia was furious over the lack of success by the police. She wondered why all of this was happening. Why was her husband killed? Why were her two nephews also killed? And then there was the peasant, Paulo. Was there some kind of a connection? What could the connection be? She decided to go and talk to her brother Vittorio. She arrived at his office at about ten in the morning. He was busy adding up the city government costs in preparation of the budget for the next quarter. He was determining the necessary income they would need from the coming harvest. That budget would determine the amount of taxes they would have to collect from each farmer and business owner. This was the job of the mayor. Vittorio was to be the next mayor but his sister would not abdicate the position. Vittorio had to do the work anyway, but he allowed his sister, Lucia, to keep the title. Besides, Lucia controlled her younger brother, Alfredo, who was chief of police. Whoever controlled the police controlled the city. The police was the private army of the mayor. Actually, Lucia should be doing the city's accounting if she is the mayor. However, for the time being they split the job. Vittorio controlled the city finances and Lucia controlled the police.

"He is in the middle of important calculations and doesn't want to be disturbed," said his secretary. "Will you please sit and wait awhile. He will not be long."

"Does he know that it is I who wants to see him?"

"Yes, mayor," responded the secretary. "I called him as soon as I saw you dismount and tie up your horse."

"Thank you," said Lucia and sat in the chair outside his office. It was only about ten minutes later that Vittorio completed his current task.

"Please send the mayor in," requested Vittorio. Mayor Lucia heard him and walked into his office.

"Lucia," said Vittorio. "So good to see you. How are you?" "I'm fine, dear brother. How are you doing?"

"I'm sorry to make you wait. I was in the middle of an important calculation and if I let myself get distracted I would have had to start all over again. Come, please sit. What can I do for you?"

"Vittorio, I am wondering about the recent killings of our family members. I think that they are connected in someway. I'm hoping that between the two of us we can figure out if my suspicions have any merit."

"What make you think that they are connected?"

"I want to consider it just incase they are. We may prevent further deaths in our family."

"Do you have anything that would lead you to suspect a connection?"

"It just seems that they were too well planned. Whoever killed my husband and your two sons have gotten away too cleanly. We haven't been able to apprehend them."

"You say them. Do you think it is the act of more than one person?" asked Vittorio, surprised at her statement.

"I think it would require more then one. They had to have a lot of information as to our movements. It was too slick to be just the independent act of one shooter."

"How can I help?" asked Vittorio.

"Well let's put our heads together and try to think of who has something against us."

"Well that would include the whole town," said Vittorio with a slight smile on his face.

"I mean who would in particular hate my husband and your sons?" asked Lucia. "Something they did together. Perhaps while they were fishing. Did anything occur during that time? You were with them most of the time."

"Not that I can think of," said Vittorio thinking deeply. "Let's take one at a time. What has your husband done lately that would anger some one?"

"The last thing he did was to make an example of Salvatore Casolini for the benefit of anyone who considered sneaking to Enna to report our activities to the officials there."

"That would rule out my sons," said Vittorio. "They had nothing to do with the Casolini family."

"That is where you are wrong," said Lucia as if a light went on in her brain. "They were involved in the death of Stellina Casolini, my son, Biachio's, wife."

"How were they involved?" asked Vittorio with a puzzled tone. "They tied up Stellina and helped me hang her in the stable." "I thought you told us that she hung herself because she was unhappy with the marriage she was forced into?"

"No, I hanged her. Your two boys helped me."

"Why would you hang your son's wife? Did Biachio agree to it?" "No, he didn't know anything. He went crazy when he found out. I had to do it. Did you know that she was pregnant? I couldn't have little half breeds running around my house. It would ruin our blood line."

"I understand why you did it," said Vittorio after a little thought. "I can't say I don't agree with you. But couldn't you use a more subtle way to dispose of her?"

"I suppose I could have acted more discreetly," admitted Lucia. But that is in the past and I can't change that now."

"How was your son involved in this whole thing?" asked Vittorio still not seeing the whole picture.

"He started the whole thing," said Lucia beginning to get very upset. "It all started when he decided he wanted that lowly peasant girl, the daughter of Salvatore Casolini. He lost his mind over her. He wanted her so badly that Pietro, to help Biachio, killed her husband for him and framed her brother Peppino for the killing." "But didn't you go and asked for her hand in marriage for your son?"

"Yes, but I thought that it was a passing fancy," said Lucia. "It was like getting him a toy to play with. I was sure that he would tire of her and get ride of her himself. Instead, he became one of them. That's why we disowned him. He wasn't one of us anymore."

"Let me see if I understand this," said Vittorio trying to get everything straight in his mind. "Your husband killed Salvatore Casolini because he was trying to sneak to Enna. My boys and you killed his daughter Stellina because your son wanted to keep her. Pietro sent the Casolini boy to jail. What you are now thinking is that someone from the Casolini family is trying to avenge their deaths. But what has Paulo, their neighbor, have to do with it?"

"Paulo was the informant who came to us and told us about Salvatore's attempt to go to Enna."

"So, one of the family killed Paulo for being the informer. He killed your husband to avenge the elder Casolini. He killed my sons because they helped kill the Casolini girl. He killed Biachio because he started the whole thing. The question then is who of the family is left?"

"That's the problem," said Lucia. "There is no one left."

"Have you thought of the fact that there are others in the same group as your husband and my boys?" said Vittorio thoughtfully.

"What do you mean?" asked Lucia.

"I think that you and Pietro are next on his list whoever he is. You did the actual hanging and Pietro is responsible for the jailing of the Casolini boy."

"I hadn't thought of that," admitted Lucia. "He wouldn't dare." "If he dared for your husband, he wouldn't think twice to come after you. You better get a couple of police as body guards."

"That will be no problem. Alfredo will take care of that. What I would like better is to catch this culprit. First we have to find out who it is."

"How about the Casolini boy, what has become of him?" asked Vittorio.

"He should be dead by now. I gave orders for him to be moved to the dungeon."

"I read somewhere that if all other answers are false, the unlikely is the only answer left to investigate. It looks to me that Peppino Casolini is the only answer left as unlikely as it may seem," said Lucia

"Are you saying that somehow Peppino has escaped from jail?" asked Vittorio.

"In the absence of other relatives what other possibility can there be? I think we should investigate the jail and see the body for ourselves," said Lucia now knowing what she had to do.

"Let's see Alfredo and find out if it is possible."

"Thanks Vittorio, I will take care of it. Go back to your calculations.

I will tell you what I find out."

Lucia went home to contemplate the possibility that Peppino was out of jail She was positive that the jailers would not knowingly let Peppino out. Their life was too valuable to them. Besides, she knew them all and was sure they were loyal. After lunch she went to visit with the chief of police. He was in his office looking over some testimony he had received from his secret spies about a plot by some unhappy residences of the city. He got names and addresses of all involved.

"Ciao brother dear," said Lucia as she walked into his office and sat down. "What are you up too these days?"

"I have uncovered a group of unhappy treasonous peasants. I'm trying to figure a way to eliminate them before they can cause trouble. I have to do it without getting the blame and causing a revolution."

"Well I have a problem. If we can solve it, we may solve your problem at the same time."

"Keep talking, I'm listening," said Alfredo willing to listen to any solution to his problem.

"I have come to a serious conclusion about the deaths of my husband and Vittorio's sons," started Lucia. "I think it is a vendetta."

"What do you have that has led you to that conclusion?"

"Well look at the facts," continued Lucia. "My husband killed Salvatore Casolini. Roberto and Giovanni helped me hang Salvatore's daughter Stellina."

"You hanged Stellina?" said Alfredo with a look of shock. "I was told she killed herself."

"That's what we wanted the public to think," explained Lucia. "She was pregnant and I didn't want half breeds running around diluting our royal blood line. It doesn't matter. To continue, Pietro started the whole problem by killing Stellina's husband and accusing Salvatore's son Peppino. Peppino was jailed as a result. That ties everything together and has the sign of being a vendetta." The problem is there are no living relatives or close friends who are good enough to do so expertly a job."

"So what is your conclusion as to who is doing all this?"

"There is only one answer," suggested Lucia. "The only person I can think of who is capable and also a relative to the Casolini family is Peppino."

"That is absolutely impossible," said Alfredo. "I had Peppino placed in the dungeon myself. He was fed a half slice of bread and a glass of water a day. He has since ceased to accept the food or water and is assumed dead."

"But brother dear, have you seen the body? Can't you see? Even though you think it is impossible it is the only answer."

"It may be the only answer you can come up with. That doesn't make it true. Besides how does this answer my problem?"

"First of all we have looked up their family history. There is no one who would care enough to take the kind of risk this guy is taking. It has to be Peppino. How does this help you? If we let out the news that Peppino is alive and spreading havoc through the city you can take out our enemies and put the blame on Peppino."

"Let's go over to the jail and settle this once and for all," said Alfredo. They walked over to the jail and confronted the guard on duty.

"We want to know what happened to Peppino Casolini?" asked Alfredo.

"He was in the last cell for over three years. Then the request came down from the mayor to put him in the dungeon and let him die.. He hasn't eaten now for over a week."

"Is there anyway that he could escape or be exchanged with some one else?"

"Not on my watch," said the guard. "I can't answer for the night shift. That is Bruno's time here. I'm sure that it's been the same person that's been here all the time I've been here. He was not all there mentally if you know what I mean. Toto 'The bull' has replaced me when I was called for other duties by the mayor."

"Take us down to the dungeon. We want to see the body," demanded Lucia. Grabbing a lantern the guard led them through the stone entrance and down the steps to the dungeon. He opened the dungeon door. The body was quite visible by the lantern light.

It lay there on the bed as if he were asleep.

"There he is," said Alfredo. "Let's get out of here. That smell is choking me."

"I want to get a closer look," said Lucia. "I just can't believe it is him. He has to be the fellow we are looking for." Holding her nose, she grabbed the lantern and went up close to the body.

"That's not him," yelled Lucia. "It isn't his features. I don't know who we jailed but it wasn't Peppino."

"Are you sure, Lucia?" asked her brother holding his nose. "The body is terribly decayed."

"Yes but look at the eyes. They are far apart. Peppino had very strong and closely spaced eyes. By the look of this man's skin he was fat when he died. Peppino had very muscular body. Also look at where the lips have shrunk around his mouth. This fellow had half of his teeth missing. I know that Peppino was a very healthy man.

This definitely is not Peppino. How and when he was exchanged is a mystery, but this is not the man they jailed. We will have to talk to all the other guards."

"I'll take over from here," said Alfredo being convinced that his sister was correct. "I will investigate every person that has ever come to this jail. "You go spread the word and start figuring out where he could hide and come up with a plan to get him out of our way. Don't work to fast. Give me time to give him the credit for all the killings that are going to take place before we catch him. You have to spread the word how he is a notorious killer. Get the news paper to warn the people of this crazy killer. Bring out the fact that he has already killed an innocent farmer, namely Paulo, what ever his last name is. Get the paper to tag him as the Notorious Casolini." It was two days later that Gino visited Peppino and Rosina. They had seen the dust of his trail and hid in the upper cave. They spent most of their time outdoors except when one of them is cooking and even then one stays outside to watch the road from the city.

"Ciao, Peppino, Rosina, it is only me." Peppino slid down the rope first followed by Rosina.

"How are you my dearest comrade," said Peppino hugging him and kissing him on both cheeks. "We have missed you." Mean while Rosina greeted him the same as Peppino did.

"Ciao Gino," said Rosina. "You're just in time to have dinner with us. Then you can tell us what is going on in town. Peppi got two rabbits this afternoon. We were going to put the other one in the water to keep it for a later time. But now that you are here I will cook them both."

"Listen you guys," said Peppino. "I'm going outside to watch for any unwanted visitors. We will talk serious when we are eating." After Peppino left, Gino turned to Rosina.

"I brought you some staples for your fantastic cooking," said Gino. "I brought you some salt, pepper, garlic and the other herbs you asked for. I also brought you some potato and some fresh fruit. Will that pay for my dinner?"

"As if you had to pay for anything we have," said Rosina.

"How are you guys doing up here all by yourselves?" asked Gino with a smirk on his face. "Is there any hanky panky going on between you two?"

"What hanky panky are you talking about?" asked Rosina. "Come on," said Gino. "I see how you look at him. And I have never seen you happier."

"That's because at last I'm free from those horse's behinds I used to work for. I'm as free as a bird. Besides, Peppi doesn't know that I'm alive."

"I know that isn't true," said Gino. "I see how he worries about you and how he looks at you. You are a very beautiful woman. If it wasn't that I am so crazy in love with Anna I would be chasing you myself."

"You are such a sweet liar," said Rosina turning slightly red.

"At any rate I highly suggest that you let him know how you feel.

What can he do, send you home?"

"Let's go outside and eat. The rabbits are ready." Peppino had brought the table and chairs outside the main cave after Gino had left earlier in the month. From there they could eat and still watch for any intruders. After they sat down, Rosina served them their food.

"Tell us what has been going on in town?" asked Peppino.

"I have a lot to tell you," started Gino. "First of all Dona Lucia found out that the body in the dungeon was not yours. She still has no idea how it all happened. She only knows that you are at large. The paper says that you have a vendetta against the ruling family. It says you are after any one of the city inhabitants, who either worked or spied for them at one time or other. Several of the city inhabitants have been killed and you have been blamed for their deaths. The inside information is that the people killed belonged to a group that was planning a revolt against the city hall. They feel that the city is weaker now that Mayor Mario is gone. Some one must have informed on them. One by one they are being eliminated. Everything that happens from now on will be blamed on you. The news paper has named you 'The Notorious Casolini.'"

"What concerns me is if they put enough together, they may come after you. If you get the slightest indication that they suspect you are involved you come and live with us. If things get rough we may need your help anyway."

"Peppi, you know that if you need any help I'll be here," assured Gino. "Anyway I have to go and be seen by my neighbors. These days you can't trust any one. I have to look like I am coming home from the farm. I'll see you guys later."

"Ciao loyal friend," said Peppino.

"Take care of yourself," said Rosina. However, Rosina's mind was on what Gino had suggested for her to do. How could she let him know how she felt? How could she face him again if he rejected her? Gino was right. One or both could be dead tomorrow. She had to let him know. She decided to think about it for a while. She decided to look for signs of his feelings.

The next morning she made breakfast for him. She ate quickly and cleaned the main cave so that it looked like no one had been there.

They left the table and chairs out. In case of an emergency they would quickly bring them inside and climb up the rope and hide in the upper cave. To date they never had to do it. No emergency had as yet come up. Rosina kept looking at Peppino. She was looking for some indication of how he felt about her. The more she observed him the deeper in love she became. She found herself day dreaming about him. She desired to have his arms around her. She wondered how his lips would taste. Finally, Peppino notice that something was different.

"Rosie, are you all right?" he asked.

"You called me Rosie," she said. You have never called me that before."

"Do you mind," asked Peppino. "Would you rather that I call you Rosina or Rose? I don't know why I called you Rosie. I guess it's because it's shorter."

"No, I don't mind at all. It's kind of romantic." She was about to tell him how much she liked it when he noticed some dust clouds coming their way.

"Some one is coming this way. We had better hide the table and chairs and get up stairs," said Peppino as he started to move all the furniture. It was done faster than Peppino had expected. They quickly climbed up the rope pulling it up after them.

"Let's stay here in the tunnel so we can hear if anyone comes in the main cave," suggested Rosina.

"That's a good idea," agreed Peppino. "From there we have the choice of going either way. Two routes of escape if you will." As they lay down in the narrow tunnel, Rosina cuddled up to Peppino as she had done the last time they were in the tunnel together. He put his arm around her and they waited. She looked up at his face. As she did her lips were only about an inch away from his. She was very disturbed. She wanted to kiss him and tell him how much she loved and adored him. He looked down at her and smiled and then looked away. It didn't seem to bother him. Rosina, in one way was excited and thrilled to be this close to him with his arms around her. On the other hand, she was hurting badly as a result of his lack of attention. He didn't seem to be affected by her closeness. They heard horse activity for about a half hour. Then they heard them ride away.

"We better stay here for a while," said Peppino. "We don't know which direction they went. They may be searching the other sides of the mountain and will be back. We are safe here and our horses are safe. No need for us to move. I could go to sleep right here." Peppino meant that he was very comfortable. Rosina took it to mean that he was bored. They stayed in the narrow tunnel for about another hour. Peppino got up and went outside with his spyglass. He could see five trails of dust. They were all going back to the city. "I think we are safe now," he said to Rosina. She didn't pay attention to his remark. She was too deep in thought about their situation.

"Tell me something," she said to Peppino. "Is there anything you like about me?"

"What are you talking about?" he asked.

"It's a simple question," she responded. "Is there anything you like about me? Is there anything about me that excites you?"

"What has prompted this outburst?" he asked, puzzled and surprised by her unhappy attitude.

"It's just that you are so cold toward me. Isn't there anything about me that attracts you?"

"I like everything about you," he said in a defensive tone. "You are very intelligent. You are a very strong and tough person, yet you are very gentle and sensitive. You are very affectionate but have fantastic control of yourself. I mean you are not apt to becoming over emotional. You are a very amazing person. You are very special to me. I have great respect for you. On top of all that, you are very beautiful. Of course, I'm very attracted to you. I don't know anyone who is like you. You have gone through so much and yet you have survived to be a better person. I'm not cold toward you."

"Why then haven't you shown any affection toward me? I mean why haven't you made a move toward me?"

"I didn't want to offend you. I thought if I made a move toward you, I would spoil the perfect relationship we have. Besides I don't feel worthy of you. Why would you care about me? I'm nobody. Any way I wouldn't know how to start. Gina and I grew up together. It was a thing from the beginning. I don't know what to do!"

"Maybe I can help you get started," she said as she moved so close to him that their bodies touched. Her lips were so near he could feel her breath on his face. "I just loved the time we spent in the tunnel with your arms around me."

"I enjoyed that time too. Why do you think I made us stay there as long as we did? I loved having my arms around you. I loved it when you put your head on my chest and snuggled up to me."

"Why didn't you do something?"

"I was afraid," said Peppino acting shy.

"I can help you get over that," she said as she wrapped her arms around his neck. "I'm so in love with you." Her lips were so close that they rubbed against his as she spoke. He didn't say a word. She could tell that his eyes softened and showed love as he closed them and pressed his lips to hers. She closed her eyes and pressed her lips hard against his. It didn't take long before her mouth opened and her tongue found his. Their passion rose to a height neither had felt before. When there lips parted he began to explain how he felt. "I think I fell in love with you the first time I saw you in your old hideout when you snuck up behind us. I was afraid to show any sign of how I felt. I was afraid that I would scare you away. I am a coward when it comes to woman. I guess that is one of my faults."

"You have another fault," she said with a smile on her face. "What is that?" he asked humbly.

"You talk too much," she said as she pulled his lips to hers. They sat on the side of the mountain with their back against a large rock. After they decided to rest their lips they sat there in each others arms cheek to cheek.

"I'm so crazy about you Peppi. I thought I was going to explode. I was afraid to tell you how much I loved you. By the way, I am the one not worthy of you not the other way around. I have never been so happy in my whole life. I know that your heart belongs to Gina. After all you have known her forever. I can live with that. I'll take what ever I can get."

"I won't lie to you. I still have feelings for Gina. She was my first love. That is hard to forget. However, she doesn't have my whole heart. You have a pretty big piece of it. Oh Rosie, please believe me. I'm crazy about you too." They stayed there in each others arms and watch the sun go down. As it grew dark the lanterns in the city lit up the sky. Peppino and Rosina were never so happy. Nothing could spoil that evening for them.

Chapter 12

THE WICKED WITCH IS DEAD

The morning found Peppino and Rosina asleep on the mountainside leaning against the large sloping rock that made a natural incline. They had fallen asleep in each other's arms there on the side of the mountain. Rosina awoke first. The sun was very high in the sky indicating that it was at least mid morning. She looked at Peppino whose arms were still around her. He was so handsome. Her heart told her that she loved him more this morning than she did last night. Full of love she started to kiss him all over his face. She kissed his eyes, his nose, and was about to kiss his lips when he woke up.

"What?" was all he was allowed to say because Rosina sealed his lips. His tongue found hers and they played with each other until they decided to exploring the inside of each others mouths. After a few minutes they came up for a breath of fresh air.

"What is this?" asked Peppino still half asleep. "Is this my breakfast?"

"Yes it was," said Rosina. "I expect to give you a similar one every morning for the rest of your life. Do you like it? I could warm it up a little more."

"It's the best breakfast I've ever had," said Peppino playing along. "It's the kind of breakfast I always wanted. I love it and know for sure that I will never get tired of it. But how will you warm it up?" Rosina pulled up her blouse and exposed her bare chest.

"No don't do that," said Peppino. "We don't have the right to be any more passionate than passionate kisses," said Peppino stumbling over the words.

"I know, sweetheart," said Rosina smiling at Peppino's embarrassment. "I know that you would never dishonor me. I wouldn't let you go any farther anyway. I just want to show you how you can have a warmer breakfast."

"You said warm," said Peppino recovering. "Don't you mean hot? Anyway I get the message. I could propose but what good would it do. We can't get married."

"If you love me as much as I love you, you will find a way. You will have to find a way. I know you will not be satisfied for very long with only my kisses. I am already going nuts with a desire for you." "I will never get tired of kissing you," said Peppino getting romantic. "Anyway if it will make you feel as wanted as you really are, and I can say what I really want to say, here goes. Rosina, I love you very much. I want to spend the rest of my life with you Will you marry me?" Rosina jumped into his arms and hugged him. "Yes, I will marry you. I love you too. And if the marriage can't be accomplished then at least we know how much we love each other. However, I have a lot of faith in you. I know you will find a way. If you love me as much as I love you it will happen soon."

"Boy, you sure know how to put the pressure on," said Peppino. "Now I have to find a way or you will never believe that I meant what I said."

"Good," she said and kissed him with more passion than he had ever felt before. After a few minutes of cuddling, Rosina got up and started to leave. "I think I'll start making some lunch. It's really too late for breakfast."

"That's okay," said Peppino. "I've had a great breakfast. I'll stay up here and watch for visitors." Rosina went down and cooked Peppino an excellent lunch.

Gino came home from the farm very tired. It was about two days since he had visited Peppino and Rosina. He had worked late to catch up on all the time he had missed by being with them. It was late and Gino was ready to go to bed when he heard a knock on the door. He couldn't imagine who it could be. He opened the door and to his surprise it was Don Vittorio and Donna Lucia.

"Ciao," was all he could say. "May we come in?" said Vittorio

"Yes of course, Your Excellency." He motioned for them to come in.

"What has happen?" he asked, worried as to what would bring them to his door. He was also surprised that Donna Lucia hadn't said a word. Being here was obviously below her dignity. It must therefore be very important.

"I'm sorry," said Vittorio. "It was not our intention to worry you. Nothing has happened. We just have to ask you some questions."

"How can I help you?" he said, worrying that they had found out that he had been aiding Peppino.

"You knew Giuseppe Casolini didn't you?" asked Vittorio.

"You mean Peppino?" asked Gino. "Yes, we kind of grew up together. We were good friends." Gino decided that it would be best if he told the truth on everything they already knew or could easily find out.

"When was the last time you saw him?"

"Well it was almost four years or more. I haven't seen him since he went to jail."

"You haven't seen him since?"

"No how could I. He is in jail. Is he all right?"

"Haven't you heard the news that we think he is the 'Notorious Casolini.'"

"I heard the rumor, but I think it is some one trading on his name. How could he be out of jail?"

"We think that we jailed the wrong person," said Vittorio. Gino knew that they knew better. He was aware of the fact that they could be setting a trap for him. He decided to be very careful.

"That's not possible," said Gino. "Stellina saw him many times. She brought in guests with her when she went. I'm sure they knew their own kin."

"Did Gina Fanucci ever go see him?"

"Yes she went several times," said Gino, still being cautious. "At first she believed he was innocent."

"Do you think he was innocent?" asked Vittorio.

"I don't know," said Gino acting very thoughtful. "They had several witnesses. I just didn't want to get involved. It doesn't matter. I believe that he is in jail or dead. History tells us that no one has ever escaped from that jail."

"Wasn't Gina engaged to Peppino?"

"Yes but that ended when he was found guilty. You know that Gina's mother married Peppino's father. He took care of them. But when he was killed by robbers they had no one to help them. I helped them until Gina got married. I know that she now loves her husband."

"Why did you stop helping them or even seeing them? Did you have a falling out with Gina?"

"No, we still have high regards for each other. I did still help them after I stopped seeing them. I stopped going there because her mother asked me too. People started to talk about Gina and me having an affair. That made Gina's mother very upset."

"Well we have taken too much of your time," said Vittorio. "Thank you so much for your honesty." With that, they left. Gino was still puzzled as to what that was all about.

The next two weeks were happy times for Peppino and Rosina. They were always together and even went hunting together. They spent the evenings on the hill side hugging and kissing. The got pretty passionate but except for a few times that his hands wandered they never altered from their high moral standards. They always prayed together and asked God for directions. Peppino had promised that he would never dishonor her and he kept his promise. It was on a Monday morning, as they sat on their rock, that Rosina expressed her restlessness.

"Sweetheart," she inquired. "Have you come up with a plan for our marriage? I want to marry you so badly."

"Are you missing your love making?" kidded Peppino.

"You know that I have never known a man. Biachio is the only man that tried but I know that he didn't get his way even though I was unconscious after he beat me. Girls have a way of knowing this that boys don't have. How about you, do you miss it?"

"You know that I haven't known a woman. You do, however, bring up a tremendous desire in me to learn." They both laughed. "As

254

far as the wedding is concerned I do have a plan. I will finalize it when we see Gino."

"That could be a month from now," said Rosina sorrowfully. Look, down toward town," said Peppino getting excited. "I think I see a dust trail coming this way. Have you cleaned everything down in the main tunnel?"

"I'm not sure," said Rosina. "We haven't been bothered for so long. I have been a little careless. I'd better go down and check. I'll meet you in the upper level as soon as I clean up." Peppino stayed up on the mountain keeping tract of the horse and rider coming their way. Whoever it was, was coming slowly. It was about ten minutes later that Peppino recognized who it was.

Rosina," he yelled toward the upper cave. "It's all right. It's Gino." They both hustled down to the main cave as Gino arrived.

"Ciao Gino," said Peppino. It's so good to see you. We have missed you. What has taken you so long?"

"Ciao Peppi and Rose," said Gino. "There is so much going on I don't understand. I'm still not clear as to what is going on except there is an argument between the brothers and sister. Lucia has a plan to trap you. The paper says that she plans on capturing you before the month is over. I can't get any details yet. I'm still going to try."

"Why are you here in the morning?" asked Rosina. "You usually come in the evening."

"I think they are watching me to see when I get home. A neighbor asked me why I am working so hard. She wondered why I come home so late. I also had a visit from Vittorio and Lucia." Gino gave them a blow-by-blow account of what was said. They couldn't figure out what that was all about either.

"Do you think they have some one watching you?" asked Rosina. "Yes, that's why I have to sneak here in the morning. "Forget about them," insisted Gino. "Tell me how are you guys doing?"

"We are doing great," said Peppino. "But we need your help. Rosina and I have declared our love for each other. I have proposed and we want to get married as soon as possible. That's where you come in. Can you get father Nicola to sneak in one more wedding for me as he did for my sister? I was thinking if we can meet at the shack at my land we could be married there and no one will know about our hide out here. My shack will be pretty isolated because it has been abundant for so long."

"You don't ask for something simple do you? I'll think it over. I will have to explain everything to Father Nicola. It should be all right since he has bucked the mayor before. You will need two witnesses."

"I was hoping that you could be my best man and a witness at the same time," said Peppino. As for the other witness perhaps the priest could bring some one."

"I would love to have Anna as my maid of honor," said Rosina. "She was not only my best friend but she gave me a place to live. I love her. Of course I know that it's impossible."

"Well let me investigate the idea. In the mean time, help me unload the horse. I've brought you all the herbs you may need. I also brought you two live hens and a rooster, and a dead chicken that you can eat tonight."

"Thank you, dear Gino. What would we do without you?" said Rosina as she hugged him.

"I have to leave now. I'll be back as soon as I learn something. Oh, before I forget. Knowing that Lucia is pretty smart, I am looking for a roof top that could hide us in case we have to go after her earlier then we originally planned. I found one but it is quite a bit to the side and pretty far away. I'll keep looking. Ciao you guys. I'm so glad that you have found each other. I had no doubts."

"Ciao," said Peppino and Rosina together. After he had disappeared from sight Rosina turned to Peppino.

"You did have a plan, didn't you? I was worried that you weren't in any hurry."

"Rosie, how am going to convince you that I love you. I'm dying to make love to you. Don't you know that every kiss you give me drives me crazy?"

"I guess I should reduce the amount of kisses to keep you sane," said Rosina teasing him.

"You had better not," said Peppino as he grabbed her and started to tickle her. She squirmed out of his grasp and started to run from him. She couldn't get to far away due to her heavy laughter. He was laughing also and as he reached her they both fell in the dirt laughing hysterically. He started to tickle her again but her lips were to close. Their joyous and festive laughter ended as their lips reached out for each other. Their laughter turned to passion.

"Are you getting hungry?" Rosina asked.

"Your kisses satisfy every desire I'm allowed to have and then some," said Peppino feeling festive again.

"I'm sorry but you have to eat," said Rosina trying to sound serious. "You have to keep up your strength if you are going to fight off lady Lucia."

"Go prepare brunch. It's too late for breakfast and too soon for lunch."

"You're spoiled," said Rosina. "You expect three meals a day. Don't you realize that you are a wanted bandit living in the wild country side?"

"Just wait until we finish eating. I'll show you what is meant by wild." He reached out for her to tickle her but she slipped into the upper cave and hustled down the tunnel to the lower cave where she had left her stove the night before. She found that the chickens were in the lower cave huddled by the opening. She feed them some grain and proceeded to look into the bag of groceries Gino had brought. She was surprised what she found. There was a whole roll of salami. She cut several slices and, using slices of her bread, she made two sandwiches. She found some lettuce and some tomatoes. She placed some in each sandwich and brought them on plates to Peppino above.

"Wow," said Peppino. "Those look delicious. What is in them?" "Do you know what Gino did? He brought a whole piece of salami."

"How can you not love that guy?" said Peppino.

The next morning Rosina surprised Peppino with scrambled eggs, toast and coffee she found in the bottom of the bag Gino brought. Peppino was delighted. This went on for the next three days. Early on the fourth day Peppino noticed that someone was coming. After warning Rosina he watched the men ride towards him hoping it was Gino. He was sure it wasn't the police because he could only see three riders. As he expected it was Gino. But he wondered who were with him.

Ciao," said Gino as he and the others dismounted. Rosina ran out tears in her eyes. She threw herself into the arms of the woman that was with Gino.

"Anna," cried out Rosina. "It's so good to see you. What are you doing out here?"

"Look who I brought with me," said Anna as she pointed to Father Nicola.

"Ciao Father Nicola, I hope you don't mind if I hug you," said Rosina as she hugged him. She turned and hugged Anna again.

"You told Gino that you needed a Maid of Honor so here I am." "But how did you get away?" asked Rosina.

"I got permission from the head servant to go to the wedding of my best friend. Things are so confused in the city government that he told me to go but to come back as soon as the wedding is over. Donna Lucia spends every day with her brothers. She's never home."

"I know you would like to spend all day talking but we don't have that luxury," said Father Nicolo.

"I brought you a long white dress," Anna told Rosina. "It's the best I could do in such a short notice. I hope it will do." She took the dress out of the saddlebag and showed it to Rosina.

"It's gorgeous," said Rosina. "I love it."

"Go put in on. We don't have a lot of time. We can have the wedding here in front of your home."

"I have a dark blue jacket, a white shirt and a tie for you Peppino," said Gino. "Go get ready." Rosina went with Anna to the upper cave to get ready. Peppino got ready in the main cave. When he was ready he went outside and stood by father Nicola. After a few minutes Anna came down and called Gino. Gino went in. A little while later Anna came out and stood next to Peppino. Next Gino came out escorting Rosina out of the cave. Rosina looked more beautiful than she had ever looked. The white dress fit her slim body like it was made for her. Anna had placed a white nit hanky over her head that looked like a professional veil. Peppino stood with his mouth open. He was surprised at how beautiful she looked. She walked with such grace. Peppino fell in love with her all over again.

Gino walked her up to the priest, left her besides Peppino, and walked over to stand on the other side of Peppino.

"Close your mouth," said Rosina with a lovable smile noticing how awed Peppino was. "I think you look most handsome too." "You are by far the most beautiful bride in the world. "You are more than beautiful. You are absolutely gorgeous."

"We are gathered here," started the priest, but that was all that Peppino could hear. He was looking at Rosina and the whole world disappeared. He stood there admiring her when Gino nudged him.

"What....? said Peppino still in a daze. "Do you have the ring?" repeated the priest.

"Uh, do I, Gino?" responded Peppino. Gino handed him a ring. "Place it on her finger and repeat after me. With this ring I thee wed." Peppino put it on her finger. And repeated what he was asked.

"With the power invested in me by the pope and by God I pronounce you husband and wife. Go and may God go with you." He then turned to Gino. I understand that there is going to be another wedding.

"Yes," said Gino. He took Anna's hand and pulled her into the entrance to the cave. Anna, I love you more than my own life. I don't have a life without you. Will you marry me? We have everything we need right here."

"Oh Gino, She responded. "Are you sure? You are outside and have your whole life ahead of you. There is very little hope for us. They will never let me go. We will be two married people who rarely if ever see each other. I can't do that to you."

"Are you saying that you don't love me enough to take a chance on me?"

"Gino, you know that is not true. I have zero chance of getting married in my position. You however have the whole world to chose."

"I do have the right to choose the woman I love. I chose you. I know that we will be apart. But I want to know that you belong to me forever. Please marry me."

"I will always love you more than myself. I can't do that to you." "Answer me one question," said Gino. "If your answer is yes I will forget the whole thing and we could go home right now." "What is the question," asked Anna.

"If I ended up in jail, and would never be available to you, and you are freed from your position, could you marry some one else?" "That's not fair," said Anna. "I would always hope that you will escape some day."

"I rest my case," said Gino. "I couldn't marry anyone else. I would always hope that you would be freed." Anna turned to Rosina who was listening intently.

"Rosina," said Anna. "Would you lent me your dress and be my maid of honor?" Gino broke out with a joyous yell.

"Hooray," he said.

"Do you have a ring?" asked Anna. "Yes I got two rings just in case."

"You were pretty confident," said Anna with a happy smile. She never gave him the chance to answer because she kissed him. After the kiss, he forgot what they were talking about.

"Peppino," said Gino. Could I impose on you for your clothes and would you be my best man?"

"You bet," said Peppino being as happy about the idea as Gino was. The wedding took place just as Peppino's and Rosina's wedding had. They were all joyously happy.

"I'm afraid we must go," said Gino at last. "I don't want to be a widow before the honeymoon."

"When are you going to have a honeymoon," asked Rosina. "We will have something to look forward to," said Gino. "In the meantime we will have wonderful dreams."

"Before we break up this party I need signatures from you all if you want a marriage certificate."

"How about us?" asked Gino. "I forgot about the paperwork." "I brought an extra copy just incase I messed up one. I just have to be very careful and I can get both certificates." After he filled in all the data that he needed, he had them each signed as witnesses to each others wedding. With that done they all said goodbye and reluctantly left. Peppino and Rosina hated to see them go but were excited that their honeymoon could start immediately.

Their honeymoon was so much more than they expected. Rosina thanked God every morning and every night. She was so grateful to have the man she wanted. She adored him and she could tell by the way he looked at her that he adored her too. Everything was perfect. The only time they were separated and not in each others arms was when she was cooking. That's when Peppino had to go on watch. When they were in the upper chamber they didn't have to be on watch. There they were alone and perfectly safe. No one could ever find the entrance to that cave. That's where they spent most of the time. Their love grew by the minute as they made love and explored each others bodies. In between love making they enjoyed each other if only by rubbing their nude bodies together as they kissed. They developed their kissing into an art. They were close to running out of food, but they didn't care. Rosina woke Peppino every morning with a series of kisses that some times extend all over his body. A few times they made love outside behind the big rock. They had blankets up there just in case they needed them for just such an occasion. Several days they didn't bother wearing clothes.

It was only a little over a week since their wedding. They happened to be outside when Peppino saw someone riding toward them. He was sure it was Gino. They had hoped that Gino would wait at least two weeks before he came to visit. They were dressed and had talked about going hunting for deer. If Gino had to come, they hoped that he would bring some food. They went down to the main cave to meet him. To their disappointment, he didn't seam to have carried much.

"Gino, what are you doing here?" asked Peppino as Gino dismounted. We were hoping that we wouldn't see you for at least two weeks."

"I'm sorry guys, but this is too important," said Gino being very serious. "We have a major problem."

"Why what is happening?" asked Rosina.

"Let's sit inside in the shade and talk," said Gino. They went inside and sat at the table.

"Do you want me to make coffee?" offered Rosina.

"No, we don't have time," responded Gino. "We have to start making plans."

"What's the problem?" asked Peppino noticing how serious Gino was.

"I found out what Lucia's plan is to capture you," started Gino. Peppino and Rosina listened intently and resisted interrupting him. "She has arrested Gina. She says that she knows how much you cared for her and that you were engaged to her at one time. This is her offer. She is going to bring Gina in front of the public on Friday. She will exchange her for you. If you don't turn yourself in by twelve noon on Friday she will be executed in public.

"That's two days away," said Peppino. "Do you have any idea as to where she will do the execution?"

"It looks like it will be behind the fence she has in front of her palace. I see that she has a chair and some posts set up there."

"Have you found a good place for us to hide as we did for her husband?"

"No," said Gino. "The only place is at the extreme right side. It is quite a distance to hit anything with a rifle. But there is another problem. I saw the police set up posts at all the streets that lead to her palace. From what I can see it looks like they expect to spend the night there."

"You're not thinking of trying to save her are you?" asked Rosina. "You can be killed before we finish our honeymoon. I'm your wife. You have to think of me first."

"Sweetheart," assured Peppino. I love you. You are my wife. Nothing can change that. But I can't let Gina die on my account. I still care for her. She is my friend. We grew up together."

"I don't like it," said Rosina looking very sad. "What are we going to do?" asked Gino.

"What it means is that we have to go tonight. We have to be in place before the police take their positions. Gino, you know that you don't have to come."

"Don't even think about it. You're going to need back up." "What will we need?" asked Rosina. "I can start getting things ready."

"What do you mean we?" asked Peppino. "You're not going with us."

"That's what you think," she answered with defiance. "I'm going with you. If we go down we will go down together. Especially after the short honeymoon you know that I couldn't live without you."

"Rosie, you don't understand. I'm not trying to exclude you. I need you to help in another way."

"What do you want me to do?" she asked feeling a little better. "I need you to go to Monte Mangone Friday morning. Just as you go through the mountain pass the road starts going down hill. The hill bears left and then sharply turns right. Right at the bend you will see a large fig tree on your right. Across the road from the tree you will see a large rock up the mountain about thirty feet up. From that rock you are looking directly down the road. When we escape from the city we will head that way towards you. When we pass you we will ride until we are hidden from the police that are following us we will dismount and work our way to aid you. You have to eliminate as many as you can before we come up to help you. Do you understand?"

"Yes," said Rosina. "I know exactly where that is. I have been hunting in that area many times."

"That's the place we got Roberto, Vittorio's son," added Gino. "We will need two blankets, two bottles of water and maybe two salami sandwiches. We are going to be up there a long time."

"We will need two extra rifles just in case we had to leave ours on the roof top," said Peppino. "We also want you to come with us to the edge of town. You will take our horses back with you. You will then tie them at the same place you take them on Friday morning before you head for Monte Mangone."

"I understand clearly," assured Rosina

The day struggled slowly toward evening. They ate one of the chickens for dinner. Gino promised to replace it after all was finished. It took forever to get past midnight. The three of them prepared to leave. Everything was ready. It only took a short time to get to the edge of town. It was about one-thirty. All was silent. Peppino and Gino turned their horses over to Rosina.

"I'll see you Friday afternoon," said Peppino trying to give Rosina some confidence.

"Peppi, listen to me," said Rosina with tears in her eyes. "Please come back to me. If you don't I will just stay on Monte Mangone until I die. I would have no place to go."

"Don't worry," said Peppino. "I have a honeymoon to finish."

"I promise you that I will bring him back to you safely," said Gino. They made their way down the street and disappeared in the dark. Rosina rode off with the horses. Ten minutes later Peppino and Gino were lying down on the roof Gino had chosen. It was perfect because the wall around the roof was about a foot high. The building was the highest around so that no one could see them there. Peppino set his rifle on the wall and it was perfect. He could look straight into Lucia's front yard. Now all that was left was the waiting. Peppino's thought went to Gina. His heart pounded at the thought of her. He still was very much in love with her. He wondered what would happen after he shot Lucia. What would they do to Gina? Gino had brought up the fact that her brothers were against what she was doing. Not that they cared for Gina or any one else. It was that they were worried that the people would revolt. Peppino was gambling that they would let her go. He didn't ever want to think of what would happen if he missed Lucia.

The hours to dawn slipped by very slowly. Gino was able to get a few hours sleep. The hours of the next day seemed to last for eternity. Peppino and Gino were already starting to ache all over. It was a great relief when darkness filled the sky. They had noticed that all the police had take their post on the streets. In spite of the police, they were able to sit up in the darkness. They even had the chance to eat their sandwiches. They also drank most of the water in the first bottle. That night they walked a little, being careful not to fall or arouse attention. They needed the exercise. After all activity in the streets ended they wrapped themselves in their blankets and tried to get some sleep. As the morning dawned so did the activity. People were starting to accumulate at the fence that surrounded the palace. The voices seemed to be very rebellious. Two policemen stood by the poles in front of the palace. Several police wandered the area on horse back. They seemed to be checking the top of the buildings. None went near the building

Peppino and Gino were on. The area seemed well protected. Peppino began to wonder if he could really hit Lucia from where he was situated. Apparently the police didn't think so. Peppino started to consider if he missed should he turn himself in. He dismissed the thought. He will cross that bridge when he gets there. It was about eleven when Lucia showed up pushing Gina in front of her. Gina had her hands tied up behind her. Lucia sat Gina on the chair and tied her to it. Peppino could tell that Gina was crying. He really couldn't see that far but his heart told him so. He promised himself that he would not let her die. He started to pray.

"Dear God, if it is your will let me succeed."

Lucia had a very strong voice. Peppino was surprised that he could hear her from where he was.

"Casolini, do you hear me," she yelled. "You only have fifteen minutes. Come show yourself. She will die and we will get you anyway. Give up. You don't have a chance." The crowd by now had gathered around the fence. They were yelling at her. Peppino couldn't hear what they were saying but he understood that they were angry at her by the way they were shaking their fists at her. She was not to be dissuaded. Peppino put the rifle on the wall to steady it. He couldn't get a clear shot at her. He waited. He would get a better shot if she would turn toward him. Time was running out. She was moving around to much for Peppino to have a clear shot.. She took out a big knife and placed it on Gina's throat. Time was almost out. Then Peppino noticed someone on Lucia's left yelling at her. It looked like one of her brothers. She stepped back to yell back at him. This made her turn to face toward Peppino. Peppino got a clear shot. The bullet entered just above her nose and came out the back of her neck. No one notice where the bullet came from. Peppino hesitated to see what would happen to Gina. Since their rifles only shot one bullet at a time, he wouldn't have time to reload so he had asked Gino to concentrate on any one who went toward Gina to harm her. Instead, Gino handed him his rifle.

"You are a much better shot than I am," he said. But they were surprised to see all the police at the palace run in the other direction.

Peppino also saw Nicolo jump the fence to go and rescue Gina. "Let's get out of here," yelled Peppino. "Gina is in good hands."

265

They ran to the end of the roof where they had climbed up and climbed down and ran toward the edge of town where the horses were supposed to be. Sure enough the horses were there. Rosina had not let them down. As they mounted their horses Gino noticed that fve of the police on horse back were coming at them at full gallop. "There are five police after us," said Gino.

"Yes I see them," responded Peppino as he kicked his horse in full gallop. The police fired their pistols at them. A bullet came so close that Peppino felt it as it passed by his arm. Now they had to get to where Rosina has set up an ambush. Peppino had liked to stop and take a shot at them but his rifle had not been reloaded. He had given Gino back his rifle. They just had to make it to the mountain. Peppino and Gino's horses were very fresh. Rosina had taken good care of them. After a few minutes they started to pull away from them. That gave them time to get to the mountain. They rode down the trail toward the fig tree. As they got out of sight behind the tree and were about to dismount they heard two shots very close together. Was someone shooting back at Rosina wondered Peppino. He climbed like a goat to get to Rosina. Suddenly, they heard another shot coming from the vicinity of the big rock where Rosina was hiding. That gave Peppino new hope. As he approached the rock, he noticed that three police were motionless on the ground.

"Rosina didn't you save any for us?" said Peppino as he got to her. She didn't answer because she was to busy jumping on top of him kissing him all over.

"Look at the other two run," said Gino, laughing hilariously. He was happy it was all over.

"Looks like you had all the fun," said Peppino.

"You guys were too late and too slow. You got to hustle if you want to keep up with me," she replied.

"I guess so," said Peppino. "Let's go home. We have a honeymoon to finish."

"I better get back to my farm," said Gino. "I may have a lot of explaining to do. They got on their horses and headed west so they would come in from the west and not from the east. As they leisurely rode back Rosina wanted to know what had taken place the previous two days.

"Before we tell you what we did, tell us how you got so many shots off in such a hurry," asked Peppino.

"Well I knew that I wouldn't get much help from you two so I loaded all the rifles. I brought two extra rifles for you two. I placed them on the rock, ready to aim and fire."

"Gino will you listen to her," said Peppino with a big smile on his face.

"That's a woman for you," said Gino jokingly.

"Do you guys want to hear the rest of the story or do you want to wallow in your hurt pride.

"Go ahead," said Peppino. "Get you kicks while you can." "Well when the police showed up chasing you I aimed the first rifle and before they knew what hit them I aimed the other and got another one. I would have gotten the third guy sooner but the third rifle slipped off the rock so I had to go get it before I could get the third guy."

"All kidding aside," said Peppino. "You did a fantastic job. I'm so proud of you, I can hardly contain it."

"I want so much for you to proud of me. It makes me feel like maybe I am good enough for you."

"Sweetheart, you don't have to prove anything to me. If anything I'm not good enough for you." said Peppino.

"Will you two shut up?" said Gino lovingly. "You two are perfect for each other. That's from an outside opinion" They all smiled.

"We love you too," said Rosina. "Now how did you guys make out?"

"Not much to tell," said Peppino. "We suffered two days on the roof waiting for Lucia to make her move. She brought Gina out in front of the palace and threatened to cut her throat. She turned to talk to her brother, who incidentally objected to the whole thing. I got a clear shot. I hit her around the nose. She fell over and I think she is dead. The police that were guarding her ran in the other direction. They were scared out of their wits. Nicolo jumped over the fence and rescued his wife. We ran and my faithful wife had brought our horses at the appointed place where we got on them and you know the rest of the story."

"I couldn't believe that your husband hit her from that distance.

I could hardly see her let alone hit her. He has a very sharp eye."
"You don't have to sell me on him. He is also a great lover did you know that?"

"Rosie! Wait until I get you home," said Peppino jokingly.

Twenty minutes later, they arrived at a fork in the road. The one led to Monte Uno and the other led back to town.

"This is where we part company," said Gino. "I have to establish an alibi. Listen, if you have run out of food eat the other chicken. It should last you a couple of days. I will bring you two egg laying hens the next time I come this way."

"Don't make it sooner than another week. We will hunt some rabbits and there is a little of the lamb left down in the stream. Don't make us come to town to save you now, you hear," said Peppino. "However if there is news we need to hear please feel free to come anytime."

"I'll try to stay out of trouble. I will try to see Gina if I can to see if there is any backlash." Gino left toward town and Peppino and Rosina headed for their home in Monte Uno.

"I'm hungry," said Peppino when they got back to their upper cave home. "Should I get the lamb from the stream?"

"Do you really want to eat first," said Rosina with a passionate look on her face.

"Honey, all I've had for the last two days is one salami sandwich and a bottle of water. After I get something in my stomach, I want to cuddle up with you and make love all night. By the way, I didn't get much sleep for two days either. I wasn't afraid of dying as much as I was afraid of what would happen to you. You are the greatest reason I ever had to stay alive."

"I understand," said Rosina. "Can we fill your stomach with a delicious salami sandwich? Lamb takes too long to cook."

"I would love a salami sandwich. That sounds terrific," he lied. "I'll call you when it is ready." Peppino went up to his watching post and Rosina went down to the main cave where she had her stove. About fifteen minutes later she called him down to the entrance to the cave where she had moved the table and chairs back to their outdoor position. Peppino came down immediately. He was extremely hungry. When he got down he was surprised at what he saw.

"Where is the salami sandwich?" he asked. "This looks like a meal for a king. What is it and how did you cook it so soon?"

"I cooked it last night. I just had to heat it. It's chicken legs rolled in a batter of bread crumbs and eggs. The side dish is Swiss chard, and the beverage is coffee. You didn't really think I was going to feed my fearless, heroic, and gorgeous, husband a salami sandwich did you?"

"You are something special do you know that?" said Peppino. "I'm so lucky to have you."

The week that followed was greater than the week before. They not only got to know each other better, but they also became like one. The joy they had with each other was so fantastic that they were sure they would remember the week for life. The more they enjoyed each other the more in love they became. They were convinced that this honeymoon would never be over. Peppino promised himself that he would do what ever was necessary to keep their marriage, joyful, loving, and always romantic. In her heart she also was sure that their honeymoon would be perpetual and their love would continue to grow to infinity. Although their desires for each other continued to grow, they were ready to receive visitors. As if God had heard their wish, Gino showed up early the next morning. They were still in bed.

"Get up you sleepy heads," said Gino through the entrance to the upper cave. "Get up; I have a lot to tell you." They got up and everyone met in the lower cave. "I would be eternally grateful if you will make me breakfast. I didn't have time to eat this morning."

"We ate the chickens and don't have any eggs," said Rosina. "What can I make you?"

"What a way to treat a visitor," said Gino jokingly. "I have to bring my own food." He reached into his saddlebags and retrieved about two dozen eggs. He also pulled out several packages of food and ingredients he felt Rosina might need. He also had two hens and a rooster to replace the ones they ate. "Now don't eat these."

"You are an angel sent by God," said Rosina as she started to get ready to cook.

"Don't cook now," requested Gino. "I was kidding you. I already ate and I have to get to the farm. Please sit here and listen to what I have to tell you." They all sat around the table. "First let me tell you of the cities reorganization. Vittorio was sworn in as the new mayor. He has selected Pietro as his assistant and future replacement. His brother Alfredo has recruited two new police. That makes his complete police force a group of five. He has strengthened the border patrol to prevent anyone leaving the area. Killing Lucia has, at least for the present, cooled the unhappiness of the people. Things are being stabilized by the new mayor. That doesn't mean that the rebels are forgiven. They are still punishing them by killing them and releasing enough information on their behavior to put the blame on you. You are feared by the whole city. The words 'Notorious Casolini' has everyone shaking in their boots."

"What do you mean by releasing enough information on their behavior to put the blame on me?"

"They let it slip that they spied for the mayor's organization. This is what they are selling and that is what you are punishing. The basis is the fact that you killed Bruno for spying on your father. I have to go. Here you may want to read the headline from last week's paper." He handed Peppino a newspaper. After Gino left, Peppino opened the paper and read the headline out loud. It said: "The Wicked Witch Is Dead."

Chapter 13

ALONE AGAIN

Peppino showed Rosina the headline in the paper the day Lucia was killed. They were amazed that the mayor and the police chief allowed the writers to get away with putting that in the paper. "Maybe the mayor will get even at a later date," said Rosina.

"I don't think so, said Peppino. "I'll be willing to bet they just warned them not to do it again. If they are worried about public reaction, they certainly wouldn't publicly harass the press. I think the new mayor wants to ease the turmoil of the people. Letting them get their steam off on Lucia is a good thing. After all she is dead. Let her take all the blame for being cruel and corrupt."

"They play all the angles don't they?" responded Rosina. "Do you think they will delay chasing after us?"

"Maybe for a while," said Peppino. "If they have other people to get rid of they will want me alive to take the blame. We will wait and see. Now that fall is here they are going to have a lot of work to do to catch up on their tax collecting. Besides, they only have five police. They are going to take their time to do better planning. They can't afford to look bad again. We have to be on our best guard because the next time it will not be so easy. They get smarted all the time from experience."

"Let's forget it for now," said Rosina getting a headache from all the talking. "I'm going to make you a fantastic breakfast. I have a lot of ingredients that Gino brought. Go up and watch while I cook."

"I'd rather have the breakfast you promised to serve me every morning. I didn't get it this morning because of Gino's interruption." "If I give you that breakfast I will be cooking lunch instead of breakfast."

"That's all right. Let's have the other breakfast in bed," teased Peppino.

"Yes I would love that," agreed Rosina. "That type breakfast in bed is a lot healthier." They scurried up the rope into their private lair. Their breakfast was so great that they almost missed lunch.

The days turned to weeks and the week turned to months. Peppino and Rosina had not seen or heard from Gino all winter. They were concerned for his safety. They had to hunt for food. They did manage to shoot a deer down beyond the hills of Monte Mangone. That was the only place deer were found because of the rare wooded areas. In February, they stole a lamb from a shepherd. That kept them fed through the winter and early spring. Peppino and Rosina were deliriously happy. It was as if they were on a perpetual honeymoon. However when spring plowing time came they became very worried about Gino. Although they still had the chickens for eggs in the morning, they were running out of the necessary staples. Gino normally provided them with.

"I think I will sneak into town to see what has happened to Gino," said Peppino.

"You can't go into town. Where would you look without getting seen?" said Rosina. "Why don't you go to his farm first to see if he is plowing his field? This is the plowing season. He should be out there by now."

"That is an excellent idea. It should be the first place to look," agreed Peppino. "I'll go tomorrow." That night Rosina was more passionate than usual. She was more romantic. It was different enough that it was noticed by Peppino.

"I love you so much Peppi," she whispered in his ear. "What's bothering you?" asked Peppino finally.

"You will be going tomorrow without me won't you? It will be the second time that we will be apart. I find it hard to breathe when I'm not with you. Do you know that soon it will be our first wedding anniversary? What happened to the time?"

"I know, time goes by so fast," said Peppino. "I have to go alone because it will be much easier for me to sneak around. One person can be a lot less noticeable."

The next morning Peppino ate breakfast with Rosina and then kissing her goodbye he left for Gino's farm. When he was about a quarter of a mile away he saw the dust coming from Gino's field. As he got closer he noticed that it was Gino. He was about to gallop to him when he notices what looked like two additional horses near a large orange tree. Peppino quickly dismounted and tied his horse to a shrub near by. He grabbed his rifle and the telescope he always had in his saddle bag. He slowly crept closer to the position he had seen the horses. Using the telescope he spotted two police sitting under the tree watching Gino work. Peppino realized that was the reason Gino had not come to visit. He quietly returned to the cave where Rosina was waiting for him.

"Did you find out anything?" asked Rosina.

"Yes," said Peppino. "He is being watched by two policemen. They aren't being discreet about it. They just sit under his orange tree in plain view and watch him."

"And they get paid to do that?" said Rosina in disgust.

"The result is that if we need things we will have to go get them ourselves."

"What else do we have to do today?" she asked. "At least we know where two of the five police are."

"You may be right," agreed Peppino. "It will be more exciting also. We will meander into town casually. When we get to the store we want to rob we put on one of those large kitchen towels that Gino brought us over our face so that we will not be recognized and get what we need."

"Early morning is better because fewer people will be around." They gathered every thing they would need. Rosina tied up her hair up under a hat. They both wore open jackets so they could hide pistols behind their back under their belts. The jacket would cover the pistols. They left as soon as they were ready and got to the outskirts of town around ten. They tied their horses by the side of the road on a fig tree.

Rosina headed for the drug store and Peppino headed for the grocery store.

"We will meet back at the horses," said Peppino. "Don't wait if you are chased. In that case we will meet at the cave." Peppino got to the grocery store in about five minutes. He covered his face and went in. There was only one customer in the store.

"Just fill this bag with the items on this list and no one will get hurt," said Peppino.

"Dear God," said the customer a young slim woman. "It's Casolini." At that the clerk jumped to fill the list.

"Please don't hurt me," he pleaded. "I will do as you ask." "What makes you think I am Casolini," asked Peppino of the woman,

"There is no one else around here that is your size," she said trembling. "Please don't kill me. I won't tell any one."

"The stories you hear about me killing other than the city officials is a lie," said Peppino. I never killed those people that they say I did. That was the corrupt mayor's people eliminating the people they think are planning a revolt. I only killed one of the working class and that was the neighbor that betrayed my father and got him killed. I'm only after those that killed my family."

"You're not going to hurt us then?" said the woman obviously a little relieved.

"I don't kill innocent people. I do however need to live and therefore must sometimes steal." The clerk gave him the package with the items he requested. "Thank you. If I ever get out of this alive I will try to repay you." He then left with the bag in one hand and as he stepped out of the door, two police were there in front of him. He had made a tactical error. He should have looked outside before stepping out into the street. *It's all over*, he thought. One of the police had a rifle in his hand ready to shoot him. They stood there for what seemed like a lifetime. Peppino waited for the pain of the bullet piercing his body. He thought of Rosina. She would be waiting by the horses. His whole life flashed before him. He would soon see his father and sister. He dropped the bag and was ready to lift his hands up to surrender. Then the strangest thing happened. As he started to raise his hands, the officer behind the one with the rifle yelled out loud.

"It's Casolini," At that, the one in front dropped the rifle and both turned, and running as fast as they could turned the corner and disappeared. Peppino grabbed the grocery bag and headed for the horses. As he crossed the street, he saw Rosina running across the road toward him. They mounted their horses and started for their home. To their surprise no one was following them.

"How did you make out?" asked Rosina. "Did you get everything we need?"

"Yes I did," responded Peppino. "How about you? Did you get everything you went after?"

"Yes and more," she responded. "We are set for at least another two or three months. Did you have any trouble?"

"Not too much. I only got caught by two police that caught me by surprise. One of them had me in his gun sight. I was caught with my hands tied up holding the grocery bag. He had me clean."

"What happened?" said Rosina her eyes opening wide with horror.

"It was very strange and unexpected," said Peppino trying to draw out his story "I would never have guessed what happened next." Peppino was getting a big kick out of seeing the expression on Rosina's face. He hesitated to let the situation sink in.

"Well what did you do?" insisted Rosina.

"I was trapped like a rat. I started to think about how dumb I was to just step out of the store without looking. What a stupid mistake I had made. My thoughts went to you. I was worried about you. If I was killed here you would be waiting with the horses. I was worried on how you would take my death, I decided to raise my hands and give myself up. I thought that was the only chance I had. As I started to raise my hands the strangest thing happened. They must have thought I was reaching for my gun." Peppino paused for a moment. "Okay, you stinker," said Rosina finally realizing that Peppino was playing with her. "You are making this whole story up. I don't think any part of this story is true."

"I swear on my honor that every word is true," assured Peppino. "Okay then, tell me how this story ended," said Rosina still doubting his story.

"Honestly it is really true," he said. "What happened next is absolutely unbelievable. The policeman who was slightly behind yelled, 'It's Casolini' and the one with the rifle dropped it and both ran away as fast as they could."

"You don't expect me to believe that ridicules story do you?" said Rosina with an, I don't believe you, look on her face.

"Honey I know," agreed Peppino. "If you told me a story like that I would laugh my head off. The whole city is frightened of the word Casolini. There was a woman customer in the store. She begged me not to kill her. The store clerk wouldn't get the items I asked for because he thought he was going to die. Every one in town is frightened out of their wits due to the stories and killings that the mayor's people are doing."

"What do you think we should do?" she asked. "If the whole town is afraid of you then the whole town could some day come after you."

"I would like to get Pietro for killing Tano and putting me in jail," said Peppino thoughtfully. "Perhaps we should try to sneak out of here. We could get past the guards and if there is a problem, we could fight our way out of the area. We could head for the mainland. Perhaps to Naples or Rome."

"I would love to get out of here and have a home like normal people," said Rosina. "I'm sure you could get us out of here, but I know that you could never be happy leaving the town in the hands of these animals. I'm not sure I would be either. Let's get Pietro and then we can talk about it again."

"In order to help the people we would have to get rid of Vittorio and Alfredo," said Peppino. "That would completely rid the town of the blue blood. The officials at Enna would then have to come and take over the city government. That would be the best scenario."

"I see that we are almost home," said Rosina. "Let's discuss it later. I'm getting hungry." The place Rosina referred to was only a hole in the side of the mountain. It had no furniture to speak of, and it had no similarity to a house. But to Peppino and Rosina it was home. What made it a home was love. Its interior was plastered with love.

The next few months went by quickly. They spent their first anniversary alone. It was obvious that Gino couldn't get away. He would have been there if it was at all possible. Peppino and Rosina had spent much time planning on how to get Pietro. It would have been easier if they had Gino to help them. They were missing the information on the movements of the mayor and his crew. They had to sneak into town and get what information they could dig up. Peppino didn't like the idea because Rosina was usually the one to enter the city since she was not recognized as one of Peppino's people. She could also disguise herself easier than Peppino since his size gave him away. They couldn't find a way to get Pietro. It was in late November when they got their first break. Rosina found out that Pietro liked one of the girls in town. She was a clerk in the local furniture store. Pietro would go there after it closed and pick her up and take her home. His mother and father apparently didn't object. After all, the only blue blood girl in town was his own sister. Little by little, they gathered the information they needed. They found where the girl lived. They found where there was a roof near by where they could hide until they could get a good shot. The information was obtained too late. Winter was upon them and it would be too cold to lie all day on a roof. It also was the raining season.

"We had better wait until the spring," said Peppino. "We don't have to be in a hurry. I'm very happy here with you."

"I'm happy here with you too. But the sooner we get Pietro the sooner we can decide whether to leave the area and try to make a life somewhere else or stay here and get rid of the blue blood disease." Peppino laughed at her classifying the Malavista family as a disease.

"We will talk about that later," said Peppino. "I would also like to free Anna and Gino. Those two haven't had their honeymoon yet."

"Peppi, it looks to me that you have made up your mind already."
"My mind will not be made up until you are with me in all that we do."

Spring came sooner then they expected. The weather got reasonably warm for March They had not seen or heard from Gino. It was time for Peppino and Rosina to act.

"I think I had better wander into town and see if Pietro is still seeing that girl," said Rosina. "No one is expecting me so I'll walk by at the right time."

"I don't like you to go into town alone," said Peppino.

"Why," she asked. "No one knows me except the old witch and some of the servants. The servants are not allowed to go outside the palace grounds and even if they did, they wouldn't tell on me. And the old witch is dead. So what are you afraid of?"

"I guess it will be all right. I still don't like it," he responded. "Maybe it's because I don't like to be alone by myself."

"Go take your siesta," she suggested. "I'll be back before you know it."

"It's too early for a siesta. Besides I haven't taken a siesta since I was a kid. We farmers seldom took a siesta. It had to be an extremely hot day for us to find shade to sleep in. And it was only to get by the worst part of the day."

"I don't want a history of farming," she responded with a loving smile. "It's a little early yet. I want to get there when her workday is over. Many people are going home at that time. I'll just be one of them."

"Be careful," he warned. "That is a very small town. They will be aware of a stranger since they know every one in town."

"You're a worry wart," she said as she prepared for her trip. When she was ready to go she hugged and kissed Peppino. He kissed her back passionately.

"I'll miss you," he said lovingly.

"Now don't get mushy or I'll never be able to go," she said kissing him one more time and then mounting her horse.

"I just want each kiss to be meaningful," he said. "You never know when it will be the last one." She smiled and left.

It was almost three hours later when Rosina returned. She was looking chipper. Peppino had worried about her the full three hours she was gone. He was so happy to see her that he waited for her at the main cave entrance. She dismounted and after a lengthy and passionate reunion, he walked her up to the upper cave where she tied and took care of her horse.

"What conclusions have you come to as a result of your trip?" asked Peppino.

"It was very interesting," she replied. "It looks like Don Pietro is quite a lover."

"What does that mean?" he asked, wondering what Pietro was up to now.

"It would seem that the house where he visits every evening has three or four girls living there. The one I saw him with this evening was not the same girl I saw him with last fall. I'm sure of it because this one is blonde and very fair skinned."

"Will he be there at the same time every evening?"

"I think so," she said thoughtfully. "He always brings the one girl with black hair home. He waits until who ever he is escorting to dinner gets ready and then he goes out. That gives us two chances to get him. Once when he arrives and, if we miss that opportunity, a second chance when he leaves."

"Sound great," exclaimed Peppino. "When do you think it will be a good time?"

"Right now I'm very hungry. Have you eaten dinner yet?" she asked.

"No, I was waiting for you," he responded. The truth was that he couldn't eat worrying about her.

"Did you prepare anything?" she asked hoping that she could eat soon.

"I didn't know what you wanted," he said knowing that it was a bad excuse.

"Peppi, what is on your mind?" she said looking as if she already knew. "You have to trust me and stop worrying about me when I'm out of your sight. I'm very flattered that you love me that much but it is counterproductive. You have to limit your love to bed time."

Peppino was very embarrassed. He didn't respond to her comments. He wanted to ask her how she felt if he left and she didn't hear from him for three hours. He remembered a couple of times when she was frantic worrying about him. However he kept his silence.

"Do you want me to go get some meat from the stream?" he finally responded.

"No," she said. "I got there early and went by the grocery store. When the grocer went inside to make change for a customer I grabbed a couple of green peppers from his outdoor stand. I'll slice them up and fry them in a batter of eggs and flour. We do have some eggs don't we?"

"Yes we do," he responded and went to get them.

"Bring four," she yelled down to him. He did, and they had a late dinner that Peppino thought was fabulous.

The next day they got up early. They wanted to get enough loving to hold them until their plan had been completed. The plan was for them to get positioned on the roof in the middle of the night and wait until late afternoon when Pietro came to the house the girls lived in. They brought salami sandwiches. It was the last of the salami. That would be sufficient for the day. They also brought water. Rosina got to feel first hand how uncomfortable and boring it is to lie all day on a hot roof top with the sun beating down on you. She was even afraid to scratch herself when some part of her body started to itch. Every part of her body seemed to be against her. They could count every second that went by. Finally, the day started to fade. Peppino reasoned that it was about six in the afternoon. The minutes ticked by and still no Pietro. Rosina pondered on the fact that she wouldn't be able to go through this again if Pietro didn't show up. But Pietro did show up. Peppino readied himself for the fatal shot. Pietro turned facing Peppino as he let the girl in the door. Peppino pulled on the trigger. Somehow, Pietro saw something, perhaps the reflection of the rifle as he looked up. Just before the bullet arrived he pushed the girl through the door and fell on top of her. The bullet hit the door casing just a half inch from Pietro's head. Pietro quickly closed the door. Peppino and Rosina quickly left the roof and getting to their horses left at a full gallop.

"I don't think anyone is following us," said Peppino feeling some what relieved.

"What do we do now?" asked Rosina, feeling depressed because all the trouble they went through produced failure. "We can't use that roof anymore."

"We will have to regroup and come up with another plan," said Peppino feeling depressed. He wasn't used to failure.

"Let's go home and get something to eat. I'm hungry after all that excitement," she said after seeing Peppino's face. She could tell from his voice that he was depressed. She wanted to cheer him up. But she didn't know how except with food. After dinner they went outside and sat by their favorite rock. Rosina found out how to cheer him up. It was with her kisses and her love. They went to bed that night back to their normal happiness.

It was just after the lunch hour that Peppino noticed some one coming up fast toward them. Since there was only one, Peppino couldn't figure who would be coming this fast at this time of day. He called Rosina to come up. She came up as quickly as she could.

"What's happening?" she asked.

"Look out there," he said pointing to the dust trail. "Someone is coming in a hurry. Strange it doesn't seem like he's coming from town. He's coming from the direction of Gino's farm. It has to be Gino." A few minutes later Gino rode up to them and dismounted. "Gino," said Peppino. "How did you get away from your guards?" "Ciao Peppi, Rose," he said. The guards were pulled away. Just a few minutes ago, a policeman came and they all left. I assumed that they were coming after you and I decided to come as fast as I could to help."

"It's probably Pietro," said Peppino. "We tried to get him from the roof top near his girl friend. I missed so I'm sure he decided to come after me. The best defense is an offence."

"Pietro is too smart for us just to hide in the upper cave. He would search until he found it," said Gino. I think we have to fight him."

"I think you are right," said Peppino. He will certainly head for the main cave. We can set up an ambush above and ahead of the main cave.

"I think our main goal should be Pietro," said Rosina. "I recommend that we all aim at Pietro. I'm sure that if we get him all the others will run for home."

"How can Pietro win when we have an intelligent strategist among us?" said Peppino being proud of Rosina. "That is perfect thinking. Let's set up now. If he called Gino's guards he is probably on his way." They searched the area for a good place for the ambush. They located what they perceived to be the best spot and separated themselves across the area, each choosing a large rock to hide behind. They brought all the ammunition they had in case the fight lasted all day.

They no sooner got ready that Gino who was on the highest ground spotted the group coming towards them.

"They are coming," he yelled to the others. "It looks like about five men."

"Wait until they are close enough so you can recognize Pietro. They waited until they got near enough to shoot. Pietro however was smarter than they gave him credit. When he got about a thousand feet from the cave he and his men dismounted and approached the area advancing from rock to rock. He wasn't going to take a chance that he would be ambushed. Peppino was hoping that the others would wait until Pietro was close enough for all three to shoot. They waited until they spotted Pietro. They followed him as he moved from rock to rock. The next time he left the safety of his rock to jump to the next, three shots were heard. Pietro fell. One of the other men ran up and pulled him to safety. Slowly shooting as they retreated to their horses. They threw Pietro over his horse and they all rode away.

"Well that was short," said Rosina. They all laughed.

"I wonder if he is dead, dies on the way to the doctor, or is just wounded," said Peppino.

"I don't know but I will try to find out," said Gino. "I better get back just in case the guards come back. I need to show some progress on my land. Here is an extra key to my house in case you need some place to stay. I'm going to stay at Anna's house. It puts me closer to town so I can get more information"

"Ciao Gino," said Rosina, "and thanks for the help."

"Yes thanks Gino. We owe you so much," said Peppino. "We will find a way to make it up to you."

"Ciao," said Gino as he rode away.

The months slipped by. Peppino and Rosina didn't hear from Gino or anyone from town. It was late summer when Rosina got the idea to sneak back into town and see what was going on.

"Not again," said Peppino. "I'm still not over the last time you did this."

"Sweetheart, we have to know what happened to Pietro. We also have to plan our next move which we can't do unless we know what the story is with Pietro."

"I still don't like you going into the lion's den," said Peppino. "Don't look at it that way," said Rosina teasing him. "Look at it as if you are worried for the Barrafranca Government leaders." "Don't you dare try anything by yourself," said Peppino starting to worry already.

"Stop it already," said Rosina as she started to get ready. "I'll be back as soon as I find out anything." She mounted her horses and threw him a kiss as she left. Peppino wasn't happy about that. He had promised himself that they would give each other a passionate kiss every time they parted in case it was the last one.

Rosina tied her horse in town by the grocery store as if she was going shopping. She then wandered through the streets looking to find some one she could safely talk to. She walked casually by the news stand. She pretended to look at the magazines. The clerk didn't pay attention to her. She looked at the paper. There was an article on the condition of Pietro. She started to read it when the paper was pulled out of her hand.

"If you want to read it, buy it," said the clerk.

"I just wanted to see what happened to Pietro. My husband gets the paper and doesn't bring it home until this evening."

"Well he is still in the care of the doctor. It seems that he was badly hurt," said the clerk. "I think that he got an infection as a result. They say that he will recover but it will take a few months."

"Thank you," said Rosina.

"I haven't seen you around before," said the clerk being curious.

"I don't get out very often. I have been very ill myself," she said and left in a hurry before he could ask any more questions. She went to the grocery store to get her horse when the clerk came out to meet her.

"Please forgive me, but I need to talk with you. I met your friend and he told me that all the killings that are blamed on him were lies. In my job, I know a lot about what is going on around here. I believed him. Your friend is doing a great job and I would like to help him if I could."

"Who are you talking about?" asked Rosina acting innocent. "I'm talking about the fellow who was surprised by the police who ran rather than try to capture him."

"Did that really happen?" asked Rosina who had only half-believed Peppino's story.

"Yes the police had him in his gun sights but was so frightened that he ran rather than fight."

"What makes you think that I know anything about this?" asked Rosina, surprised at his actions.

"If I can put things together I know who you are. I have never seen you around here before. I know that new people do not come here. I believe you are Rosina that had escaped from the palace several years ago. I think that you joined him and the two of you are trying to survive out in one of the caves of Monte Uno.

"Why are you telling me this?" asked Rosina suspiciously. "When the man we are talking about came here he gave me a list of items he wanted. I made a new bag of the items and would like you to take them to him, that is, if you are his friend."

"I will be glad to take it to him," said Rosina. "Thank you so much. You will never be sorry." He helped get the bag in her saddles and helped her on her horse.

"May God bless you both and watch over you," he said affectionately.

"Thank you so much," said Rosina. And as she rode away she yelled back. "I'm not his friend, I'm his wife.

Rosina got back before it got dark. She told Peppino all that she had found out and about the grocery store clerk. She showed him the items he had packed for him. There were a few things in the bag that he didn't have on the original list. One thing was a large solid link of salami.

"Boy," said Peppino. "We can surely use this."

"Honey I want to apologize for not believing you about the story of the police you encountered when you went there. I only believed half of your story. I thought you were exaggerating."

"That's okay, sweet heart. It was very unbelievable," said Peppino. "So Pietro is still alive and will completely recover."

"That's what they told me."

"We will have to plan another way to get him," said Peppino. He will be harder to get now. He will be on his guard constantly." "There is only one way," said Rosina thoughtfully. "Now is the only time he is vulnerable."

"What do you have in mind?" asked Peppino. "I usually don't like your ideas when you put it that way."

"I think I can sneak into town and finish him in the doctor's office. His office isn't that secure. I'm sure they will have a guard at night. I could find out when the guard comes on duty and take out Pietro before he gets there."

"You are going to do this all by yourself?"

"Well if you can think of a way you could help or if you have any other ideas, I will listen."

"I don't have any ideas off hand. Let me think about it." After much thought, they decided that Rosina would go into town in search of other possibilities. They really missed Gino's input. He was good at finding solutions. Rosina was gone for less than an hour. She came back much sooner than Peppino expected.

"Wow," said Peppino. "You came back so soon. I didn't expect you till twilight Did you find a better solution that fast?"

"No the solution may have been made by God," said Rosina as she dismounted.

"Pietro has taken a turn for the worse. His infection has spread. They don't think he will make it. We will have to wait to see what happens. If he dies on his own then we don't have to take a risk to get him."

"Sounds great to me," said Peppino. "Perhaps now is the time to talk about leaving the area if he dies. What are your thoughts?" "I've been thinking a lot about it," said Rosina. "It seems a shame to leave with the job not completely finished.

"It depends on what you consider is the job," said Peppino. "If the job is to take care of the people that killed my family, Pietro is the last one. If the job is to free the city from these so called blue bloods then there are two more to take care of after Pietro or when things get so bad that Enna gets involved."

"I'm for freeing all our friends," said Rosina. "I'm sure that one of these days the information will get to Enna even before we get the other two. Remember that two of the people we will be freeing are

Gino and Anna." They decided to talk more about it after Pietro has been taken care of.

The fall and winter went by without a single word from any-one. Neither did anyone come looking for them. Peppino and Rosina were so happy that they almost forgot their goal. Every once in a while Rosina would go into town and the clerk at the grocery store gave them a large bag of supplies. He also informed her that Pietro was still hanging on. They got most of their meat from hunting, something they loved to do together. It was late in the spring when Rosina went to town that she was told that Pietro had survived his infection and was scheduled to go home soon. Now was the time to act.

"Peppi, honey," she said. "I need to go into town and finish Pietro before he goes home. It will be more difficult to get him if he leaves the doctors building. At the doctor's they will probably only have a nurse and a guard."

"I think I should go," said Peppino. It's too dangerous." "Nonsense," she responded. You are too easily spotted. They will never suspect a woman. I can dress as an older woman. I'll be smart about the job. I will not do it if it's too dangerous."

"Perhaps I should go and wait for you outside of town."

"No, I don't think so. I may have to wait a day or so if it looks dangerous. I may have to investigate and study the situation. Since Gino gave us the key to his house I'll stay there if I have to stay over night. I'll leave after dinner. I want the nurse to be gone by the time I get there."

Rosina got to town about eight in the evening. She put on her old ladies clothes with a black shawl over her head. She walk past the doctor's office and was surprised that there wasn't a guard outside. She walked up to the door and found that it was open. Was this some kind of a trap? She wondered. She walked inside with her hand on her pistol under her apron. There was a light on in one of the rooms. She looked inside. There was a bed there but it was empty. As she was about to leave she hear a noise behind her and was about to bring her pistol out when she noticed that it was a nurse.

"Can I help you?" the nurse asked.

"I was looking for Pietro. I understood that he was here."

"No he was sent home yesterday. He will need about three months to recuperate but he wanted to do it at home. That's why I'm here this late. I stayed to clean up. I'm usually home by six."

"Is Pietro home with his family?"

"No, he has a house of his own. He felt he was too old to be tied to his parents."

"I didn't know that," said Rosina acting surprised. "Do you know where his house is located?"

"I don't," said the nurse. "I'm sorry"

"Thank you anyway," said Rosina. "Ciao." She left the doctor's office and went to Gino's house for the night.

The next morning Rosina went to the grocery store to talk to the friendly clerk.

"Ciao," she said. "What do you have for me today?"

"I've got the usual plus a special surprise," he said as he brought out two large bags of food.

"Tell me," she asked. "I understand that Pietro has purchased a small home for himself. Do you happen to know where it is located?" The clerk got a piece of wrapping paper and drew a little map on it showing where Pietro's house was.

"You didn't get this from me," he said whispered while slipping the paper to her. "I don't really know were he lives," he said out loud.

"Thank you very much," she said and left. After looking at the paper, she was confident that she knew where it was. That evening just before it got dark, she put on her disguise and went to the area where the house was. Sitting outside on a stool was a policeman as a guard. Apparently, they were confident that he was safe. The policeman was asleep. Rosina crept silently along the wall of the house and came up behind the guard. A hand on his mouth and a quick knife in his heart soon made him motionless. She tried the door but it was locked. However, a window was open. She slithered through the window and soon found Pietro lying in bed.

"Who's there?" he asked.

"I'm the ghost of Stellina," she said as she plunged the knife into his chest. "I come to avenge the death of my husband." She left quickly and walked to Gino's house, which was located at the edge of town.

She picked up the groceries and was back home with Peppino before midnight.

"Pietro is now with his cousins," said Rosina to Peppino. "We are almost finished. Two more to go."

"Let's celebrate in bed," suggested Peppino. "I have missed you so much. We have two days to catch up on."

"But I was only gone for one day," said Rosina with a pixy smile. "Interest," said Peppino as he led her to their bed.

Two days went by and they were happier than they had ever been. It was on the third day that the surprise attack took place. Peppino came out in the morning to his favorite look out spot. Rosina went down to cook breakfast. He bent down to get his telescope when a bullet came so close that it tore his sleeve.

"Rosina." He yelled out. Bullets rained all around him. Rosina came out with three rifles and as much ammunition as she could carry. From behind the rock, they began shooting back. It was obvious that they were out numbered. The chief of police had outsmarted them. He and six of his men had quietly moved in during the night and taken positions around where they had suspected they were hiding. After a few rounds, they started to charge up the hill towards them. There was a man on their right and a man on their left coming in for the kill. Rosina managed to get one man as he charged toward them.

But the man on their right got a bead on them. A shot was heard and the man fell. Two other men fell as the shooter from the right side came to their aid. It was Gino. He had arrived in time to get the man on their right flank. The man on the left however charged and got a shot off toward them. Rosina saw him first. Her gun had just been fired and was unloaded.

"No," she screamed as she threw herself in front of Peppino. The bullet entered in her back between her shoulder blades. Peppino got the man as he came toward them. Gino got one more man as he jumped besides Peppino. Peppino, forgetting about the attackers, bent over to help Rosina.

"Rosina, are you hurt?" he said as he turned her on her back. Her shirt was full of blood. She was barely alive.

"Gino," he yelled. "We have to get Rosie to the doctor. She has been shot."

"Wait Peppi," said Rosina. "It's too late. Please listen to me. There isn't much time. I love you with all my heart and life. I told you I would die for you. Not many women have had the happiness I've had. I have no regrets." Her breathing was getting very shallow. Peppino's tears were streaming down his face like a two small rivers. Gino in a fit of anger go up and charged the remaining attackers out in the open. As one got up to shoot, he shot him first.

"I'll get every last one of you if it's the last thing I do." Tears were running down his face. He was out in the open firing both pistols, one in each had. The remaining two attackers ran for their horses and left at full gallop. Gino went back to Peppino and Rosina. It was obvious that Rosina was taking her last breath.

"How is she?" asked Gino. He got no answer.

"I wouldn't change one second of my life," continued Rosina. "Don't leave me," cried Peppino

"Kiss me one last time," requested Rosina. Her voice was so low that Peppino could hardly hear her. Peppino kissed her hard on her lips. Her arms which were wrapped hard around his neck suddenly fell to the ground. Peppino felt the life drain from her lips.

"No, Rosina," he cried in anguish. "Please don't leave me. Rosie I can't go on without you. Please Rosie, don't leave me."

Chapter 14

PAID IN FULL

Fino left Peppino to grieve over his beloved wife. He tied the dead police to their horses as he usually did after an attack.

He then swatted the first horse, which headed for home. The rest of the horses followed. After about a half hour Gino approached Peppino where he was still hugging Rosina.

"Peppi, dearest friend," he said as gently as he could. "You have to let her go. She is with God now."

"Oh Gino, how could I go on without her. I don't know what I will do without her."

"You are a strong person. You will survive. Remember when we first came here it was just the two of us. It will be the same as it was before you met her."

"She was such a lively, upbeat person," said Peppino sorrowfully. "She could handle anything. She made life up here enjoyable. What do I have to live for?"

"You have to finish the job she wanted you to finish," said Gino trying to give him a reason to go on. "The least you can do is get the man who killed her."

"You're right," said Peppino getting angry. "She would want me to free the people from these animals. Did you see who it was that was leading this attack?"

"Yes, said Gino. "He stayed in the rear of the action so that he was safe. I tried to get him but he escaped. I did see who it was however. It was Chief of Police Alfredo. He is fired up to revenge his son's death."

"I can't let Rosie go. If I let go I will never see her again," said Peppino hugging Rosina's body tightly.

"You will see her again when your time comes. For now, we have to give her a decent burial before the police return. She is getting cold and this heat will affect her body." Gino slowly pulled Peppino's hands from around Rosina.

"There is an old shack not too far from your land. I think it has been abandoned," said Peppino.

"Yes," said Gino. "The family was wiped out by the police. I don't even know why. Why do you bring it up?"

"I think it was made from large boards. I can use the wood to make a box for Rosina."

"That's a good idea," said Gino. "I have to go back before I'm missed. I'll come back as soon as the guard leaves." Peppino tearfully released Rosina. He got a blanket and covered her. He rode to the land where he had seen the wooden shack. It was very old wood but was still sturdy. It was nut wood from the type that grew in the area. Peppino took it apart saving the nails. Back at Monte Uno, he built a box for Rosina. He dug a hole just beyond the cave opening. It was a shallow grave. He placed a cross at the head of the grave, which he built from the wood that was left over. He also placed a plaque on the grave which read; "Rosina, the joy of my life sleeps here" He spent the night until morning praying and weeping over her grave.

Gino got back to his land just as the guard got there.

"Where have you been," he asked seeing him on his horse carrying a rifle.

"I saw a deer behind my shack. I grabbed my rifle and chased it. It got away but I think I wounded it."

"It doesn't matter," he said sadly. "I probably won't be back." "Why what is going on?" asked Gino, acting innocent.

"The chief is bringing everyone in, even the road guards. I also was told to be ready to go with them and fight. I'm not a gun fighter.

I'm just a guard. The chief is determined to get Casolini even if it kills all of us."

"I thought you were always left behind to guard the city?" "That's what I usually do, but the chief wants everyone out there."

"Is that wise?" asked Gino. "Who is going to guard the city?" "No one," he answered innocently. "They aren't worried about the town people. They are all like scared rabbits. Come to think of it so am I. Casolini has killed a lot of police. I pray I'm not one of them."

"When is all this supposed to happen?" asked Gino beginning to worry about Peppino. "Why do you go? Why don't you just go to some other town?"

"I got to get back at twelve or they will come after me," he said showing his fear.

"Well I hope you will be all right. I enjoy your company. It gets pretty lonely working out here alone," said Gino. "I better get back to work. I got a lot of work to catch up on." It was about a quarter to twelve when the guard said Goodbye.

"Good luck," said Gino. As soon as the guard left, Gino got on his horse and rushed back to the mountain to warn Peppino.

Peppino was at Rosina's grave when he saw Gino riding up fast. He stood up and watched Gino jump off his horse and approach him.

"Peppino," he said, "the police chief has rounded up every one of his people and even the road guards to come after you."

"How did you find this out?" wondered Peppino.

"The guard that watches me told me. Even he had to leave to join the group."

"Doesn't he usually go back and be one of the city guards?" "Yes, but this time the police chief wants every available hand in this action," said Gino. "I think we are going to have a big, and maybe our final, battle."

"Tell me?" asked Peppino deep in thought. "Who is guarding the mayor?"

"No one," said Gino. "Why do you ask?"

"Because that's where we will be," said Peppino. "We have to dispose of the new mayor." Peppino got his horse and both of them rode to the edge of the olive grove. From there they could see when the police group left town. It was about twelve-thirty when they saw the group leave town. There were about ten riders.

"I though that there would be more then that," said Peppino. They had about twelve road guards alone. I wonder if this is a trap." "I don't know," said Gino. "All I know is what the guard told me. It's my guess that since they saw where you were the last time they came that they figure that they will catch you as you come out after lunch."

"We have to take the gamble," said Peppino. They got on their horses and slowly rode into town. They tied their horses at a hitching post near city hall and approached the city hall hugging the sides of the buildings. The city people who saw them ran inside and locked their doors.

"Stay here in the safety of the building," Peppino told Gino. "We don't want anyone to recognize you." Peppino stepped out into the open in front of the city hall and called out to the mayor.

"Mayor Vittorio, Come out," he yelled. "I have something to tell you. Or are you the coward that I think you are?"

"I'm not a coward nor am I stupid," said the mayor stepping out from a building behind Peppino. He had a pistol aimed at Peppino's head. "Now turn around slowly and if you drop your rifle you may live a few seconds longer."

Peppino turned slowly and dropped his rifle. "Did you really think I was so stupid not to figure if that nut head brother of mine left the city unprotected that you wouldn't be around. Now if you like, say a prayer to that mystical God of yours." Alfredo lifted his pistol getting ready to fire. "Say ciao to your father and sister for me. A shot echoed through the street. However, it was Mayor Vittorio who fell. Peppino ran up to him. "How?" is all the mayor could say.

"You didn't think I would walk out into the street with out a back- up?" The mayor's lungs were filling with blood and he couldn't breathe. "Say ciao to your murderous sons." The mayor died. Peppino picked up his rifle and he and Gino left the area and headed to the olive grove where they waited for the attackers to return.

Several days later, Peppino was sitting at his usual place by his observation rock. He was talking to Rosina as he usually did as part of his mourning.

"Rosina, honey, there is only one more to go and I will fulfill your last request. And, God willing, I will come and join you." As he was telling her how much he missed her, he saw the dust from what looked like two horses. He prepared his rifle to defend himself. As the riders got closer he recognized that one rider was Gino. He put down his rifle and climbed down to meet them.

"Anna," he yelled, surprised to see her. She jumped off her horse and landed in Peppino's arms. "Anna what is happening? What brings you two out here?"

"It's a long story," said Gino. "Can we sit down over a cup of coffee and we will tell you all the details."

"You can sit down but I'm sorry I don't have anything to give you," said Peppino apologetically.

"You have a lot of coffee and lots of food," said Anna as she emptied her and Gino's saddlebags. "Our loving clerk is worried about you. Peppino," she then added sadly, "I was so shocked and saddened when I heard about Rosina. I felt I lost part of my body. I loved her like my own sister. I'm so sorry Peppino." Tears appeared in Peppino's eyes, which set them off in the other two.

"Tell me what is happening?" said Peppino.

"You tell it, honey," said Gino. "I'll make the coffee." "Yesterday, Mayor Vittorio's widow called all the servants of the mayor's house together. She told us that she was saddened at the death of her husband although they had not been in the best of terms for a long time. She told us she didn't approve of the crudity of the Malavista family. She didn't know what she was getting into when she married Vittorio. In a way, she was freed and said that she was going back to Syracuse. She has family there. Then she told us that anyone who wanted to leave the job as servant at the Mayor's house would have her blessings. She knows that some of the young ladies would like to get married and raise a family of their own. As soon as she left, I packed up the little that I had and ran to my husband. So here we are."

"What are your plans now?" asked Peppino.

"Well we haven't had a honeymoon yet," said Gino as Anna's face got red. "Anna has relatives in Naples. They own a grape and olive pressing business. Anna thinks they will give me a job there. First however, we are going to spend some of the money we have from selling her house to spend some time around Sicily."

"I am so happy for you both," said Peppino. "It couldn't happen to two more wonderful people."

"We intend to leave tomorrow morning unless you feel that you need me," said Gino.

"You have to be kidding," said Peppino. "I am so happy for you two. You know that I love you both. I am going to leave soon myself. I just wish I could go with you. I should have insisted that Rosina and I leave this place. I could have gotten us out."

"We are going to go to my house," said Gino. "We will not have time to sell it. Since it's at the edge of town it could be a good place for you to hide. You have a key so help yourself."

"By the way," added Anna. "Did you know that Angelina LaFonti is going to marry Nino? I met her on the way to Gino's place."

"That is wonderful," said Peppino feeling a little of the joy he had brought to others.

A week had passed since Gino and Anna left, and Peppino never felt so alone. He almost wished they would come after him. He was getting tired of the whole situation. He wanted to leave the area but couldn't bring himself to go. He remembered that the man who killed Rosina was still alive. Peppino kept himself busy planning on how to get the chief of police. He thought that it had to be a surprise attack. He also realized that he would not survive. He sure could use Gino's help. He went up to his observation rock to think in the open fresh air. As he looked out he saw a cloud of dust coming his way. It was a large group of men. He guesses that the police chief had determined to get him at all costs. Peppino knew that his time was up. He only prayed that if it was his time that he could at least take chief of police, Alfredo, with him. He had four rifles. He loaded them all and did what Rosina had done. He had them all lined up on the rock. The men came to the bottom of the mountain and all dismounted and got behind a rock. There must have been about twenty of them. Peppino using his spy glass looked for Vittorio. He couldn't find him. Suddenly three shots were fired then another and the firing stopped to Peppino's surprise.

What were they up too? Then as he waited for their next action, he saw a white cloth tied to the barrel of a rifle.

"Peppino Casolini," said the man in front. "Let's talk."

"What is there to talk about?"

"I would like to discuss your freedom and ours," said the man. "Who are you?" asked Peppino.

"My name is Giacomo Camio. My wife is the woman you spared in the grocery store. You told her that you were not doing the killing of the towns' people. She believed you and so do I."

"Where are Chief Alfredo and his police?" asked Peppino. "The chief and three of his police are dead. The shots you heard were for them. We are the common town folk who were drafted by threatening our families. The chief called in all the road guards. Only three showed up. The rest skipped town and are probably out of Sicily. Seven of the police he had assigned for this duty have disappeared. We have a group of men who are on the way to Enna. We will probably have a new government soon." Giacomo stepped out into the open and walked up to Peppino and stuck out his hand in a friendship motion. "I want to thank you personally for freeing our town from the Malavista family."

"I only wanted to punish the criminals that killed my family and in the process took out the murderous police that did the mayor's dirty work." About twelve of the other men came up and shook Peppino's hand and thanked him for his part in freeing the city.

"I understand from the grocery clerk that your wife was killed. We are so sorry. The grocery clerk cried when he told us. We would like to celebrate our freedom but I suggest that you disappear from these parts. We don't know what the new people will do."

"I think my job is completed here, thanks to you. The man who killed my wife is dead. That is the last of the Malavista blue blood. I think I will leave soon. It will take some time for the new government to get settled."

"If you get caught there are more than a dozen people who will testify in your behalf."

"Thank you," said Peppino. "I thought I was finished when I saw you coming."

"I'm sorry about that. We had no choice until on our way here the police started to disappear from our ranks." Turning, he addressed the others. "What do you say we go home to our families?" They all agreed and soon were gone. Peppino stood still shocked at what had taken place just a few minutes ago. He went to Rosina's grave. "Honey, the job here is completed. What you desired has been accomplished. The town is free. But now I have to leave our home.

You will always be in my heart. I'll come before I leave.

The next morning Peppino packed all that he needed to travel. He walked through every inch of what had been his and Rosina home for over two years. He was now twenty-eight. He had to start a new life. He packed Rosina's horse with food and other items he thought he would need and set out on his journey. He planned on going to Monte Mangone and taking the north road to Valguarnera and then take the road to Catania. There are a lot of fishing fleets from there to Messina. He figured on getting a job with one of them. The plan was good but it didn't work out. As he passed through Valguarnera he was stopped by a local policeman.

"Will you keep your hand away from your rifle and dismount," said the officer.

"Why are you stopping me," said Peppino. "I'm just passing through."

"Well I think you are the one who robbed the Bank di Roma. I've been chasing you for the last hour," He lifted his rifle and aimed it at Peppino's head. "Get down on your own or must I shoot you." Peppino dismounted and walked toward the officer.

"You have made a big mistake," said Peppino. "I don't know anything about your bank."

"Stop where you are and hand me your rifle."

Peppino did as he was told. "Why don't you search my possessions and see if I have your bank's money."

"You could have hid it with the plan to come back for it later. Now come with me peaceably."

"Wait a minute," said Peppino. "Don't you want this too?" He reached behind his back and pulled out his pistol. The officer was stunned. *My life is over* he thought. But then to his surprise Peppino hand him the gun handle first. "I don't think I should walk into your police station with this in my possession."

"Thank you," said the officer. "You could have disarmed me or shoot me and escaped. Why didn't you?"

"I'm innocent of your robbery and I never shoot an innocent person." The officer took him to the police station where the bank clerk was there to identify him.

"That's not the man," he said sounding very disappointed.

"I told you that I was innocent," said Peppino. "May I get my horses back and leave?"

"I'm very sorry to inconvenience you," said the arresting officer. "I'll get your things and send you on your way."

"Wait a minute," said the police chief. "Don't I know you?" "I've never been through here," said Peppino. The chief pulled out his gun and pointed it at Peppino.

"I do know you. I have a picture here of you. You're wanted in every providence in Sicily. You're Notorious Casolini. Put your hand above your head."

"What?" said the arresting officer. "You could have shot me. If I had known it was you I would have run to the other side of town. "I never killed an innocent person. I only killed the ones that killed my father, my sister, and my wife. Besides I'm tired of killing." "Call Judge Rini," said the chief. "He will know what to do with him. Judge Rini came as soon as he was summoned. The chief explained to him who Peppino was and how he happened to be captured.

"I don't know what to do with him," said the judge. "This is too big for us. We can't handle this. Let's send him to Enna. They are more prepared for this kind of problem."

Three police were assigned to take Peppino and all his possessions to Enna. When they got there the three delivering officers were relieve to turn Peppino over to the Enna police. Peppino was jailed and told that they were going to investigate after contacting the official now in Barrafranca. The Barrafranca officials being new took time to obtain information from the residents. They took affidavits and sent them to Enna with all the records they had at the city's office on Peppino Casolini. It was three weeks later that Peppino was summoned to the cities court. He was brought before a three judge panel.

"Mr. Casolini," said the presiding judge. "We are here to determine the extent of your crimes. We have affidavits from some of the residents of Barrafranca. They all pretty much say the same thing. It is their opinion that you acted in self-defense against a cruel and murderous city government. However, the city records show that you have also killed city residents. What are your comments on this?" Peppino related how he was jailed on a false charge after the son of the chief of police killed his brother-in-law to widow his sister. He told how his father was killed and how his sister was hung by the mayor's wife.

"I never killed the city residents. That was a plot by the ruling people to rid the city of a group of men that were planning to revolt. It was easy to blame all on me." He told how they had killed his wife.

"Yes, we have an affidavit from a Giacomo Camio," said the judge. "He claims to be the head of the group. We will take this all under advisement and get back to you." Peppino was taken back to jail. It was four weeks later that he was brought before the three judges.

"We want to tell you that it was a very difficult decision," stated the head judge. "Under our law a person who has killed some one will normally get a verdict of death by hanging. Under some conditions, a person could get life in prison. We have toiled over your case for these weeks. We all couldn't agree on the verdict. We however have come to a compromise. Some of your killings were justified. And some of your killings were considered self defense. However, we can't excuse all the killings. It is therefore our verdict that you be sentenced for thirty years." That was it. Peppino was to serve thirty years in the Enna prison.

In prison, Peppino kept to himself. There was a ruthless criminal in the jail who acted tough and intimidated all the other prisoners. However, because of Peppino's size and his intimidating stare he left Peppino alone. The time pasted slowly. Peppino adjusted and spent his time reliving his past.

It was two years later that Peppino got his first contact with the outside. It was a letter from Gino. Gino and Anna had traveled to Barrafranca to visit with Nino and Angelina. While in Barrafranca he found out that Peppino was in jail in Enna. He told Peppino that they had a little girl and Anna was expecting again. If it was a boy, they promised to call him Peppino after their best friend. He also told Peppino that Gina had two boys, that they had visited them and that they were all fine. Gino promised that the next time they are in Sicily they would try to visit him. This gave Peppino a new perspective on life. He now had something to look forward too. The letter also caused him to become friends with the guard on his cellblock. His name was Bruno. He had no family. He was very interested in Peppino's letter. Peppino let him read the letter and after some conversation, Peppino told him his life story. That brought everything back as if it was yesterday. Bruno started to bring a newspaper into the cell and let Peppino read it. It let Peppino know what was going on outside of the prison. Peppino would let Bruno read his letters from Gino. Later that year Bruno agreed to mail letters that Peppino wrote to Gino. This made time go by more rapidly. It was several years later that Bruno came in one morning very excited.

"What are you all excited about," asked Peppino.

"There is a war going on in all of Europe," said Bruno. "It's Germany and Austria-Hungry against France and Great Britain."

"What are they fighting about," asked Peppino.

"I think it started because of the murder of an Archduke Ferdinand.

"So what," said Peppino. "I got over ten more years to go, about twelve, to be more exact. Unless it comes here I can't care less."

"Well it's news anyway. Here take the newspaper and read all about it."

"Thanks," said Peppino. It was time for his one hour in the courtyard which he used every day to get some exercise. He decided to read it later.

For the next year, Peppino would get news of the war until one day Bruno came in with exciting news.

"You said once that you didn't worry about the war in Europe because it didn't affect you, isn't that right?"

"That's right, so what?" said Peppino.

"Well things have changed," said Bruno. "This morning, Italy has declared war on Austria. They are calling young men to arms. They are also giving pardons to prisoners who are willing to go to war." "I'm too old to go in the army," said Peppino.

"They are calling men forty and below if you don't have a family to support."

"That's not true is it?" said Peppino. "You are just making that up." "I don't know," said Bruno. It could be true."

"It doesn't matter; I'm forty-six. How about you? Are you ready to go? You're still in your low thirties aren't you?"

"I hope not."

That year Peppino got a letter from Gino. Both of his boys were in the army. He asked that Peppino to pray for them. He also informed him that he had been writing to Gina. Gina had written that both of her boys were also in the army. She also told him that she had lost her youngest son. He was killed in Austria. He was saddened with that information.

"Poor Gina," he said to himself. "Hasn't she had enough pain in her life?"

All year Bruno kept Peppino up to date on the war. A year later, he informed Peppino that the United States had entered the war "Since the United States is in the war and so is Canada they are calling it a World War," said Bruno. "I hope that the war ends soon. The men they are calling are getting older every day."

"I wouldn't worry if I were you," said Peppino kidding Bruno. "They only want strong men. You wouldn't make the grade." Bruno could tell by Peppino's expression that he was kidding him.

"Keep that up and I won't tell you anything." They both laughed. Bruno did keep Peppino informed and they were both happy when almost a year later the war ended. The next big news that Bruno brought him was the rise of Mussolini in Italy. With the change in politics, new rules were coming into being. The newspaper reported that there was a movement in Italy to pardon political prisoners.

Upon reading this Peppino voice his hope to Bruno "Do you think that I could be considered a political prisoner?" asked Peppino.

"I don't see why not. You were fighting a political group," said Bruno. Without Peppino's knowledge Bruno did some investigating. He found that some of the city officials were being replaced with Mussolini's party. The changes had reached Sicily. The leaders of Palermo were being investigated. Bruno wrote a note to the new leaders in Palermo. He told them about the unfair treatment that was given to his area. He didn't hear back but it may have had an effect. It was two years later beforePeppino was called before the new party in Enna. There were three men in the review group. They were looking over his records.

"So do you think you are a political prisoner," asked the oldest of the group.

"I rebelled against the ruling family that was inflicting cruel punishment and performing terrible and painful killings of the people. If those are the papers that tell my story you can see that they killed my entire family just because the mayor's son wanted my sister for his playmate."

"Yes I see that you have been victimized. But why did they give you thirty years? That information is not clear."

"The ones that were actually performing most of the cruelties and killings were the mayor's personal police. The panel of three judges couldn't agree. From what I have been told one of the judges wanted me hung. I think if you investigate you will find that one judge had a relationship with the Malavista family whom I shot one at a time. The thirty years was a compromise."

"Yes, I see that here," said the investigating official. That on the surface looks like a cruel miscarriage of justice. I see here that you have been in prison for twenty-four years. We will have to look at it and if we determine that you were wrongly imprisoned we will look to get you some sort of compensation. We will let you know our decision after we review all the documents we have." Peppino was brought back to his cell. When he got there, he was surprised to see Bruno standing by his cell with a big smile on his face.

"Did you eat your neighbor's chicken," asked Peppino in jest. "No, but I have a surprise for you," he said. "It isn't generally done except for one's family or his attorney." "What in the world are you blabbing about?"

"Come with me, because, if I tell you will not believe me," he said. "By the way if you are interested, I'm the one that wrote the letter that brought those guys here to try to release you."

"When we come back from where you're taking me remind me and I will kiss you."

"When you come back from where I'm taking you, you will not remember anything."

"There you go blabbing again," said Peppino.

"Just go through that door in front of you. I'll be here when you come back out." Peppino had no idea what Bruno was talking about. He opened the door and went in. tears filled his eyes.

"Gino, Anna," was all he could say. He hugged them both at the same time. "What a wonderful surprise. How, what, where did you guys come from? What has brought you here?"

"A fellow named Bruno wrote us to tell us that you were going to have a hearing that could set you free. So here we are to testify in your behalf."

"Let me catch my breath. How are you guys? How is your daughter? I would love to meet her. How are your boys? Did they both get back safely?"

"One question at a time, please," said Gino. "We are fine. Our daughter is great. You will meet her if you come up and visit us. Our boys both have come home safely. Any more questions, Peppi?" "Yes, how have you two managed to stay looking so young? You two look exactly as you did the last time I saw you."

"Thanks, you look good two except you are a little thinner. But then when you love some one as we love you, they will always look beautiful."

"Anna," said Peppino hugging her again. "Why haven't you said anything?"

"I'm afraid if I speak I will start to cry," she said tears appearing in her eyes. It's like twenty some years have just been wiped away and we are back where we were at the cave at Monte Uno."

"How long are you guys going to stick around?"

"We are going back home from here," said Gino. "I have a job to go back to. I got a special approval from my boss to come here. This is the busiest time of the year." They talked about old times until the guard came in and told them that their time was up. They kissed goodbye and Peppino went back to his cell. That was the best day he had in twenty-four years.

A few days later Peppino was called back to meet the special officials.

"We have good news" said the official. "We have saved you six years and we apologize for the days you have spent here. We also have obtained for you a fair sum of money. Invest it wisely and you will be able to live on the dividends. We have obtained two horses for you and some items you will need for your trip. We got the items from a list of things you had when you were apprehended. The actual items you had have all disappeared over the years. Here is your bankbook. The guard will see you to your horses. Goodbye and good luck."

"Thank you for everything," said Peppino, trying to keep the bitterness out of his voice. Bruno led Peppino to his horses.

"Bruno, you have been the only good thing I've had happen to me in all the years I've been here. I feel like you're part of my family.

I will never forget you. I couldn't possibly thank you for all you have done and most of all your company."

"I'll miss you too. You made my time pass very pleasantly. Remember, Barrafranca isn't that far away that you can't come and visit a friend."

"You'll understand if it isn't too soon," said Peppino.

"I know," said Bruno. They hugged and said goodbye. As he rode away Peppino felt all alone again.

Peppino headed for Barrafranca. His desired to get a job with a fishing fleet had faded. After twenty-four years of living in a small room, suddenly everything happened so fast it was hard for him to comprehend. He rode passed Barrafranca and went directly to the last place he called home, Monte Uno. When he got to the cave, it was all cleaned out. There was no table no chairs, nothing but dirt. He went around to the upper chamber and to his surprise, no one had been there. It was just as he had left it. Even the mattress was still there. It was starting to get dark. He went to Rosina's grave. The city had built a little monument where he had placed a cross. The cross now was imbedded in the monument stone with the words he had placed on the plaque engraved on the front. Peppino was very taken by their thoughtfulness. He soon realized that he couldn't stay there. There were too many memories. It was too depressing. He knelt down and prayed. After praying, he talked to Rosina. He explained why he couldn't stay there. He promised to visit soon. He decided to stay at Gino's house. He searched the upper chamber of the cave and found the key. He slept there that night and traveled to Gino's house the next morning. He was surprised at how clean it was. He assumed that Gino and Anna had stayed there during their visit. Then he found the note on top of the table. He read it out loud.

"Dear Peppino, I hope you decided to stay here. Anna and I cleaned it up for you. I know that you couldn't stay at Monte Uno. Please make yourself at home. We are leaving now to testify in your behalf. We will try to see you before we leave for home. Incidentally, if you decide to farm your land all the equipment I used is stored in the stable. Feel free to use it. It is yours.

All our love Gino and Anna"

Peppino drove out to his father's land. The shack was still there but it was empty. It looked like it had been used recently. The land had been used for the summer planting. Peppino wondered if the land now belonged to someone else. He got on his horse and decided to report to the city office. The new mayor was there. It was Giacomo Camio.

"Peppino," he said as soon as he saw him. "I'm so glad to see you. How are you?"

"I'm fine, but what are you doing here?"

"I'm the newly elected mayor," he said. "What can I do for you?"

"Well mayor, I was wondering who owned my father's land.

I thought I would do some winter planting. But it looks like it belongs to some one else."

"No," said the mayor. "The Enna officials bought the land back and signed it over to you. It's yours. And Peppino, please call me Giacomo."

"I'll see you later then," said Peppino. "I have a lot of settling to do."

"See you later, Good luck and welcome back."

Peppino got back to Gino's house and decided to wait until next spring to start working his land. It was getting to late to start. He had to bring all the equipment to the shack. He also had to get a lock for the shack. He would take care of all this in the winter months. He wanted to enjoy the rest of the good weather while it lasted. He got into the habit of walking down the west dirt highway every evening after dinner and sit on the wall looking down the olive orchard. He did this every evening for a month enjoying the view and the evening breeze that blew across the high ground of the road. It was an evening just as this when as he sat in deep thought that he heard a voice behind him.

"Is this a private place, or can you have visitors?" said the voice. Peppino turned around thinking that he was fantasizing. It sounded like Gina's voice. He could never forget her voice. His heart stopped. He found he had a lump in his throat. His eyes were blurred, but he could see that it was Gina. He slid down and stood before her.

"What are you doing here?" he asked almost instinctively. "Well you didn't come to me so I came to you. I wanted to thank you for saving my life from the wicked witch. Thank you."

"I couldn't let her hurt you," said Peppino his voice projecting the love he had in his heart for her.

"It's so nice to see you, Peppino."

"It's nice to see you too," said Peppino. "I'm sorry about your son. How is your other son?"

"My oldest son is on his way to America. They gave visas to any one who fought on the allied side. On his way, he stopped to visit Gino and Anna. You know I think he and Gino's daughter have fallen in love. I think when she finishes nursing school he will come back and marry her. They may both go to America."

"How beautiful you are," said Peppino still feeling stunned "You haven't changed a bit! You look as young as you did the last time I saw you."

"You look very handsome," said Gina. "You look just like I remember you. However, there is one difference. The old Peppi would have had me in his arms as soon as he saw me."

"Why are you doing this to me? Why are you tearing my heart in pieces?"

"Is it because you want to put your arms around me and kiss me?" said Gina lovingly.

"It's because you have a husband and a family," said Peppino with tears in his eyes.

"Oh dear Lord," said Gina. "Of course you haven't heard. That's why you haven't thrown your arms around me. Don't you know? Nicolo was ten years older than I. He passed away three years ago."

"Oh I'm so sorry, Gina. I didn't know."

"Did you think I was going to cheat on my husband?" asked Gina. "Did you love him as much as you loved me?" Before she could answer, he had her in his arms and his lips were searching for hers. He kissed her passionately.

"Did you ask me something?"

"I don't remember," said Peppino and kissed her again. He wrapped his arms around her so tight that she could hardly breathe. "You feel so good in my arms," said Peppino. "You fit perfectly. I think we were made for each other."

"I know," said Gina and kissed him again. When their lips parted, she remembered what he had asked her. "I think you asked me if I loved Nicolo as much as I loved you. You were married too. I saw what you wrote on her tombstone."

"I won't lie to you, Gina. I loved her very much. She was a very special lady. She was agile, smart and a better shot than any man I know. Yet she was very gentle and affectionate. But she never crowded you out of my heart. I have never loved any one as I love you. You were my first love. I cried when Gino told me about your wedding. There is a magic that flows through my body when I touch you."

"I know I feel it too," said Gina. "To answer your question I did love Nicolo, but it was a different kind of love. I have never loved any one as much as I loved you. And Peppi, I still love you so much that it almost hurts. I've missed you every day of my life."

"You had children with Nicolo," said Peppino showing his jealousy."

"Would you believe that when we were making love I would close my eyes and pretend it was you?"

"I want you to understand that I still want to visit Rosina's Grave now and then." She was my wife for two years.

"I understand," said Gina. "I would like to visit Nicolo's grave also."

"I think we are talking too much," said Peppino as he wrapped his arms around her with his lips wanting to swallow her lips and her tongue. After the kiss, Gina put her hands on his chest and let her eyes feast on his face.

"I see that you are still wearing your wedding ring," said Peppino. "I am not wearing a wedding ring," said Gina. "Look closer to my finger."

"Is that…" stuttered Peppino. "Is that, the engagement ring I gave you?"

"Yes it is and I have the matching wedding rings on the necklace I have around my neck."

"What are you trying to tell me?" asked Peppino.

"What I'm saying is that I feel that we are still engaged. You're not trying to break our engagement are you?"

"Not on your life," said Peppino. "Do you want me to propose again?"

"No, you promised to marry me. Now don't you think that thirty years is too long an engagement?"

"Yes I do, it's thirty years too long. I would like to keep my promise."

"Then let's go find a priest and set a date," suggested Gina. "Are you ready?"

"I've been ready for a long time," They walked hand in hand down the road towards the church at the Piazza at the end of the road.

"How much do you want to marry me?" asked Gina.

"I've never wanted any thing more in my whole life," answered Peppino.

"How soon do you want to marry me," asked Gina. "Yesterday would not have been too soon."

"Then why are we walking?" asked Gina.

"As I hold your hand my feet are barely touching the ground.

With you holding my hand I think I could fly." "Then love of my life, let's fly to the church."

The End

www.ingramcontent.com/pod-product-compliance
Lightning Source LLC
Chambersburg PA
CBHW070907120626
46546CB00001B/165